The author—their thought M000072814 character—is indistinguishable from the works they write. That's why you want to read *Authenticity*; Chad speaks from an intimate and abiding walk with Christ, and he's spent years teaching and coaching others in doing the same. Strangely, this is a unique book as it's written from the perspective of an experienced discipler—not pastor, not blogger, not counselor, but someone skilled in the art of personal, biblical discipleship—someone who traffics daily in the netherworld between orthodoxy (right belief) and orthopraxy (right practice) where all of us live.

Rick James
Publisher, CruPress
Author, *A Million Ways To Die* and *Jesus Without Religion*

After working closely with Chad for a few years, he demonstrates an authentic relationship with Christ on a daily basis. People are naturally drawn to Chad because they desire to have the same genuine relationship with God that Chad has. In this book, not only does he articulate an "authenticity" that is exemplified in his daily walk with the Lord, but he does a great job of conveying these vital relational truths in a simple and understandable fashion. This book is a great guide in growing closer to the Lord!

Tom Heinemann
Major League Soccer player, currently with the
Columbus Crew

Chad combines his insight into Scripture with his tremendous storytelling ability to produce a must-read for students desiring a truly authentic walk with Christ.

Bill Jones
President, Columbia International University,
   Columbia, SC
Author, *Putting Together the Puzzle of the Old Testament*
   and *Putting Together the Puzzle of the New Testament*

In this intensely personal and yet universal book, Chad Young has written of what it means to let oneself see through the inauthenticity it sometimes seems surrounds the church. By turns memoir, devotional, instruction manual, and just plain good storytelling, *Authenticity* is a must read.

Bret Lott
English professor, College of Charleston
Author, *Jewel*, an Oprah's Book Club selection

Chad takes you through his journey in the way that the guy next door would. He discusses how he has overcome many of the challenges that we all go through on a daily basis, and as a result, he could not be happier living for the Lord. This was a refreshing and informative look at ways that we can change our outlooks and ultimately change our lives.

Bryce Florie
Former Major League Baseball pitcher

Rarely does the title of a book perfectly match the subject matter AND the author. Such is the case with *Authenticity* by Chad Young. In my 25 years of working with college students I have encountered many campus leaders who made a significant mark for Christ and his Kingdom among the campus community. Among these Christ-followers, Chad Young stands out in remarkable ways. I believe *Authenticity* is the first of several books the Lord will give Chad to enlarge his influence and ministry as a disciple-builder among emerging adults. *Authenticity* should be required reading for every Christian high school and college student who is serious about spiritual growth and leadership."

Dr. Rick Brewer
Vice President, Charleston Southern University

After spending time with Chad, one thing that you learn very quickly is that he has a desire to live his life in a way that glorifies God. I have been able to witness first hand through Chad's life some of the fundamentals Chad shares in this book. In *Authenticity*, you find a book that is open, honest, and straightforward, just like Chad. Within the pages of this book are resources that can help guide anyone who has a true desire to know and follow God down the path of authentic Christianity.

Nelson Akwari
USL PRO and Major League Soccer player, currently with the L.A. Blues

AUTHENTICITY

REAL FAITH IN A PHONY, SUPERFICIAL WORLD

Chad Young

Transforming lives through God's Word

Transforming lives through God's Word

Biblica provides God's Word to people through translation, publishing and Bible engagement in Africa, Asia Pacific, Europe, Latin America, Middle East, and North America. Through its worldwide reach, Biblica engages people with God's Word so that their lives are transformed through a relationship with Jesus Christ.

Biblica Publishing
We welcome your questions and comments.

1820 Jet Stream Drive, Colorado Springs, CO 80921 USA
www.Biblica.com

Authenticity
ISBN-13: 978-1-60657-087-6

Published in 2011 by Biblica, Inc.™

A catalog record for this book is available through the Library of Congress.

Printed in the United States of America

Contents

Acknowledgments

No one has read this book more times than my beautiful wife, Elizabeth. Her patience, encouragement, and editing spurred me on to complete this book.

I also want to acknowledge Blythe Daniel of The Blythe Daniel Agency. She is truly authentic, and this book is a result of her taking me in and helping to sharpen me as a writer.

I would also like to thank Volney James and John Dunham with Biblica for believing in this project and helping to shape it along the way.

David Jacobsen took a raw, rough draft and coached me and helped me produce this final product. I've grown as a writer as a result of his hard work and expertise.

I'd like to thank my friend Rick James for coaching me along the way, always being so encouraging, and giving helpful advice. Along the same lines, I'd like to thank Keith Davy, Gilbert Kingsley, Tony Arnold, Eric Pederson, and Nick Corrova for their help and encouragement.

There are so many others who have helped with editing along the way, including my aunt, Lil Duncan, and my father, Herb Young, who helped edit the entire book. Others who have helped with ideas and editing include Mary Mena Koches, Nancy Snowden, Gin and Anne Edmunds, Doug Schutz, DJ Horton, Bret Lott, and Dr. Rick Brewer. Thank you all.

Last but not least, I thank my Lord Jesus, who gave his life for me, changed my life, led me to write this book, and worked behind the scenes during this entire writing and publishing process.

C hristianity has an image problem. I was recently on campus at Colorado State University in Fort Collins, Colorado, and got into a spiritual conversation with a student we'll call "Amanda" in the Student Center. When I asked her what she believed about God, Amanda hesitated.

"Well," she said slowly, "I do believe in God, and I've heard stories about Jesus. However, I had a lot of friends in my high school that went to church, and their lives didn't seem to be anything like the life of Jesus. In fact, some of the kids who went to church had the worst reputations in my school. Several people have tried to talk to me about Christianity, but it's hard for me to believe in something that doesn't seem to have much of an impact on your life."

There wasn't much more I could say. I simply apologized to Amanda for the lack of authentic Christian faith in her high school. I confessed to her I was like her friends when I was in high school. I called myself a Christian, but I lived a hypocritical lifestyle. I asked her to forgive me for the way I acted when I was in school, and she did. The last thing she told me was that our conversation seemed so genuine, and it made her think maybe there is something authentic about Christian faith.

Recent studies by Campus Crusade for Christ and The Barna Group reveal Christianity's image problem is widespread. David Kinnaman writes, "You may be astonished to learn just how significant the dilemma is—and how the negative perceptions that your friends, neighbors, and colleagues have of Christianity will shape your life and your culture in years to come."[1]

According to Barna's three-year study, only 16 percent of people between the ages of sixteen and twenty-nine have a positive impression of Christianity in general—and a mere 3 percent of that age group has a favorable impression toward evangelical Christians! When I read this, I recalled that 3 percent is within the margin of error in most polls—is it possible that *no* young person has a positive impression of evangelical Christianity?

Why all the hostility? We'll dig into the reasons for this throughout the book, but let's glance at them here. According to this study, there are six major reasons why postmodern young adults have a negative view toward Christianity, which is perceived as being:

1. *Hypocritical.* Most teens and young adults are skeptical of Christians' morally superior attitudes. "Christians pretend to be something unreal, conveying a polished image that is not accurate."
2. *Too focused on getting converts.* Postmodern teens and adults wonder if Christians genuinely care about them. "I feel like a target rather than a person."
3. *Antihomosexual.* They say Christians are fixated on "curing" homosexuals and on leveraging political solutions against them. "Christians are bigoted and show disdain for gays and lesbians."

4. *Sheltered.* Christians are thought of as old-fashioned and out of touch with reality. "Christians are not willing to deal with the grit and grime of people's lives."
5. *Too political.* Christians are perceived as being too conservative politically. "Christians are overly motivated by a political agenda. They're right-wingers."
6. *Judgmental.* Young adults doubt Christians really love people the way they say they do. "Christians are quick to judge others."[2]

What's even more alarming about these statistics is that from this age group—you and your peers—will come the next generation of leaders of our communities, our churches, and our country. Yet most of the young adults your age have opted to reject Christian faith, and these studies indicate young men and women are running from Christians. Meanwhile, we are so busy "being" Christians and "doing" Christian activities in our churches that we are not relating to non-Christians or even each other as believers.

How can we be the solution and not the problem? How can we become more genuine for ourselves and for others who are looking for Christ in us? Does Christ really matter in today's culture, and if so, why?

You may know people who are confused about the existence of God and frustrated by a lack of authentic Christian faith. Perhaps you or someone you know is turning to sexual relationships, drug and alcohol abuse, and worldly lifestyles in search of significance and satisfaction. If the generation that you are a part of, who will lead our country in the coming years, does not find authentic faith, what will become of our country?

The good news is that there is a spiritual movement growing on college campuses throughout the country, and lives are being transformed by the life-changing power of Jesus. Students like you are pursuing authentic Christian faith and are making a difference by impacting tomorrow's leaders on their campuses.

I asked a number of students from different campuses to define authentic Christian faith, and the following are some of their responses:

> Authentic Christian faith is selflessness; understanding that it's not about us at all. Just as Christ gave his life for the whole universe, we can show that love in selflessness to one another.
>
> — *Lee from Charleston Southern University*

> An authentic Christian is so overwhelmed and overjoyed by their relationship with Christ that they don't simply do good works just for their own benefit but namely for his glory.
>
> — *Todd from Marshall University*

> Authentic Christian faith is living a Spirit-filled life of worship. It is not self-seeking, but outward-seeking and looking toward Jesus alone.
>
> — *Josh from N.C. State University*

> Authentic Christian faith is surrender. It is surrendering to God, his will, his ways, and his plans. It is letting go of self and independence. It is casting off worldly ways of thinking and being. It is embracing the kingdom of God. Through this surrender salvation is received, the Holy Spirit is given, and lives are transformed.
>
> — *Eric from the College of Charleston*

Sadly, authentic Christian faith is something that most people never see. I didn't see it until college, and

I grew up in the church. When it is lived out, you see peace, vulnerability, and an authentic love for God and for others that can only come from Jesus.

— *Ty from Morehead State University*

When I was a college student a number of years ago, I had a negative view toward Christianity that was similar to the views most young people have today. Although I would have called myself a Christian if someone had asked me my beliefs, I was seeking purpose and satisfaction in other things besides Christ.

Toward the end of my freshman year in college, an older brother in Christ helped me discover a road that has helped me find my purpose and deep satisfaction in Jesus. Like all roads, there have been many bumps along the way, and at times I have taken detours. However, God has always been there with me and has helped me get back on the right road. There are some key truths God has taught me along the way, and he has placed in my life many people who have helped me survive on the road during my journey. My appreciation for all God has taught me and my desire to help others along their way have driven me to write this book.

I want to reemphasize that I haven't arrived at my destination yet. The Lord is still refining and changing me. I don't have all of the answers, and this isn't a book about everything you need to know about being a follower of Christ.

It *is* a book about some of the key things I've learned so far and feel led to pass along. My hope and prayer are that this book would help you overcome obstacles and travel well on the road toward authentic Christian faith.

> *Let this be written for a future generation,*
> *that a people not yet created may praise the LORD.*

—Psalm 102

PART 1 | The Great Commandment
Love God

> *Hearing that Jesus had silenced the Sadducees, the Pharisees got together. One of them, an expert in the law, tested him with this question: "Teacher, which is the greatest commandment in the Law?"*
>
> *Jesus replied: "Love the Lord your God with all your heart and with all your soul and with all your mind." This is the first and greatest commandment.*
>
> —the Gospel of Matthew

God created us to know him personally. When we lack an authentic relationship with him, we cease to fulfill our overarching purpose. When we fall in love with God as we were created to do, the other relationships and areas of our lives cannot help but become more authentic as well.

CHAPTER 1 | Don't Drink and Mountain Climb

N ear-death experiences are sobering, even when you've had too much whiskey to drink. During my freshman year in college, my fraternity brothers and I took a weekend road trip to Boone, North Carolina, to visit one of the local tourist attractions, Linville Falls—located on the Blue Ridge Parkway about thirty minutes south of Boone. Staff at Linville Falls say the falls were used by local Native Americans to execute criminals. Reportedly, no one has survived a plunge over the final section of the falls.

My memory is fuzzy because of the shots I thought would be a good thing to drink after breakfast, but I remember rock climbing and taking pictures on top of a cliff with more than a hundred-foot drop. Always the life of the party, I ignored the caution signs and crossed a fence in order to stage a funny picture near the drop. I hung my feet over the cliff and raised my hands into the air as if I were falling. "Quick—take a picture!" I called.

Suddenly, I slipped and began to fall. Just before I plummeted to the rocks far below, my right hand grabbed a rock.

I was instantly sober. My mouth was so dry I could barely swallow. Sharp pain flooded my arm as my right hand clenched a large rock with jagged edges above my head. The roaring sound of the water crashing on the rocks of Linville Falls overwhelmed all other sounds except the pounding of my heart. With one hand holding the rock above and the other hand dangling below, I looked down with a helpless feeling and thought, *That's it. My life is over.*

I needed someone to save me, but it was too late. I had fallen too far.

My right arm and hand grew numb. Just as I was about to let go, I looked up one more time and saw the face of hope. Kevin, one of my closest friends and my fraternity brother, reached down to grab my hand. What I couldn't see was that two other fraternity brothers, including my future brother-in-law, Jim, had created a human chain and were holding Kevin's feet so that he wouldn't fall off the cliff. These brave friends risked their own lives to pull me back to the top of the cliff and save my life.

I could have easily died that day, and I shudder to think of the amazing journey and adventure I almost missed out on living.

Missing Out on Real Living

One of my greatest adventures has been working full-time for Campus Crusade for Christ, a Christian organization that tries to help students grow spiritually on college campuses. Each year, we survey college students, asking them two questions: Who is Jesus? What do you believe is the message of Christianity? Year after year, many answers confirm some of the major misconceptions people have about Christianity.

College students are the next generation of leaders of our communities, our churches, and our country, yet most of them reject

Christianity. According to a recent study, their number one reason is a lack of authentic Christians among their peers.[1]

I was on campus with a student named Daniel recently, conducting a spiritual interest survey using artistic photographs taken by college students. We met a student named "Kristen" who stopped to chat with us. Daniel asked Kristen to pick out a photograph that best represented her spiritual life, and she chose a picture of a man passed out on the floor in a train station.

When asked about her choice, Kristen said, "All of my life, my parents made me go to church when I didn't want to go. Yet all of my friends who went to church were hypocrites. They said they were Christians, but then they didn't act anything like Jesus. When I came to college last semester, I wanted to get as far away from church as possible. So I joined a sorority and started living a lifestyle that I knew my parents would never want me to live. Now I think I might be an alcoholic. When I go to class every day, I can't stop thinking about how I want to be back in my dorm drinking."

Kristen was a beautiful young woman, if you looked past the dark circles beneath her eyes. She had long brown hair that curled around her shoulders and a tanned complexion. The look of exhaustion and hopelessness on her face, however, made her look several decades older than her nineteen or twenty years.

"Can you pick a picture that best describes what you *wish* were true?" Daniel asked. She pointed to a photograph of a little girl laughing and running, holding a cluster of balloons. Looking at the picture, Kristen replied, "She seems so happy. I wish I were that happy, but I usually feel miserable. I want to find a relationship with God that will bring me joy and happiness like that little girl is feeling."

Kristen's boyfriend was standing next to her, conducting his own survey. When he heard her say she was miserable, his attention turned toward Kristen. "What? I don't make you happy?" he asked her. Kristen stared back at her boyfriend and answered, "No, you don't make me happy. No one makes me happy. I feel miserable and frustrated with my life." She looked upset, as if she was about to cry.

At that instant, Kristen's boyfriend took her hand and led her away. His face was red and mottled, probably from a mixture of fear, anger, and embarrassment. As they walked off, I heard him say, "Come on. We don't have time for this. We need to go study." Kristen glanced back, almost desperate, as if she wanted to stay and talk, but she allowed herself to be pulled away from the table and into the crowd of busy college students.

My heart was heavy. Kristen was living the same kind of lifestyle I experienced while in college, and she seemed ready to turn to God to find the happiness she desired. Her glance toward me as her boyfriend led her away reminded me so much of the helplessness I felt as I hung over the cliff that day at Linville Falls. The difference was that someone had rescued me and then pointed me toward Jesus. No one was there for Kristen, and her boyfriend seemed determined to pull her away from anyone who could help her find God. I never saw Kristen again.

Working in full-time campus ministry for nearly a decade, I have met many "Kristens"—students tired of living their lives in their own strength, desperately searching for significance, purpose, and happiness. Many of these students believe there is be a God, but they remain skeptical of Christianity because they haven't met a Christian their age who seems authentic and honest.

Few college students can say that they've met a Christian who fits the definition of authentic Christianity given by Ty, a student at Morehead State University: "Sadly, authentic Christianity is something that most people never see. I didn't see it until college, and I grew up in the church. When it is lived out, you see peace, vulnerability, and an authentic love for God and for others that can only come from Jesus."

I wish I wasn't part of the problem, but unfortunately I spent years living as a hypocritical Christian who turned others away from God. I was part of the problem.

I was fortunate to have grown up in a home with parents who loved Jesus and did everything they could to model an authentic relationship with him. When I was twelve, I attended a summer camp where the message of Christianity was clearly explained to me. I recognized that I was separated from God and that I desperately needed a Savior. One night alone in my room, I prayed and asked Jesus to come into my life. I was willing to do anything to follow him. I even sensed that professional ministry would be in my future.

However, as time passed, the worries and busyness of life distracted me. My schoolwork and my football, basketball, and baseball commitments consumed my time and thoughts. Upon graduation from high school, I planned to attend Clemson University in South Carolina, and after that I hoped to go to graduate school so that I could earn a lot of money.

During my first semester at Clemson, I pledged a fraternity and quickly found myself living a lifestyle I knew wasn't right. There was a massive divide between how I lived and what I claimed to believe, and the difference was incredibly frustrating. Something had to give. One night soon after my near-death experience at Linville Falls, I prayed, "Lord, please help me. I'm tired of living *my* way. I don't have any Christian friends and don't know where to start. *Please help me.*"

God answered my prayer when I met a young man named James who was on staff full-time with Campus Crusade for Christ.

He was starting a Bible study for guys in fraternities and asked if I'd like to be a part of it. For the next three years, James mentored me. He showed me what an authentic walk with Jesus looks like. Slowly but surely, my life began to change. The lifestyle I was living that almost sent me over the edge of Linville Falls was replaced by a devotion to Jesus. As I spent more and more time with Jesus, reading the Bible and praying, my faith grew, and I began to experience a relationship with God that was real and deeply satisfying—far more so than the hypocritical years of distraction and partying!

The fundamentals of authentic Christianity that James taught me during those years are the same principles that every believer needs to understand and practice. An intimate relationship with God, nurtured by these fundamentals, is the only way that we can become the men and women God intends. A Christian life that doesn't look any different from the world's way of living is falling far short of the fulfillment and happiness that God longs for us to have—and it is probably turning off people to God's good news as well!

Before we explore these fundamentals in the following chapters, however, it's important to understand *why* intimacy with God is so important. We're bombarded by countless messages each day about what we should do and where we should go. There's only one person who knows what is best for us and who knows the best way for us to get there.

We're All on a Journey

When I was a teenager, I attended a youth retreat at the YMCA Blue Ridge Assembly outside of Asheville, North Carolina. I went on a day hike with some friends up the mountain, and I was enjoying the view from the top. These mountains were named the Black Mountains because of the surrounding dark spruces and firs, and in the distance we could see Mount Mitchell, the highest peak east of the Mississippi. The sun looked like it would be setting in two or three hours. Realizing I was late for an event with my group at the conference center down below, I decided to hike back down by myself.

From the top of the mountain, I spotted a path that looked like the path I had used earlier. A couple of hours later, I reached the bottom of the mountain, only to discover the conference center was nowhere to be found. I figured it had to be close and searched for another hour. By this time, it was dusk. I knew if I retraced my steps, it would be dark before I reached the top of the mountain.

When a teenage boy from Alabama is alone for several hours in the Appalachian Mountains, he starts to believe every rustling of bushes or leaves is a charging bear—or something worse. I was beginning to feel a rising tension in my stomach. Every few minutes, I heard a stick snap or a bush rustle twenty or thirty feet from me. I felt that same feeling I had as a child when I would dash to my bed at night, diving under the covers to prevent the monsters under my bed from grabbing my feet. I could feel my heart pounding through my chest, and I tried to keep my mind from imagining there was a bobcat walking in circles around me, slowly closing in for the kill.

After what seemed like an eternity, I stumbled upon a house in the middle of the wilderness. A beat-up truck sat in front of the house, deer antlers decorating its hood. By this time it was almost nightfall. Either I could risk getting eaten by a bear in the dark, or I could take a chance that someone in that house could help me.

I knocked on the door and thought I heard the sound of glass shattering inside the house. The door flew open, and a man with a rugged face and the longest beard I'd ever seen emerged from the shadows. I explained in a trembling voice that I was looking for the YMCA Blue Ridge Assembly. He burst out laughing like a hungry hyena.

Then the man picked up his keys and walked out toward his truck. "Well, ya coming?" he called. I walked slowly toward the truck and opened the door, not entirely sure what I was getting into. "How in Sam Hill did you get clear over here?" he asked. "The Blue Ridge Assembly's more than an hour away. I sure hope I have enough gas."

An hour later, we arrived at the camp, despite my fears that he was driving me deeper into the woods. I gave him some gas money, thanked him, and as he drove off I wondered if he was an angel of the Lord.

Have you ever thought you were heading toward the right destination, only to find yourself completely lost? We wonder what our careers are supposed to be, which friends we should choose, who we're supposed to marry, and what our purpose is in life. Sometimes the only thing that seems certain is that we don't know what to do!

Yet we often put on a face of false confidence and pretend to know where we're going. We pretend to be people we're not, walking with a swagger deeper and deeper into the woods.

This lack of authenticity spills over into our spiritual lives. Because we don't want people to think less of us, we put on the mask of a much wiser and more authentic Christian than we are. Instead of asking questions and trying to learn like children, we act as though we know all the answers. Other people see right through this however—when our pious prayers don't translate into action the next day, our authentic witness withers and blows away. Jesus knew we'd struggle with this, which is why he commands us to take off our masks and get real: *Truly I tell you, unless you change and become like little children, you will never enter the kingdom of heaven.*

Every year, many students ask me what it means to be an authentic Christian. One of the best places to discover an answer is Matthew 19. Jesus had just entered the region of Judea, and large crowds were following him. He healed people, and everyone was in awe of his power. Excitedly, a rich young ruler came to Jesus and asked what he needed to do to have eternal life. Jesus said, *"If you want to be perfect, go, sell your possessions and give to the poor, and you will have treasure in heaven. Then come, follow me."*

The rich young ruler walked away sad, but that doesn't have to happen to us.

To become authentic followers of Christ, we must count the cost of being a disciple. Jesus demands that we give him what is most important to us, and he promises in return to give us a life of confidence, purpose, and joy. For the rich young ruler in Matthew 19, money mattered more than anything, and Jesus called him out. Our cost may be popularity, or pride, or self-indulgence. Mine—revealed that day at Linville Falls—was my worldly lifestyle and alcohol abuse. Whatever Jesus is calling us to give up, we can be sure of this: we'll never be authentic Christians until we smash our idols, turn our backs on the pieces, and walk toward Christ.

What in your life is keeping you from taking steps of faith with God?

Counting the cost of following Jesus and then deciding to follow him may involve changing our lives. Habits, friends, hobbies, schools, significant others—letting go of any of these *may* be part of the cost. What would this look like for you?

A few years ago, I went to a country in central Asia on a mission trip. This country was primarily an Islamic nation, hostile toward America and Christianity. I was amazed to meet some college students who had decided to follow Jesus despite persecution and hardship that most of us couldn't even begin to imagine. One young man told me that he hid his Bible every day from his parents, because if they found the Bible, he would likely be executed for his faith. A young woman whose father was a government official shared that her father had beaten her unconscious on numerous occasions because she professed to be a Christian. These students count the serious cost of following Jesus every day of their lives—and still they choose to follow him with joy.

If we clearly understood the joy and peace found by following Jesus every day, the decision to be an authentic Christian would be easy. Perhaps the blatant persecution suffered by some Christians in our world clarifies the issue. For us, the distractions of this world and the temptation to do things on our own make the right decision harder.

Like Kristen, the student whose story we discussed earlier in this chapter, we fill our lives with unhealthy relationships and damaging lifestyles in search of satisfaction and significance. When these things don't fulfill us, we look for something greater. A crisis may cause us to search for God, but we forget that we don't have to wait for something bad to happen to seek him. People who have authentic Christian faith understand that the cost is worth it, because the life that God has for them is so much more rewarding than anything they had to leave behind.

Thankfully, Jesus is waiting to be found when we look for him. *"Ask and it will be given to you; seek and you will find; knock and the door will be opened to you."*

Everything we hear from the world tells us that the direction of our lives is up to us. There are as many human opinions about what brings happiness as there are humans—no wonder there are so many people who feel lost in the woods! Only our Creator, the One who made us *and* the world we live in, knows the destination that will bring true joy and satisfaction and purpose. He sent his Son to show us and to walk beside us along the journey.

Being Honest with Ourselves

It isn't enough to be honest about the destination of our life and to count the cost of following Jesus. To do these things, we have to be honest about who *we* are, or else we'll be chasing a truth with a lie.

Unfortunately, being completely authentic in our relationships is nearly impossible. We fear that if our friends knew our struggles or our faults they would desert us. It wasn't always like that, however. As children, we were all completely authentic. We didn't worry about what people would think about us when we cried in public places. We didn't care if our diapers were dirty when we were at restaurants or grocery stores. We were who we were, and we didn't bother trying to hide it. We said what was on our minds and didn't try to edit our thoughts.

One summer when my son Wyatt was three years old, our family spent six weeks in Fort Collins, Colorado, attending training provided by our employer, Campus Crusade for Christ. To save money, we decided to rent an apartment with some close friends of ours, Ron and Celia. Ron and Celia had a son, "Little Ron," who was born within a few weeks of Wyatt, and these two boys quickly became best friends.

That summer, Wyatt and Little Ron became quite popular in our apartment complex. Every day while our families were in the apartment, the two boys would stand outside on our second-floor balcony and holler happily at people down below, asking them their names, what they were doing, and why they were doing it.

One day while "Big Ron" and I were chatting in the living room of our apartment, solving all of the world's problems (in our minds only, I'm sure), our boys were out on the balcony as usual. At one point, I noticed that it was unusually quiet outside. What did I see when I opened the door to the balcony? Two bare bottoms of two little boys with pants pulled down to their ankles!

I quickly discovered both boys were urinating off the balcony and watering the flowers below.

Needless to say, Wyatt and Little Ron got into big trouble for that incident, but Big Ron and I burst out laughing together after we disciplined the boys. There was something authentic and carefree in how our boys were acting. Boys will be boys! They weren't concerned with what people thought—they were simply being themselves!

How far that often is from our realities! Most of us worry about people's reactions. Somewhere along the line, we've been hurt by someone who didn't love us unconditionally. We try not to attract too much attention, hoping to avoid criticism—or we overcorrect the other way and attract way too much attention. We create false selves, hoping to control how other people treat us, all the while keeping our true selves hidden. To ensure we are not hurt again, we push relationships aside—including our relationship with God—or pretend to be someone who's stronger, more intelligent, more faithful, and more respectable. The end result is that our lives are based on lies and that real joy and peace will forever escape us.

Wyatt and Little Ron "let it all hang out," and we need to do that, too. Not literally, of course—I think that's illegal! But we need to figuratively "let it all hang out," building relationships with God and others in which we present our honest selves. This means we can, perhaps for the first time in our lives, open up and share our hopes and dreams, as well as our successes and failures. Authentic Christianity begins with authentic people who are willing to be themselves, relate with real love toward others, and—most importantly—enjoy a genuine relationship with God.

We need to ask ourselves: Is my relationship with Jesus authentic? Am I experiencing the life-changing power of Christ in my life? Am I too busy to notice? Do I care more about my family, my schoolwork, or my job than who Christ is in my life? Choosing to follow of Jesus many years ago doesn't automatically mean we are experiencing God in our lives right now. The Holy Spirit produces fruit in the lives of authentic believers: *love, joy, peace, forbearance, kindness, goodness, faithfulness, gentleness, and self-control.* Do those words describe us?

The book of Revelation tells the story of the church in Laodicea—a church that was struggling with authenticity. To them, Jesus said, *"Look at me. I stand at the door. I knock. If you hear me call and open the door, I'll come right in and sit down to have supper with you"* (MSG).

Is Jesus knocking in your life? If so, read on to find out what it means to be an authentic follower of Christ. The first step of authentic faith might be the hardest, because most of us don't understand that it changes every other aspect of our lives. Don't miss out on learning the importance of spending time with God, because time is the most precious gift God has given us while we're here on earth!

CHAPTER 2 | Real Relationships Take Time

Have you ever had a good plan go very, *very* wrong?

One spring evening when I was eighteen, my parents left town for the weekend, leaving me in charge of the house. Two of my buddies, "Bill" and "Carl," had been over playing card games with me, enjoying a parent-free evening. We decided to stock up on frozen pizzas at the local grocery store in our small town of Valley, Alabama. Bill and Carl ran in while I waited in the car.

Suddenly an old friend approached and asked if I could give him a quick ride home. I hesitated because I knew "Tim" was trouble. I hadn't seen him since we played summer baseball a few years earlier. Since then, Tim had been in and out of a juvenile detention center for selling drugs.

I fumbled for words and said, "I don't know, Tim. We just stopped to get some pizzas."

Tim pleaded, "Oh, come on, Chad. We're old friends. I only live five minutes away. You'll be back before they're done shopping."

I looked at Tim intently, searching for any indication of dishonesty in his face. *Should I trust him?* Finally, I said, "All right, get in the car."

Tim directed me to a nearby neighborhood where many of my friends and classmates lived. *I didn't know Tim lived here,* I thought to myself. As we pulled in front of a house with no lights on, Tim barked, "Stop the car. Stay right here!"

He left the door open as he rushed into the darkness. I thought I saw Tim crawling into some bushes in front of the house. Everything was silent except for the typical Alabama night sounds of chirping crickets and croaking tree frogs. A minute or so passed before I saw a shadow emerge from the bushes.

"Let's go!" Tim exclaimed as he jumped into the passenger's seat and slammed the door. He had a large video camera in his hands, and he placed it down at his feet. At that time, video cameras were very expensive, not to mention heavy and the size of a sewing machine.

Bewildered, I asked, "Go where? I thought I was taking you home."

Tim replied, "That *is* my home. My dad just gave me this video camera for Christmas, but I need to sell it. I need some cash. I came to get it after dark because I didn't want to hurt his feelings by letting him know I'm selling it."

Although I didn't believe Tim's explanation, I didn't know what to do. Tim had a history of violence, and I wasn't sure how he would react if I didn't do what he wanted. Even though I had other options, at that moment I made a decision to play along with Tim because it seemed the easiest thing to do.

Finally, after I insisted we return to the grocery store, Tim and I arrived to pick up Bill and Carl. As they approached, a station wagon suddenly pulled in front of my car.

A nicely dressed middle-aged man ran to my passenger-side door. He opened the door, grabbed Tim by the arm, and lifted him out of the car. The man looked down at me and asked in an angry voice, "What is that video camera doing in your car?"

I paused, not knowing what to do or say. Everything seemed to be happening so quickly, and I was trying to figure out the right answer to this man's question. I glanced at Bill and Carl, who were standing a few feet behind the man, but they, too, looked dumbfounded. In an innocent-sounding voice, Tim responded to the man, "That's his video camera. He was just giving me a ride home."

The man continued to look at me for an answer to his question. *He must be Tim's dad*, I thought to myself. The man asked, "Is that true? Is that your video camera?" I nodded, figuring it was easier to play along with Tim than to tell the truth.

At that moment, Tim jerked his arm from the man's clutches and took off running. The man started shouting and running after him. Bill, Carl, and I looked at each other in astonishment.

Bill asked, "What in the world was that all about?"

"That was crazy! Just get in the car, and let's go back to my house."

On the ride home, I was relaying the story of what happened during my adventure with Tim when we passed nine police cars, with their blue lights flashing, on the side of the road.

Bill shouted, "Drug bust! Somebody's busted!"

We all started singing, "Bad boys, bad boys, whatcha gonna do? Whatcha gonna do when they come for you?"

As we passed the cluster of police cars, one of the police officers pointed his finger at us and started shouting. All of the police officers jumped into their cars and sped after us!

Bill, Carl, and I were taken to the police station. One of the officers knew my father, who was a pastor in our small town. He said that we were in serious trouble, that I was an accomplice in a robbery, and that I would have to bring my father to the police station the next day for a statement. The next day, the top story on the local news reported that Tim was involved in a shoot-out with a number of police officers. Fortunately, no one was hurt, and Tim surrendered.

When my father returned home, we headed to the police station. I felt ill when I discovered who would be taking my statement. It was the nicely dressed man who had approached my car the night before at the grocery store and had run after Tim. He explained he was an undercover cop, not Tim's father, as I had foolishly thought. After I gave my statement, this officer shared that my story lined up perfectly with Tim's story. Fortunately, Tim had told the truth. The police officer also explained that the man whose house Tim had robbed was the father of one of my classmates. The son vouched that I was a good student whom he respected, and all of the charges against me were dropped.

And it all started with a plan to grab a stack of frozen pizzas!

I jeopardized my future by taking the easy way out with Tim. There were points all throughout the evening when I could have pursued truth and done what was right—but I didn't, because it seemed easier to go with the flow. I didn't realize at the time what I was jeopardizing: my scholarship to college, my future career, and, most importantly, my freedom.

You've probably never had to think about what to tell a police officer. Yet, in a similar way, we jeopardize our futures every day when we don't pursue the truth about God's plan for our lives. If I had known Tim's intentions, I would have steered clear of him that night. But what about God's plans? If we claim to believe that God exists, shouldn't it be our top priority to determine the truth about what God wants our lives to look like?

According to the Bible, there are two key truths about God that should concern us: God loves us, and God has a plan for us. And both of these take place in the context of a relationship with God, as we see in John 17:3. *"Now this is eternal life: that they may know you, the only true God, and Jesus Christ, whom you have sent."*

I used to fret over God's will for my life. Who should I marry? What career should I pursue? How should I spend my time? Eventually I learned that all of these concerns were insignificant in comparison to the overriding reason I was created: to be in a loving relationship with my Creator. When this relationship is solid, we can begin to understand every other area of life.

Oddly, however, we often want to know God's specific will for the details of our lives *before* we have a relationship with him. We cannot develop this relationship with God if we don't spend time with him. Instead of getting to know him intimately and understanding this purpose he has for our lives, we often neglect God's best and settle for what *we* think is best, which is always a poor substitute. We choose what *we* want, say a quick prayer, and hope God "blesses" what we already intend to do anyway.

Every day, we make relational choices that affect our lives and our relationship with God in some way. Some friendships lead us toward God, while others lead us away from him—and it isn't always our friendships with other Christians that lead us toward God, or vice versa! What matters is that Christ is at the center of all we do, including all our relationships. I've noticed that when I share Christ with others and see him work in their lives, my intimacy with Christ grows. That's why putting Christ in the center of all of my relationships is a good use of my time, and why spending time with God is the first of the fundamentals of authentic Christianity.

Often our greatest struggle involves spending time with God. Students have an almost unlimited number of ways to *not* spend time with God: video games, partying, social networking, watching porn, fantasy sports—the list goes on and on. All are unsatisfying substitutes for authentic relationships.

A few years ago, while I was on campus at Charleston Southern University passing out free water bottles to students, I met a freshman football player named Josh. We formed an instant friendship, and I began mentoring him. I recently asked Josh, now a junior in college, to share about his struggle to become an authentic Christian as he has learned to use his time wisely and invest it in a relationship with God. This is what he said:

> Throughout my high school years I tried to feed my heart with exciting but empty satisfaction. I would go from thing to thing, searching for that joy and intimacy that my heart desired. While in that search I suddenly found myself addicted to drugs, alcohol, sex, popularity, and everything else that the world had to offer me. I was the master of disguise when it came to hiding these things from my family and Christian friends. As time progressed, I became more and more disgusted with myself.
>
> In one of my meetings with Chad, I told him that something was keeping me from being in love with Jesus Christ. Because Chad's background was similar to mine and because he had mentored other guys like me, he always knew more about me than he would reveal and began to explain my situation to me. He began by asking the question, "How does a man get to know a woman and fall in love with her?" I responded with, "By spending time." He said the same thing is true about getting to know God and falling in love with him. He also said my battle with addictions couldn't be fixed by any self-help books

or doing anything on my own. In order for anything to happen, I would have to make Jesus not just my Savior, but also my Lord as I surrender my life to him. He said it is difficult to surrender my life daily to a God whom I barely know and am not in love with.

In the next few months as I spent more time reading my Bible and praying, I ended up giving Christ more divinity and began to love him deeply. I found that at this point I was able to surrender my addictions and struggles to him and him alone. I have to admit that setting time to spend with Christ in a disciplined manner is not easy, but it's vital to any Christian's pursuit of authenticity.

So is it simply spending real time with Jesus that leads to transformation? Let's look at what Jesus promises in John 15:5: *"If you remain in me and I in you, you will bear much fruit; apart from me you can do nothing."* The answer is yes—it is only when we spend time with Jesus, remaining in him, that we are transformed into people who bear the fruit of the Spirit in our everyday lives.

I just spent a week with Josh during a trip to New York City. I saw him lead four college students to Christ, and the day after he returned to his own campus he led his best friend of eighteen years to the Lord! Josh is beginning to have a huge impact on those around him, and it all started with a decision to spend time with Jesus and put Christ at the center of his relationships.

As Josh now knows, having an intimate relationship with Christ brings us joy and satisfaction that other activities can never bring. Time is the greatest treasure we have on earth, and we must consider how damaging it can be to passively waste precious time. If we are to live the life of joy God has planned for us, we must begin by changing the way we spend our time.

Keeping Good Time in Light of Eternity

My personal story is similar to Josh's story. While a college student at Clemson University, I desired an authentic walk with Jesus. However, it was years later before I began to understand the importance of spending time with God. After graduating from Clemson, I received a graduate degree from Georgia Tech and soon began working for a paper company in Chillicothe, Ohio.

I had a strong work ethic in grad school, and I took that work ethic with me to Chillicothe. Besides working over sixty hours per week, I somehow found time to be a leader in the youth group at church, a teacher in the children's program, a worship leader, and a Sunday school teacher. If that wasn't enough, my wife, Elizabeth, and I also found time to attend a Bible study with some other young couples at our church, and we had teenagers from the youth group over to our house two to three nights each week. Every hour of every day was filled with important work or church activities, and we felt proud that we seemed to be accomplishing so much with our talents and hard work.

After we lived in Ohio for a few years, I accepted a position with another paper company and moved to Macon, Georgia. Within several weeks of moving to Macon, I met a young pastor who was planting a church right down the street from our house. We decided to join his church and help him start a youth group, and I agreed to be a worship leader in the worship band. Once again, Elizabeth and I filled our schedules to overflowing with "good" activities. We had well-paying jobs, and things seemed to be going just great—but I bet you can guess where this story is headed.

About a year after we moved to Macon, Elizabeth and I began to feel worn out. I struggled to spend time with the Lord each week. My schedule was so hectic that many nights I would feel too tired to open the Bible. Prayer was difficult. Spiritually, I was starting to feel the effects of trying to do too much. I became impatient with Elizabeth and started to develop a critical attitude toward my boss and coworkers.

Guilt was quickly becoming my companion—guilt for these sinful behaviors, guilt for not continuing to do enough good things, and, to top it all off, guilt for not spending enough time with God! One night as I was spending time with the Lord, I confessed my sin. I heard a voice in my head telling me I should get up early the next morning to spend time with Jesus. For me, this was a tough request because I was already getting up early to get to work by 6 a.m. However, I was so tired of my guilt and frustration that I decided to listen. I got up early the next morning and spent time with Jesus, reading and listening and praying. My soul felt so refreshed and revived that I got up early again the next day . . . and the next day . . . and the next day.

Over the next six months, I spent time with Jesus the first thing in the morning nearly every day. Slowly I became a more joyful person, and friends and coworkers commented on how much more of a peaceful, loving person I had become.

It was during that time in my life that I began to understand a bad habit in my life that was keeping me from having an authentic relationship with God. For several years, I had been so busy "doing" Christian activities that I had stopped enjoying "being" in a relationship with God. I had been so focused on helping others know Christ that I stopped growing in my own personal relationship. In other words, my overriding purpose of being in a loving relationship with God was being forgotten while I tried to be a hero and help others.

What I learned during that time in my life is that any "Christian activities" I do are going to be hypocritical if I don't truly know

God. Everything has to start with a genuine relationship—and when my relationship with God is real, I can't help but share him with others!

Later that same year, Elizabeth and I sensed a calling to full-time college ministry. Perhaps that calling was already there, but we hadn't taken the time to listen to God and develop real intimacy with Him. With God at the center of our daily lives, the calling became clear, and our passion grew to help college students discover authentic Christian faith. The next year, we joined staff full-time with Campus Crusade for Christ.

What if I had never learned the importance of spending time daily with the Lord? For one thing, you wouldn't be reading this book! Listen to what Paul says to the church in Romans 12:1–2 (MSG):

> So here's what I want you to do, God helping you: Take your everyday, ordinary life—your sleeping, eating, going-to-work, and walking-around life—and place it before God as an offering. Embracing what God does for you is the best thing you can do for him. Don't become so well-adjusted to your culture that you fit into it without even thinking. Instead, fix your attention on God. You'll be changed from the inside out. Readily recognize what he wants from you, and quickly respond to it. Unlike the culture around you, always dragging you down to its level of immaturity, God brings the best out of you, develops well-formed maturity in you.

Are you beginning to see the importance of relationship to authenticity? A real relationship with God isn't just a good thing—it's the *only* thing!

Josh, whose story was told earlier in the chapter, recently asked if he could stop by my house. I had a million things to do, but I told him to come on over, trusting that prioritizing relationships was the right thing to do.

That night Josh opened his heart to me. He shared his spiritual concern for his father and brothers and how he cried almost every day for them. We prayed together, and at the end of the prayer, Josh gave me a hug and told me he loved me as a spiritual father. On his way out the door, he thanked me for my time and said it meant the world to him. If I hadn't stopped what I was doing to spend time with Josh, I would have missed out on the joy I received from our time together.

What God-given joy are you missing out on?

Think of the events that have shaped you and defined you. How many did you see coming ahead of time? For me, I think about a recent knee surgery I had to undergo because of an old football injury. I had just finished a busy and intense semester working on campus and had to stop everything to have the surgery. Little did I know how badly I needed to slow down and just enjoy God, my family, and life! Though I experienced pain and suffered from the surgery, I felt the Lord restore me spiritually as I came to him for rest. Jesus says, *"Come to me, all you who are weary and burdened, and I will give you rest."*

Do you hear his voice calling us to rest in him? When we rest in Jesus, we remember that spending time with him and sharing our lives with others are the things that last for eternity. Listen to Jesus's words from Matthew 6: *"Don't hoard treasure down here where it gets eaten by moths and corroded by rust or—worse!—stolen by burglars. Stockpile treasure in heaven, where it's safe from moth and rust and burglars. It's obvious, isn't it? The place where your treasure is, is the place you will most want to be, and end up being"* (MSG).

There's no activity we can do on this side of heaven that is as important as spending time with Jesus and leading others toward him. I don't say that to sound legalistic—it's simply true. Remember, we shouldn't tell others about Jesus just because we think we have to, or we feel guilty, or we want to add another "Christian" activity to our resumé. Everything starts with our relationship with Jesus. We spend time with him first, and everything follows from that.

Jesus invites us to spend time with him: *"Let anyone who is thirsty come to me and drink. Whoever believes in me, as Scripture has said, rivers of living water will flow from within them."*

Spending time with the Lord is also personal and intimate. If we didn't spend time with our friends, our spouse, or our family, we would never develop intimacy with them. And it takes time. In one of Jesus's parables, a man had a fig tree planted in his vineyard. He went to look for fruit on it but did not find any. He said to the man who took care of his vineyard,

> *"For three years now I've been coming to look for fruit on this fig tree and haven't found any. Cut it down! Why should it use up the soil?"*
>
> *"Sir," the man replied, "Leave it alone for one more year, and I'll dig around it and fertilize it. If it bears fruit next year, fine! If not, then cut it down."*

Spiritual growth doesn't happen overnight. It takes time. The only thing that can produce spiritual growth is an intimate relationship with Jesus, and only by spending time with him can we discover that intimacy.

Before we end this chapter, I'd like to share a few tips I've learned over the years that can make it easier to spend time with Jesus. You don't have to do all of these, but let's be honest—spending quality time with another person requires us to be intentional, so tips like these may be exactly what we need to help us spend our precious time in the best way:

- Try to spend time with God every day, and at the beginning of the day if possible. Talking to God throughout the day and before bed is great as well, but when we start the morning in the presence of God, it can transform the rest of our day.

- Come with a spirit of expectancy and obedience. Like any relationship, listening is vital, as is a willingness to change. As Max Lucado has famously said, "God loves you too much to leave you exactly the way you are!"
- Remember that God speaks to us through the stories, prayers, letters, and poems of the Bible—so read all of it! It's easy to dwell on only familiar passages, or to skip around almost at random, looking for passages that happen to appeal to us. But God is a big God, and *the whole will of God* (Acts 20:27) has something to teach us.
- A relationship isn't a race, so take your time. Some people pride themselves on covering a certain number of chapters each day, or praying for a certain number of minutes. But God may be asking you to read a single verse over and over for a month!
- Prayer is a conversation with God, and we can't have a relationship without it. There are many kinds of prayer, too: praise, thanksgiving, confession, asking for understanding, praying for the needs of others . . . the list is almost endless. The important thing, as in any relationship, is to keep the focus on God and to keep it real.
- Keep a prayer journal. In a blank journal or notebook, write down the prayers you've prayed and the prayers that have been answered. Your faith will grow as you see God answer your prayers!
- Finally, don't forget that the intimate time you spend with God has *everything* to do with the rest of your day! Whether you're walking to class, studying for your calculus exam, texting the cute sophomore in the front row of

your history class, or heading out for a night on the town, *take what you learned in your time with Jesus with you.*

But what if we don't even *want* to spend time with God? There are times in my life that I have gone through dry spells and have lost the desire to know Christ better. During those times we can pray and ask the Lord for the desire to spend time with him, and he will rekindle this desire according to a promise he gives in 1 John 5:14–15: *This is the confidence we have in approaching God: that if we ask anything according to his will, he hears us. And if we know that he hears us—whatever we ask—we know that we have what we asked of him.* We know beyond any doubt that God's will is for us to remain in him and to spend time with him. When we pray according to his will, he answers our prayers and gives us that desire.

This is one reason that it is important to have committed Christian friends. If we are going through a time where we find it hard to desire God or to spend time with him, our friends can help us. Ask a friend to meet you for breakfast every week and commit to memorizing a verse together each time. Request prayer from a friend. Buy a buddy a coffee, and ask him what God has been teaching him lately. All of this will reinforce your desire to spend time alone with God.

As you begin to spend regular time with Jesus, no doubt you will begin to crave a deeper understanding of God and what it means to live a Spirit-filled life, which is the topic we'll look at next. What is your understanding of the Holy Spirit? Have you ever experienced an entire day when you've felt the Lord guiding you and directing you? How much confidence would you have that you are in the center of God's will if you felt God's presence and direction for an entire month? Let's explore the answers together.

CHAPTER 3 | Striking It Rich!

I n 1915, entrepreneur and Texas rancher Ira Yates traded his thriving dry-goods store in Rankin, Texas, for a huge ranch on 16,640 acres. By 1926, his ranch was losing money fast—and he was about to lose everything. In a desperate attempt to stay afloat and provide for his family, Yates convinced Transcontinental Oil Company to drill on his ranch. Everyone said that was a fool's errand that far west, but Yates had no other choice. After a few exploration wells, the drillers began their final hole, having found no oil.

That final hole hit the edge of the largest oil deposit in Pecos County, thereafter known as the Yates Pool. Ira Yates had been living in poverty for more than a decade, while hidden beneath his property was a resource worth tens of millions of dollars. Almost overnight, Yates became one of the richest men in the country.[1]

Ira's problem wasn't that he didn't *have* what he needed—it was that he didn't *know* he had what he needed.

Sound familiar? If you're a Christian, you already have the power of the Holy Spirit . . . but it may be hidden, waiting to be discovered and used.

When a person decides to follow Christ, he or she experiences a rebirth as the Holy Spirit becomes part of that new life.

He saved us through the washing of rebirth and renewal by the Holy Spirit, whom he poured out on us generously through Jesus Christ our Savior.

The Holy Spirit, God himself, offers us power beyond measure. *For the Spirit God gave us does not make us timid, but gives us power, love and self-discipline.* However, if a new Christian doesn't understand or experience this power, he or she will live a life of spiritual poverty and bankruptcy.

Understanding and experiencing the Holy Spirit is vital to traveling toward authentic Christian faith. It's like my car parked in the driveway. There have been numerous times I've been ready to leave for work, only to realize I'm missing my car key. My car possesses all the power I need to get to work on time, but without the key, all of that power is untapped.

The Holy Spirit is our key.

The Holy Spirit's Job Description

Although I started to follow Christ at the age of twelve, I spent the next seven years living as a frustrated, defeated, and fruitless Christian. I lived in spiritual poverty, not knowing the vast resources of God available to me. As a young believer, I viewed Christianity as more of a religion than a relationship with God. Instead of feeling encouraged after visiting church, I often left overcome with guilt because of how often I succumbed to the temptations of the world. Sometimes I would repent and turn away from my sins, but my "spiritual high" lasted only until my own strength ran out. Christianity seemed like a roller-coaster ride of good times and bad times.

In college, when I finally began to live in the endless resources of God's love, I felt like Ira Yates after he struck it rich! Once I discovered the life-changing power of the Holy Spirit, my

Christian life became about trusting in God's strength instead of my own effort, and my relationship with God became rich, intimate, and fruitful.

For example, seven years ago, Elizabeth and I experienced the loss of a child when she miscarried. There was no way we could have experienced joy and peace through that difficult circumstance on our own. When we placed our trust in God and prayed, asking him for peace and comfort, the Holy Spirit delivered, giving us a peace, joy, and comfort that went beyond human ability or understanding. God was already there for us, waiting to be asked.

Remember how we looked at relationships and discovered that we cannot make them a priority unless we first make it a priority to be honest and authentic with ourselves and with others? In the same way, we cannot truly experience the power and joy of the Holy Spirit in our lives unless we first have a general understanding of who the Holy Spirit is and why He was sent to us.

After the resurrection of Jesus, he promised his disciples a helper for when he was gone. When he ascended to the Father, the Spirit was sent to continue his work on earth—loving, healing, transforming, empowering—through those who follow him. The Holy Spirit, our promised helper, is the Spirit of God, fully God as Jesus is fully God. On the night of his crucifixion, while still in the upper room, Jesus said to his disciples, *"But the Advocate, the Holy Spirit, whom the Father will send in my name, will teach you all things and will remind you of everything I have said to you."*

This promise was kept when the Holy Spirit came into the believers' lives on the day of Pentecost. *Suddenly a sound like the blowing of a violent wind came from heaven and filled the whole house where they were sitting. They saw what seemed to be tongues of fire that separated and came to rest on each of them. All of them were filled with the Holy Spirit and began to speak in other tongues as the Spirit enabled them.*

Our lives may seem pretty far removed from the multilingual chaos of that day of Pentecost two millennia ago, but the Holy Spirit is as active as ever. This takes many shapes in our lives as believers, so don't get discouraged if it takes you awhile to understand or experience all of these roles in your life. I've been growing in my relationship with God for many years, and I'm still learning new things about the Holy Spirit every day. If we were writing a job description for the Holy Spirit, it would look something like this:

1. *Convicting us of our sins.* The Holy Spirit convicts both the unbeliever and the believer of sin. Without his conviction, we wouldn't know how badly we need a Savior. *"When he comes, he will prove the world to be in the wrong about sin and righteousness and judgment"* (John 16:8).

2. *Baptizing and regenerating.* In simple terms, this means we become new people when we receive Christ into our lives. We become alive spiritually. *Therefore, if anyone is in Christ, the new creation has come: The old has gone, the new is here!* (2 Corinthians 5:17).

3. *Indwelling.* When we experience new life in Christ, the Holy Spirit actually comes and lives inside of us for the rest of our lives to guide us and help us. *And you also were included in Christ when you heard the message of truth, the gospel of your salvation. When you believed, you were marked in him with a seal, the promised Holy Spirit, who is a deposit guaranteeing our inheritance until the redemption of those who are God's possession* (Ephesians 1:13–14). The Spirit of God permanently indwells all believers in Christ (John 14:16–17; Romans 8:9).

4. *Revealing truth to us.* The Holy Spirit inspired the men who wrote the Scriptures (2 Timothy 3:16; 2 Peter 1:20–21), and he reveals what those Scriptures mean as we read the Bible (1 Corinthians 2:10–16). Only the Holy Spirit can

give us the insight we need as we read the Word of God, and only the Holy Spirit has the power to help us apply these truths to our lives.

5. *Praying on our behalf.* Because we do not always know what we ought to pray for, the Holy Spirit intercedes for us and talks to God on our behalf as we pray. However, later in this chapter, we will discuss the need for intimacy with the Holy Spirit in order to have this intercessory prayer take place. *And he who searches our hearts knows the mind of the Spirit, because the Spirit intercedes for God's people in accordance with the will of God* (Romans 8:27).

6. *Helping us bear fruit.* The fruit of the Holy Spirit in our lives is *love, joy, peace, [patience], kindness, goodness, faithfulness, gentleness, and self-control* (Galatians 5:22–23). We cannot bear fruit without the Holy Spirit working in our lives. Jesus says, *"If you remain in me and I in you, you will bear much fruit; apart from me you can do nothing"* (John 15:5).

7. *Gifting.* The Holy Spirit gives different spiritual gifts to different Christians in the body of Christ. The purpose of these gifts is to glorify Christ and to help build others in their faith, not simply to satisfy ourselves (1 Corinthians 12).

Worshiping in the Spirit and in Truth

While I was in college, my relationship with Jesus became more intimate, and I began a diligent search for his truth. Of course, I could explain it the opposite way: I searched for God's truth and my relationship with Jesus became more intimate. This circularity highlights an important reality of a Spirit-led life, discussed by Jesus when he spoke with the Samaritan woman at the well.

In this story found in John 4, Jesus was traveling through a place called Samaria. He sat down by a well and got into a conversation with a Samaritan woman and told her, *"If you knew the gift of God and who it is that asks you for a drink, you would have asked him and he would have given you living water."* He said, *"Everyone who drinks this water will be thirsty again, but whoever drinks the water I give them will never thirst. Indeed, the water I give them will become in them a spring of water welling up to eternal life."*

By this, Jesus was referring to the Holy Spirit. The truth is God's Word, but intimacy with God comes from the Holy Spirit. As Jesus was explaining what he meant when he said he had *"living water,"* he told the Samaritan woman that simply knowing the truth isn't enough for us to experience eternal life. He said, *"A time is coming and has now come when the true worshipers will worship the Father in the Spirit and in truth, for they are the kind of worshipers the Father seeks. God is spirit, and his worshipers must worship in the Spirit and in truth."*

Clearly, then, we need to worship and live in the Spirit and in truth. We need both the fire of the Holy Spirit and the light of the Word of God (the truth). However, there have been times in my life that I have put too much emphasis on one and too little on the other. I would describe myself during these times as being either a truth-centered believer or a Spirit-centered believer, and both extremes are hazardous to an authentic Christian life.

When I struggle with being a truth-centered believer, I tend to focus solely on sound biblical doctrine, and so fail to rely on the power of the Spirit of God inside me. I often succumb to the temptation of living the Christian life in my own power, becoming "religious," focusing on the rules, and constantly noting who else is righteous and who else is failing.

When I struggle with being a Spirit-centered believer, I become preoccupied with the subjective benefits of my faith, such as spiritual gifts, rather than focusing on the person and plans of Christ. I sometimes glorify the gifts of the Giver more than the

Giver of the gifts. Just as overemphasis on truth leads to the pride of knowledge and personal effort, overemphasis on the Spirit can lead to the pride about my own spiritual gifts—even when I'm too busy being spiritual to actually use them!

Rather than vacillating from one unhealthy extreme to the other, we need to become followers of Christ who worship in the Spirit *and* in truth. This is what Jesus was saying when he was talking to the woman at the well.

When power and truth, experience and explanation, manifestation and maturity are combined, Christ is glorified.

Filled with the Holy Spirit

One of the most common descriptions of the Holy Spirit in the New Testament church is being *filled with the Holy Spirit*. When I first heard this term as a freshman in college, I felt skeptical—it sounded pretty weird! In fact, I was tempted not to write about "being filled with the Holy Spirit" in this chapter because it's seldom used in our postmodern culture. However, the fact remains that this term is used frequently in the Bible. If we are to study and understand what the Bible says about the Holy Spirit, we must understand what this phrase means.

And it gets even weirder. Paul gives the command to the Ephesians: *Do not get drunk on wine, which leads to debauchery. Instead, be filled with the Spirit.* In this verse he uses a present-tense imperative verb that could be more explicitly translated, "Be continually being filled with the Holy Spirit," thus implying that this is something that should repeatedly be happening to Christians—and when we're repeatedly filled with God, we can expect God's sort of things to start happening in our lives.

In his book *Systematic Theology*, Wayne Grudem writes, "It is appropriate to understand filling with the Holy Spirit not as a one-time event but as an event that can occur over and over again in a Christian's life. It may involve a momentary empowering for a specific ministry, but it may also refer to a long-term characteristic of a person's life. In either case, such filling can occur many times in a person's life."[2]

The New Testament distinguishes between the *inward work or filling of the Holy Spirit* and the *outward work or filling of the Holy Spirit.* The former produces Christlike character and spiritual maturity. When I'm inwardly filled with the Holy Spirit, my life looks quite different, as my wife can attest! I'm patient with the kids, I don't get stressed out as easily, I love to sit on the porch and talk to God, I'm filled with joy and inner happiness, and I love other people, including those who aren't believers or are hard to love. In short, I'm the man I want to be!

When I'm not being filled inwardly with the Holy Spirit, however, things start to go wrong. I lose patience quickly, snap at my family, try to do everything in my own strength (and fail!), worry about the present and the future, consider only myself, and turn my back on other people, especially non-Christians. Without the inward filling of the Holy Spirit, I'm a mess!

The outward work or filling of the Holy Spirit involves divine empowerment for ministry and service. Whether God is equipping me for a one-time ministry or challenge, or whether he is giving me a gift with which I can serve for my whole life, certain characteristics define God's work. When I am outwardly filled with the Holy Spirit, I can sense him leading me to pray for certain people; I am filled with God's love, which overflows to others in ministry and relationship; and when I share Christ with others, I am authentic and patient, and I allow them to be the same. Holy Spirit-led ministry is the only genuine kind, and through it we will bear fruit without burning out.

When I try to do this kind of outward ministry on my own, my focus is often on my needs instead of the needs of others. I lack authenticity because I don't care about others as much as I care about myself, and when I try to share Christ with others, I simply toss a load of spiritual truths at them, without discerning whether they are open to spiritual things or how I can love them first. Such self-powered ministry is *never* what we're called to as Christians!

You Can Be Filled with the Holy Spirit

Faith, which is trust in God and his promises, is the only way a Christian can be filled with the Holy Spirit. Spiritual breathing is a powerful word picture that can help you experience moment-by-moment dependence upon the Spirit[3]:

> *Exhale*: Confess your sin the moment you become aware of it—agree with God concerning it and thank him for his forgiveness, according to 1 John 1:9 and Hebrews 10:1–25. Confession requires repentance—a change in attitude and action.

> *Inhale*: Be filled with the Holy Spirit. Surrender control of your life to Christ, and rely upon the Holy Spirit to fill you with his presence and power by faith, according to his command (Ephesians 5:18) and promise (1 John 5:14–15).

As you seek to be filled with the Holy Spirit, there are three important questions you must ask yourself. You're not just trying out the latest diet or a new study schedule—you're readying yourself to be filled by the very Spirit of God! When you think you are ready, ask yourself: Am I ready now to surrender control of my life to our Lord Jesus Christ (Romans 12:1–2)? Am I ready now to confess my sins (1 John 1:9)? Do I sincerely desire to be directed and empowered by the Holy Spirit (John 7:37–39)?

If you answer all three of these questions with a yes, claim the fullness of the Spirit according to his command and promise. God commands us to be filled with the Spirit (Ephesians 5:18), and God promises he will always answer us when we pray according to his will (1 John 5:14–15).

Sincere prayer is one way of expressing our faith. The following is a suggested prayer for praying to be filled with the Holy Spirit:

> *Dear Father, I need you. I confess that I have sinned by directing my own life and living on my own strength. I thank you that you have forgiven my sins through Christ's death on the cross for me. I now invite Christ to take his place at the center of my life. Please fill me with the Holy Spirit as you commanded me to be filled, and as you promised in your Word that you would do if I asked in faith. I pray this in the name of Jesus. I now thank you for filling me with the Holy Spirit and directing my life.*

As I've learned to pray this prayer often—every time God reveals sin in my life—I've found myself growing closer to him. As I stated earlier, I didn't learn everything about the Holy Spirit and how to experience him in my life all at once. At first when I discovered what it meant to live a Spirit-filled life, I simply prayed and asked God to direct my life. As I've done this over and over through the years, I've come to understand and love the Spirit more and more. I no longer have to live in spiritual poverty, and I no longer have to try to live the Christian life on my own strength. I can trust in and rely on the unlimited power of the Lord.

Don't live like Ira Yates, so near to a source of power that was completely hidden from him. If you are a follower of Jesus, now is the time to call on the power of the Holy Spirit to help you live an authentic, God-directed life!

CHAPTER 4 | A Conversation with the Creator

About a year ago, I received a phone call from Nelson Akwari, the team captain of our local professional soccer team, the Charleston Battery. He shared with me that he had previously been involved with Athletes in Action, a Campus Crusade for Christ ministry for athletes. He felt the Lord had called him to Charleston to play for the Battery. He wasn't aware of any other Christian players on the team, and he needed help getting a ministry for the team started. Nelson asked me if I would consider being the team chaplain.

At the time that Nelson called, my work plate was full. I was leading a growing staff team, raising funds for our ministry, mentoring college guys, traveling to multiple campuses, and fulfilling dozens of other professional obligations. However, I told Nelson the same thing I've learned to tell everyone who asks me to help them with a project: "I'll pray about it and see if the Lord would have me drop something else in order to help you start a new ministry."

During the next month, I prayed and sought counsel from a number of Christian leaders in the Charleston area to learn their thoughts regarding this new ministry. The overwhelming response was that I should accept Nelson's request since God had opened a door.

As I evaluated the responsibilities on my plate, I prayerfully decided to postpone a time-consuming project that had hit a major snag—okay, more like crashed into a brick wall! After much prayer, the Lord granted me peace about waiting on him to open the right doors for this other ministry while I took a step through the giant door he had opened with the soccer team.

I contacted Nelson, and we immediately began meeting weekly to pray for God's wisdom and guidance. There were some huge barriers to overcome in order for us to move forward. The coaches and top leaders were skeptical about having a Christian ministry as part of the team. The season would be ending soon, and we weren't even sure Nelson would be retained. Instead of worrying about what might happen, we placed our faith in God and continued to meet and pray.

After the season, Nelson and I continued to pray for four specific things: that the Lord would provide another Christian on the team so that Nelson would have fellowship; that we would be able to start a team Bible study; that guys who weren't believers would be drawn to the Bible study; and that God would soften the hearts of the coaches and team administration and allow us to have a "Faith and Family" night during a game, where Nelson and other Christians could share Christ at the stadium.

During the off-season, the professional team in Atlanta, Georgia, the Silverbacks, folded, and a strong Christian player on that team moved to Charleston to play for the Battery. Then another young Christian player made the team, just in time for us to start a team Bible study during the first week of preseason. During the next few weeks, several other players began coming to the Bible study, and the team Bible study grew from three to nine!

Nelson recently called me with more good news. The team president has been having conversations with a local radio station about partnering together to co-sponsor a "Faith and Family" night during the season. Recently, we also discovered two of the players who come to Bible study each week are not yet believers, but they are interested in learning more about Christianity. Another player indicated that he gave his life to Christ earlier this season after getting involved in the Bible study!

God is as amazing as he is surprising!

By seeking God's wisdom, waiting for his clear direction, and then asking him to do specific things according to his will, I have experienced his goodness and love through this ministry with the Charleston Battery and have come to know him better.

When Nelson first contacted me to ask me for my help, my instinct was to decline because I had too much on my plate. However, when I prayed and waited for God's guidance, God called me to plant this ministry and then gave me the wisdom and powers I needed to make it happen, through being filled with the Holy Spirit.

It all starts with prayer. Prayer *is* communicating with God, but it's more than that, too. Prayer is an act of faith that God is who he says he is and can do greater miracles than we can ever imagine.

How we pray reveals our view of God and also affects our view of God. If we were truly convinced that *"everyone who asks receives; the one who seeks finds; and to the one who knocks, the door will be opened,"* then we would probably be praying all the time! This is why prayer is possibly the most essential ingredient in becoming a more authentic follower of Jesus, as we seek to see God as he truly is and promises to be.

Prayer Reveals Our View of God

Most of us can be classified as a cat or dog when we speak to God in prayer, a surprising insight I gleaned from a book I read recently.[1] A dog says, "You pet me, you feed me, you shelter me, you love me, you must be God," while a cat says, "You pet me, you feed me, you shelter me, you love me, I must be God."

Does that sound familiar? Cats pray for the things they desire, the things that will make life more comfortable and easier. John Piper has referred to this type of prayer life as a domestic intercom, by which a family can ask for requests from the kitchen. For example, the prayers of someone with cat theology usually begin with phrases like, "Dear Lord, please give me . . . please let me . . . please bring me."

Dogs, on the other hand, pray for the things God desires, the things that please him and bring glory to him. Someone with dog theology would pray: "Father, let *your* glory shine in this sickness. Allow *your* glory to shine in how I'm treating my parents, my spouse, my kids."

As I reflect on my life, I realize for years I was more like a cat in the way I viewed God—that he existed to serve me. Of course, I never said this out loud, but this internal view revealed itself in the way I prayed. Even in Sunday school classes, we rarely prayed for God's wisdom but were quick to pray for instant healing for our sicknesses or our family members' sicknesses. When I was in college and began spending personal time with Jesus, I usually prayed for myself, that I would do well on tests, but rarely prayed for my friends in my fraternity who didn't know Jesus.

However, several years ago, after studying the Lord's Prayer in Matthew 6:9–13, I realized I wasn't following Jesus's model for prayer. I felt led to start my prayer time at least once per day by praying the Lord's Prayer slowly in my own words. If you've been stuck praying cat prayers, perhaps the following model will help you.

"Our Father in heaven, hallowed be your name."

Praise God for his attributes. Think about his goodness for a moment. When God created the heavens and the earth and the land and water in Genesis 1, he said it was good. What would this world be like if we could not experience God's goodness? What are things God has done for you that you have taken for granted? Thank him! Praise him for his attributes he doesn't share in common with others, such as his omnipresence, unchangeableness, and sovereignty. Also praise him and acknowledge the attributes we can experience and take part in, such as his knowledge, mercy, justice, and love.

Over the years, by putting God first in my prayers and saying, "Hallowed be your name," I've found myself praying less and less for myself during times of trials and spending more time praising him. Recently I had my seventh major knee surgery from old football wounds. It was my worst surgery yet, and I experienced complications of deep vein blood clots after surgery. I personally felt like God was using the surgery and pain to refine me, and I felt led to give him praise and thank him for the trial each day. In the midst of the pain, I experienced joy and satisfaction in my relationship with Christ.

That's the kind of thing that sounds crazy from the perspective of the world. Praising God and thanking him for intense, ongoing pain in my knee? Come on! But in reality—in God's reality—it's perfectly possible. An authentic relationship with God transforms everything. We have to count the cost of following Christ, but we shouldn't forget to count the blessings!

"Your kingdom come, your will be done, on earth as it is in heaven."

This part of the Lord's Prayer is an opportunity to reflect on his will. You may read Scripture to meditate on his will communicated through its pages, or you may just pray for his will based on the Scripture you already know. For example, it's his will that you have wisdom in your decision making because James 1:5 says, *If any of you lacks wisdom, you should ask God, who gives generously to all without finding fault, and it will be given to you.* You also know he loves everyone in the world because John 3:16 says, *For God so loved the world that he gave his one and only Son, that whoever believes in him shall not perish but have eternal life.* Spend time praying for people you believe don't know the Lord.

An example of praying for God's will to be done is the story of how I started a new ministry with the Charleston Battery soccer team. At first, my will was to tell Nelson I had too much on my plate and didn't have time to help him start a ministry with the team. However, as I prayed, "Your will be done," the Lord placed on my heart the idea to put a project that wasn't going anywhere on hold. When we pray, "Your will be done," the Lord will guide us in our prayers and reveal his will to us.

"Give us today our daily bread."

Pray for the Lord's provision as well as for his desire for justice in the world. Praying for his provision may mean asking the Lord to put food on your table, or it may mean providing a job or enough money for college. Praying for God's justice is praying for his provision and healing for others in the world. It's God's will that we care for the orphan, the widow, and the immigrant. It's also his will that broken families are healed, that oppressive political and corporate systems end, and that the rich share their wealth with the less fortunate.

As we pray for justice, it's only a matter of time before the Lord starts putting ideas into our minds on how we can be a part of bringing his justice to the world. This is an area in which I've grown a lot these past few years. Praying this prayer every day will help us grow in our compassion for the needy, and compassion will move us into action. When Elizabeth and I moved to Charleston several years ago, the Lord used our growing compassion to lead us to join a church that helps the needy. Our local church was planted in a part of town where the crime rate was the highest. During the past three years, we've seen the crime rate drop 30 percent in the part of town where our church is located, and many hearts have been transformed by Christ and the compassion of his followers.

"Forgive us our debts, as we also have forgiven our debtors."

Think for a moment, and ask God to reveal any sin in your life that you haven't confessed to him. Sin grieves God and causes our fellowship with him to be broken. Take some time and confess your sin to God. *If we confess our sins, he is faithful and just and will forgive us our sins and purify us from all unrighteousness* (1 John 1:9). This time of confession gives the Lord the opportunity to reveal sin you haven't thought about yet.

Next, spend time reflecting on whether or not there are others you haven't forgiven. If the Lord reveals someone to you whom you haven't forgiven, pray and ask God to help you forgive that person. Ask him if you need to talk to that person. More often than not, an action point you will take from this prayer is sitting down with someone and sharing how he or she has hurt you, or sharing with someone else how you have hurt him or her.

"Lead us not into temptation, but deliver us from the evil one."

There is a spiritual battle taking place around us at all times, and the apostle Paul tells us there are spiritual forces of evil trying to distract us and discredit us as we follow Christ: *For our struggle is not against flesh and blood, but against the rulers, against the authorities, against the powers of this dark world and against the spiritual forces of evil in the heavenly realms.* When we give in to the temptations of the world, we lose our authentic faith and become hypocrites who push people away from God. Therefore, we must pray daily for the Lord to help us in this spiritual battle.

Several years ago, a spiritual battle was taking place on one of the college campuses where I serve in ministry. I confronted a young man because I found out he was being abusive to a female student on campus. This young man didn't appreciate being confronted, and he did everything in his power to discredit our ministry on campus. He made up lies about the leaders in our ministry and even met with someone in the administration in an attempt to have us removed from campus. I prayed with our student leaders, and we asked the Lord to help fight this spiritual battle for us. In the end, the administration took our side, and the reputation of our ministry became great as a result of how we handled this conflict. We believe the Lord rescued us from harm because we turned to him and prayed during this spiritual battle.

A common thing I've seen when students on campus pray the Lord's Prayer is that they make decisions based on what they feel the Lord wants them to do rather than on what they *want* to do. Earlier this year, two freshman girls, Ashlyn Reeves and Ashton Schultz, approached me about a decision they had made. Ashlyn had just begun a relationship with Jesus, and Ashton had recently recommitted her life to the Lord.

Both girls were living off campus at home because it was so much cheaper than living on campus. It was a huge financial sacrifice to move onto campus, but Ashlyn and Ashton felt the Lord was leading them during their prayers to live on campus. This is what Ashton said to me as she was processing the difficult decision:

"Chad, I want to share something the Lord has been doing in my prayer life. I have grown spiritually so much this year, and I know I wouldn't have grown so much if I hadn't had an older sister in Christ mentoring me and helping me to grow. I've also grown so much in the area of prayer as I've attended our prayer meetings. I feel like the Lord is calling me to live on campus and be a good big sister in Christ to the freshman girls next year.

I've been praying all year, asking God if it was his will for me to live on campus. At first my parents weren't supportive. They thought living on campus was a waste of money because we lived so close to the school. I continued to pray and ask God to give me a clear answer. During our student leadership retreat, the Lord spoke to my heart during my prayer time and made it clear he was leading me to live on campus. Once I was sure God was leading me in that direction, my parents started praying about it. Chad, God has changed their hearts, and they are now sure I should live on campus just in time for me to sign up for housing. He is always right on time! I know it will be a sacrifice, but I'm convinced this is what the Lord wants me to do."

Did you catch that last part? Ashton was praying for God's will to be done in her life, and she was listening to him. As a result, both Ashlyn and Ashton moved onto campus this fall, and they have had a huge positive impact. Ashlyn just led a freshman girl to the Lord a couple of weeks ago!

When I was young, the Lord's Prayer was recited and prayed every Sunday during our church service and every Friday night before each football game. The prayer became mundane because I didn't think about what I was saying. However, as I have learned to pray the Lord's Prayer in my own words, the prayer has taken on meaning. The prayer has become authentic. I encourage you to read it in as many versions as you can find and then to pray it in your own words. Make it your own, and you'll see it begin to transform your days. After all, Jesus taught us this short, powerful prayer for a reason.

There are other formats people use when they pray, and reading books on prayer can be very helpful. The important thing is that when we pray, we put God and his will first. When we begin to pray in a way that puts God first, thus revealing who we say God is, our view of God is affected for the better, and our lives are transformed.

Prayer Affects Our View of God

The way we pray and the things we say to God during our prayers ultimately answer the great faith question: *Can I trust God?* When we pray believing the answer to that question is yes, God moves in a way that is very clear to us, helping us to trust him more and grow deeper in our faith—and it all starts with the way we pray: *your* kingdom come; *your* will be done.

Kenneth Boa describes the difficulty of letting go by saying, "We want control and security on our terms, yet the Scriptures tell us that the only true security comes from abandoning the illusion of control and surrendering ourselves unreservedly to the person and purposes of God."[2] We're used to controlling our own lives, and nothing fires up our passions more than the chance to control something—or times when we understand we have *no* control.

After all, God created us to be passionate. That's why it's so easy to get passionate about football, having a boyfriend or girlfriend (or the thought of having one), and getting good grades in school. Because passion is in our DNA, the best way to combat the passions of this world is by passionately pursuing Christ, fighting passion with passion.

There was a time in my life when I was an *overly* passionate Clemson Tigers football fan. I followed the recruitment of high school players. I counted down the days to National Signing Day when high school seniors filed letters of intent, binding their commitment to play football at a particular school. When that day arrived, I studied the players to figure out how good they were and dreamed about how they would one day be future football stars at Clemson. If a potential "star" chose another school over Clemson, I felt devastated. These were only eighteen-year-old high school seniors who weren't even Clemson students yet! I am still a passionate Clemson fan, but I've learned to draw boundaries that prevent eighteen-year-old football players from affecting my joy in the Lord!

As we begin to grow in our prayer times and focus more on God, we become more passionate about his purposes. As the Bible says, we are transformed by the renewing of our minds. This is seen in the book of Job, which I once thought was a book about suffering but now realize is a book about God, his sovereignty, and his trustworthiness.

In the first chapter, God gave Satan permission to test Job. Job lost all of his wealth and then lost his children in a horrible accident. When he found out about the loss of his children, he tore his robe, shaved his head, and then fell to the ground in worship and said, *"Naked I came from my mother's womb, and naked I will depart. The LORD gave and the LORD has taken away; may the name of the LORD be praised."* Job realized his life was not all about himself, but that the purpose of our lives is to glorify God.

As you grow in your prayer life, be careful that your prayers are Christ centered, not self-centered. Listen to these words God spoke to Job and his friends at the end of the book of Job:

> *"Where were you when I laid the earth's foundation? Tell me, if you understand. Who marked off its dimensions? Surely you know! Who stretched a measuring line across it? On what were its footings set, or who laid its cornerstone—while the morning stars sang together and all the angels shouted for joy? Who shut up the sea behind doors when it burst forth from the womb, when I made the clouds its garment and wrapped it in thick darkness, when I fixed limits for it and set its doors and bars in place, when I said, 'This far you may come and no farther; here is where your proud waves halt'?"* (Job 38:4–11)

Prayer reveals our view of God, whether we praise him and seek his will, or whether we simply present a wish list of personal wants. As we learn to pray God-centered prayers, our view of God is affected, and soon we come to see that his way is the best way. Our passion for God burns brighter and brighter as we trust him in faith and watch him fulfill what he promises. As we move toward prayer that is more authentic, God centered, and trusting, we discover something amazing—our faithful prayers can change the way the King of the Universe acts!

Prayer Can Move God

After Elizabeth and I decided the Lord was leading us to be in full-time Christian work with Campus Crusade for Christ, our most difficult task was to resign from our full-time jobs and trust God to provide for our salaries as we raised support for our ministry. Little did we know that this step of faith would take us to the next level of intimacy and faith in God! I am so thankful to God that he gave us front-row seats to see him provide for our family in miraculous ways!

One of my favorite stories from our support-raising adventure occurred a few nights before Christmas. Our job while we were raising support was to find people who had a heart for college students and missions and to share our ministry with them. It was difficult getting appointments with anyone during the holidays, and one evening Elizabeth and I were feeling discouraged. Raising the support money we needed was going slowly, and we wanted to finish so we could report to campus and begin our ministry. We prayed together one afternoon that the Lord would provide for us.

That night, as we were preparing to go to bed, the phone rang. When Elizabeth picked up the phone, a man's voice on the other end said, "Is this Chad and Elizabeth Young's residence? I'm a truck driver out here on the interstate, and I was just listening to Bill Bright talk about Campus Crusade for Christ on the radio. Then someone on my CB started talking about your ministry and said they supported you financially. I just became a Christian recently, and I feel like the Lord was telling me in my heart that I should start giving to your ministry financially."

Elizabeth was shocked. No one had ever *called us* out of the blue to tell us they wanted to support our ministry, much less a truck driver who randomly heard about us on his CB radio. She thought it might be a prank call but took a deep breath and said, "Would you like me to tell you about our ministry?"

"Naw," the man said, "I trust ya. Just tell me where to send the check each month."

This man ended up becoming a very dear friend of ours. We've been there for him during a couple of times of crisis he has had, and he's been there for us when we've had tough times. His story is one of many reminders to us that prayer affects the way God acts.

James tells us, *You do not have, because you do not ask God.* By saying this, he is implying that our failure to pray deprives us of what God was ready to give us. Jesus said, *"Everyone who asks receives; the one who seeks finds; and to the one who knocks, the door will be opened."* In this verse, Jesus is saying that when we pray and ask, God responds.

We see this happening many times in the Old Testament. When God sent Jonah to Nineveh to warn them that God was about to destroy them, the people of the city listened to Jonah and led a citywide fast, dressing in burlap to show their repentance. *When God saw what they did and how they turned from their evil ways, he relented and did not bring on them the destruction he had threatened.* When God threatens to punish his people for their sins in 2 Chronicles, he declares, *"If my people, who are called by my name, will humble themselves and pray and seek my face and turn from their wicked ways, then will I hear from heaven, and I will forgive their sin and will heal their land."* If and when God's people humble themselves in repentance and pray, *then* he will hear and forgive them.

Does this mean God always gives us everything we pray and ask for? Of course not! Chances are we won't get a million dollars or a brand-new car if we pray for them. God *does* promise, however, that when we pray according to his will, he will give us what we ask of him. *This is the confidence we have in approaching God: that if we ask anything according to his will, he hears us. And if we know that he hears us—whatever we ask—we know that we have what we asked of him.* That's why it's important to pray, *"Your* will be done," and not, "Send me the answers to my English final"!

We've already spent some time looking at how we can use the Lord's Prayer to guide the time we spend with God each day. As we get ready to move on in our journey toward authentic Christianity, I'd like to share a few tips with you that I've learned over the years. Perhaps some of these will help you in your own prayer life, just as they have helped me.

- **As you pray, maintain an attitude that says, "*Your will be done.*"** This is the way Jesus taught us to pray in Matthew 6:10, and he himself gives an example when he prayed in the garden of Gethsemane, *"My Father, if it is possible, may this cup be taken from me. Yet not as I will, but as you will"* (Matthew 26:39).

- **Pray continually throughout the day, as commanded in 1 Thessalonians 5:17.** This doesn't mean you shouldn't talk to anyone but God. It just means you should try to develop a lifestyle of praying often while you are alone and also praying with friends as you spend time with them. A habit I've developed is often to turn off my radio while I'm driving in order to talk to God, and I also try to pray as I walk back and forth across campus.

- **Be full of faith as you pray.** Remember when you ask something according to his will, you know that he hears you and that he will answer you. The Lord wants us to have faith and believe he can answer our prayers. *But when you ask, you must believe and not doubt, because the one who doubts is like a wave of the sea, blown and tossed by the wind* (James 1:6).

- **Obedience is a key to effective prayer.** Since prayer involves a personal relationship with God, anything in our lives that displeases him will be a hindrance to prayer. Imagine if your boyfriend or girlfriend wanted to chat with you, but only moments earlier he or she had done something that really hurt you! The psalmist says, *If I had cherished sin in my heart, the Lord would not have listened* (Psalm 66). Confession of sin, which involves agreeing with God and turning away from sin, is necessary before we can fellowship with him.

- **Spend time waiting on the Lord and listening to him.** What if I asked someone to come over to my house to have dinner with my family, but then before they could answer me, I rushed off? It sounds ridiculous, but that's how we are sometimes when we pray. We pray and ask the Lord to give us wisdom about something, but then we don't wait on him to lay an answer on our hearts. The psalmist writes, *LORD, I wait for you; you will answer, Lord my God.* Sometimes, in order to allow the Lord to speak to our hearts, we simply need to sit in silence while we are praying.

- **Be humble as you pray, and if you pray with others in a group, don't feel obligated to pray out loud.** It's normal to feel uncomfortable praying out loud when others are present. It's just as effective when you agree silently with someone else who is praying out loud.

- **Last but not least, be thankful and full of praise toward God.** The Lord's Prayer begins with: "*Hallowed be your name*" (Matthew 6:9), and that's how we should always begin. Thankfulness should not be shallow or hollow but should reflect a deep appreciation of what's in our hearts. Practice writing a list of things for which you're thankful.

As my prayer life has become more authentic, I've realized more and more that God is relational. In other words, he created us to have a personal relationship with him, and he loves to have conversations with us! I don't have to be eloquent in my conversations with him. I can talk to him as if I'm talking to a friend or my wife, Elizabeth.

As your occasional prayers become more of a daily habit, your love and concern for other people will grow. In the next chapter, we'll discuss the important role relationships with other believers play in our lives. They not only provide encouragement and accountability, but also join us on exciting adventures as we live with passion and joy!

PART 2 | The Second Great Commandment

Love Others as Yourself

And the second is like it: "Love your neighbor as yourself."
—the Gospel of Matthew

In order to truly be authentic, we must value healthy relationships more highly than we value work or any other activities. We must love others as much as we love ourselves—and not just the people in our lives we know, but also the people in the world we don't know. When we reach a point where we are helping others anonymously, or at least unselfishly with God as our only audience, we have reached a place in our lives where we are truly being authentic.

CHAPTER 5 | **An Epic Fireworks Battle**

Several summers ago, unintentionally, I almost found myself in big trouble with the law! Elizabeth and I were helping to staff a summer project with Campus Crusade for Christ in Daytona Beach, Florida, and I was leading a Bible study with five great college guys. One night, we decided to ask another men's group to participate in a "creative battle" with us. We picked the group with the strongest men and challenged them to an epic battle.

That Friday night, twelve men, including me and my college guys, jumped into a few cars and headed to the nearest fireworks store. We purchased bottle rockets, Roman candles, and protective eyeglasses. Because we knew it was illegal to shoot fireworks inside of Daytona city limits, we headed toward a secluded park just outside of town. We knew we were in for a memorable night.

What we *didn't* know was that an armed robbery would be occurring directly across the street at a convenience store!

We had a wild time shooting Roman candles at each other, running for our lives, and doing our best gunpowder-aided *Braveheart* impressions. Bright lights flickered in the dark, and young men screamed as balls of fire whizzed past their heads.

Suddenly, a booming voice yelled, "Stop what you're doing! Put your hands in the air!"

While we were busy shooting fireworks, a police SWAT team had arrived at the convenience store to investigate the armed robbery. Hearing what sounded like gunfire across the street, they surrounded the park and closed in on us. Fortunately the police recognized pretty quickly we weren't the armed robbers they were hunting! They set us free, told us to be careful, and allowed us to return to our hotel.

For the record, I can't officially recommend that you try any of the above activities. (Unofficially, however, it was a pretty cool idea!)

Despite the SWAT team and threat of a real gun battle—or perhaps because of them—the twelve of us guys became like family that night. We bonded, and we genuinely loved each other. While it doesn't take shooting fireworks at others to create authentic, lasting friendships, real Christian community is an essential element of living a Christ-centered life that is honest, passionate, and full of joy.

We Need Each Other

If we try to walk the road toward authentic Christianity alone, we'll miss out on the adventure and joy of traveling with friends. One of the greatest travelers of the New Testament, Paul, had many traveling companions along the way, such as Barnabas, Silas, Timothy, and many others. Like Paul, we must find at least one person who can travel alongside us during each stretch of our journey.

One of the reasons we need each other is that God has designed us to be relational. We're made to have real friends, friends who may even stick closer than our own brothers and sisters, and relate to those friends at the deepest level of emotional and spiritual reality.[1] We can't be healthy individuals unless we're part of a healthy community.

Why is our need to bond with others so strong, and why can our failure to bond lead to a disaster for our emotional well-being? The answer can be found by studying God and his attributes.

God is a relational being, and he created a relational universe. He exists and always has existed in relationship. He is three persons in one—Father, Son, and Holy Spirit. This relationship we refer to as the Trinity is hinted at in the first chapter of Genesis when God says, *"Let us make mankind in* our *image, in* our *likeness"* (emphasis added).

Jesus also talked about his connection to the Father: *"I pray also for those who will believe in me through their message, that all of them may be one, Father, just as you are in me and I am in you. . . . I have given them the glory that you gave me, that they may be one as we are one—I in them and you in me."*

God is also love. *God is love,* writes the apostle John. *Whoever lives in love lives in God, and God in them.* When we understand that the foundation for our existence lies in relationship, we can understand our need for bonding and for loving friendships.

Thinking about that epic fireworks battle that summer, I can still remember the deep connection I felt with those guys in my discipleship group. I've kept in touch and have developed closer friendships with some of them. Without having deep friendships, I'd be missing a key ingredient needed for my own personal growth—and I help their lives grow, too. The ways in which we help each other in relationship are almost endless, but in this chapter we'll focus on four: we help keep each other safe, we help keep each other accountable, we encourage and comfort each other, and we experience the fun and adventure of God's plan together.

Stay Safe

When I was a child, I lived close to my paternal grandparents, Grandpa and Grandma Young. Grandpa fittingly was born in Hazard, Kentucky, a town some of us are familiar with because of *The Dukes of Hazard*. One of seven wild brothers, Grandpa spent a few years of my dad's childhood in the Ohio State Penitentiary for armed robbery.

When Grandpa Young was at home, my dad's safety was often in jeopardy. My father was just a few weeks old when Grandpa and one of his brothers used him to play "keep away" from Grandma out in the front yard. Dad was wrapped in a baby blanket and was tossed like a football while Grandma was yelling and screaming, trying to catch her newborn. Yes, this is a true story!

Grandma Young was the "safe haven" for my father, and it's likely he survived in this household because of her protection. One time, Grandpa shot my dad with a BB gun, and Grandma ran to rescue him. She snatched the gun from Grandpa, pumped it several times, and yelled, "How would *you* like it if someone shot *you* with a BB gun?!" She then shot Grandpa at point-blank range in the leg—way to save the day, Grandma!

Fortunately, most of us don't have grandfathers who are armed robbers, but we all need someone to protect us and keep us safe. As Paul states in Ephesians 6, there is always a battle taking place around us in a spiritual realm: *For our struggle is not against flesh and blood, but against the rulers, against the authorities, against the powers of this dark world and against the spiritual forces of evil in the heavenly realms.* We must have "teammates" who can pray for us and also be there for us when we are struggling spiritually, just as Dad had Grandma for protection, and I had my teammates to protect me during our epic fireworks battle.

Even Jesus needed and desired the safety of being in close proximity to his disciples. In Matthew 26, right before he was arrested, he took his disciples to the garden of Gethsemane to pray. His most trusted disciples, Peter, James and John, came with him even farther into the garden, where he fell with his face to the ground and prayed. Before Jesus began praying, he said to them, *"My soul is overwhelmed with sorrow to the point of death. Stay here and keep watch with me."*

Jesus understood the need to have companions who can "hold the wheel" for you when you cannot. The road toward authentic Christianity has many bumps, curves, and other hazards along the way. God created us as relational beings who need traveling companions to keep us safe and alert on the road.

The most practical way our friends can help keep us safe is through prayer. On one of the college campuses where I spend a couple of days each week, Charleston Southern University, students have embraced prayer. About a hundred students gather every Tuesday night to pray for each other as well as for other students on campus. Many students have prayer partners who meet them at breakfast each morning to pray together and spend time with the Lord. Students are falling deeply in love with the Lord on that campus as a result of prayer.

Be Accountable

Accountability involves opening your life to a few carefully selected, trusted, and loyal confidants, and then allowing them to speak truthfully to you about what they see. They have the right to examine, ask the hard questions, and give counsel. Preferably, these need to be people who help create a safe environment by loving you unconditionally.

In Galatians 2, Paul describes a time in which he provided this kind of accountability for the apostle Peter. *When Cephas came to Antioch, I opposed him to his face, because he stood condemned. For before certain men came from James, he used to eat with the Gentiles. But when they arrived, he began to draw back and separate himself from the Gentiles because he was afraid of those who belonged to the circumcision group. The other Jews joined him in his hypocrisy, so that by their hypocrisy even Barnabas was led astray.* Knowing how important Peter was to the authenticity of the early church, Paul felt compelled to help Peter get back on the road toward authentic Christianity.

I don't know about you, but I can think of countless times I've needed other people to help me get back on the road when I've lost my way. One of those many times occurred one night during my first semester as a college student. I was struggling to find the road toward authentic Christian faith, and I was at a fraternity party drinking too much alcohol.

A friend at the party who knew I was a Christian saw me intoxicated and approached me. "You call yourself a Christian, but look at how you're acting," she said. "You're not acting like a Christian!"

The embarrassment and conviction I felt the moment I heard her words were unbearable. I knew in my heart I was living as a hypocritical Christian, but this was the first time anyone communicated disappointment in me. Immediately, I left the party, went back to my room, and began to ask Jesus to change me, which became a turning point in my life.

Accountability to one another is healthy and helpful. When we are regularly accountable, we're less likely to stumble, more likely to see truth accurately, and less likely to get away with sinful and unwise actions.

Several men hold me accountable in the area of purity, making sure that I avoid sexual immorality and stay true to Elizabeth. A few others hold me accountable for how I use my money, and my boss holds me accountable by making sure I'm working hard in my job. A couple of close friends, including my boss, also hold me accountable by making sure I'm not working so hard that I'm neglecting my family. They make sure I always put family above ministry. Accountability to one another is both helpful and healthy in our pursuit to become more authentic.

Who in your life is holding you accountable? If you aren't sure, it's time to find someone. The road of life is too dangerous to travel on your own!

There are four qualities to look for in accountability: vulnerability, teachability, availability, and honesty. How willing are you and your accountability partner to be open and transparent? Are you willing to be teachable if he or she calls you out on something? Are you both willing to set aside time regularly to meet? Are you both willing to be completely authentic and honest?

If you find someone who has all four of these qualities and is someone you can trust to be confidential, invite them to lunch or coffee and discuss your need and desire for accountability. Tell them the areas of your life in which you need accountability, and ask them if they would be willing to meet regularly to help hold you accountable in those areas. Examples of areas in which you might need accountability include spending time with the Lord, praying, sexual purity, dating relationships, or any other area in which you might need help.

Encourage and Comfort

In the book of Job, our need for the encouragement and comfort from friends is emphasized. In one single day, Job lost his sons and daughters in a natural disaster, as well as his vast wealth of animals. Then, on another day, God allowed Satan to afflict Job with painful sores from the soles of his feet to the top of his head.

When Job's three friends, Eliphaz the Temanite, Bildad the Shuhite and Zophar the Naamathite, heard about all the troubles that had come upon him, they set out from their homes and met together by agreement to go and sympathize with him and comfort him. When they saw him from a distance, they could hardly recognize him; they began to weep aloud, and they tore their robes and sprinkled dust on their heads. Then they sat on the ground with him for seven days and seven nights. No one said a word to him, because they saw how great his suffering was. (Job 2:11–13)

I mentioned in chapter 3 that my wife, Elizabeth, and I were expecting a second child a number of years ago. Sadly, she miscarried, and we both felt deep disappointment. We continued to hope and pray we would have another child, and a few months later, we rejoiced when Elizabeth became pregnant again. As time passed by, we started dreaming about the birth of our new child and even started picking out possible names.

When Elizabeth had a second miscarriage, we were completely devastated and heartbroken. We took the day off work and just sat together in silence. We were too saddened to talk about it, but it was comforting to be together.

Do you know someone who could use encouragement? Perhaps a friend is struggling in school with his or her classes or is having a family crisis. Maybe you know someone who has just lost a close relative. Or perhaps you are going through a difficult time, and you're struggling emotionally. You are tempted to just hang out by yourself and try to get through this time alone, but you need the encouragement of a friend. When you're struggling, those are the times you must find someone who can be there for you to listen, comfort, and encourage.

Traveling companions are crucial to our journey. When the road toward authentic Christian faith hits tough terrain, we need traveling companions to encourage us and to point out the smooth pavement ahead.

Friends in Fun and Adventure

The final reason for friendship is simple: traveling alone just isn't as much fun as traveling with others! Growing up, I always had two best friends, Gene and Eric. We did everything together, and fun and adventure were our specialties. Every day after school, we played basketball and Ping-Pong at my church, and on weekend nights, we played cards for hours. High school baseball and football were shared activities. Gene and Eric joined my church and attended youth retreats with me. We even got tattoos together—Japanese symbols that stood for brotherhood—much to our parents' dismay.

When Elizabeth and I were married, I had two best men instead of one; I couldn't choose between Gene and Eric! Over the years, we've continued our friendship and have traveled great distances to spend time together.

Last year during spring break, I had the opportunity to go to Argentina on a mission trip. I knew mostly college students would be attending the trip, and I would be the only "old guy" there. So I gave Gene a call and said, "Guess what? You're going to Argentina with me!" Gene jumped at the opportunity. Not only did we experience Argentina together, but we also saw a young Argentine medical student place his faith in Christ. It's a memory we will not forget.

The abundant life—the life of fun, adventure, and a sense of fulfilled purpose—doesn't happen just by going to work or class, eating dinner, watching TV or playing video games, studying, and then going to bed. The God who created us in his image and breathed life into us never meant for life to be that mundane. We must find other believers who share our same interests and get involved! Join a community group or Bible study. Find a group of friends to hang out with on the weekends that knows how to have fun and live a life full of authentic faith at the same time. Take a road trip! Go on an overseas mission trip while you're young. When you have children, you may not have the same opportunities to travel. Get to know a neighborhood, and dream about how it could be transformed. Mentor a high school student. Nothing is more adventurous than real, authentic relationships, and nothing lasts longer.

The road to authentic Christianity is everything we could ever imagine and desire! In order to experience the joy of that abundant life, we must find other people with whom we can share our journey. Who knows? You may even find yourself taking part in an epic fireworks battle—but you didn't get that idea from me!—or some other adventure with stories to pass along to your children and grandchildren. And as you journey down the road, it is your authentic relationships that will keep you on the road and out of the ditch.

CHAPTER 6 | Living in a Ditch

I was fourteen years old when I ran away from home. My pal "Ben" and I had talked for weeks about living out in the woods on our own, but honestly it was just talk. We both knew that we were fortunate to have loving parents and that we'd be foolish to run away, but we continued to talk and dream about it.

One winter evening, however, our foolish dream became a reality after I made my sister late for a basketball game. My family waited in the car while I puttered around my bedroom, taking my sweet time. They decided to leave without me, and my father's last words became etched into my mind: "*You're going to be in big trouble when we get home.*"

After they pulled out of the driveway, I picked up the phone and dialed Ben's number. When he answered, I asked in a serious voice, "Are you ready? Tonight's the night. I'll be there in a couple of hours. Just be ready like we talked about."

After I hung up the phone and packed a small duffel bag, the reality that I was running away began to sink in. Something in my conscience tried to tell me to stop what I was doing and abort the plan, but I shrugged off those thoughts. As I started for Ben's house, I felt my heart racing as a newfound sense of adventure pushed me forward.

For the next hour, I stayed away from the main road through our small town. I knew that my sister would finish her basketball game soon and that my parents would travel back home on that road. I wanted to stay out of sight.

The back roads were familiar to me, but at least one dog was barking at me at all times. I was so tense my heart felt as if it would thump out of my chest. After an hour I arrived at a gas station. I figured my parents had gotten home by now and were looking for me. Finding a pay phone, I dialed Ben's number.

He answered in a hushed voice, almost whispering, "Hello?"

"It's me," I said. "Is everything okay on your end?"

Ben was silent for a moment and then said, "Gotta go. Your parents are looking for you. Get here as soon as you can." He hung up the phone.

Still only a quarter of the way to Ben's house, I knew I needed help to make it the rest of the way. Ignoring my parents' advice to never talk to or ride with strangers, I approached a man pumping gas and asked if he could give me a ride to the Wal-Mart near Ben's house. When the man questioned me and asked where my parents were, I told him that they were dead and that I lived with my elderly grandmother.

At first, he looked at me suspiciously, but then with a shrug of his shoulders, he said, "Sure. Hop in the back of the truck."

After hitching a ride, I walked the last stretch of road to Ben's house. I could see him in his driveway and moved toward him slowly. His eyes met my eyes, and he immediately shook his head and gave me a stern look. His dad walked out the front door and toward Ben.

I ducked behind a parked car and then into a ditch to keep his dad from spotting me. I lay in the ditch for what seemed like hours, waiting for Ben, but he never came.

At this point, reality began to sink in. It was a winter night, and I was in a ditch! The air grew colder and colder. It must have been below forty degrees, and my thin coat was next to useless. I thought about my loving parents and regretted my decision to run away. Exhausted from my journey, I drifted off to sleep.

A few hours later, at two in the morning, I awoke to the sound of an approaching car. Feeling disoriented, I thought my running away earlier was just a dream. As I came to my senses, I realized I was soaking wet from the dew, and I was still in a ditch! I so wanted to be at home in my warm, dry bed! As the approaching car slowed and stopped in front of Ben's house, I lifted my head curiously.

My mother's familiar voice called from the car: "Chad, is that you?"

My parents took me home, gave me some dry clothes, and sent me to bed. My mother didn't say anything that night about my running away, but my father and I had a short but sweet one-way conversation before I went to bed. I'll never forget the words my father said to me on that night:

> "Chad, your mother and I love you with all our hearts, and we have respect for your intelligence and your judgment. We are not going to punish you by turning this house into a jail. God has blessed us with two wonderful children and has given us the responsibility to bring you up in his loving way. That means we are your parents and do our tasks the best way we know. If you don't want us to be your parents anymore, we

can help you find other ones. That would be much better than you trying to run away or our keeping you locked up in the house. Now, if you run away again, you will have to suffer the full legal consequences of your decision."

Now that I am a father, I cringe to think about what I put my parents through that night. If my own son pulled a foolish prank like that, I don't know if I would respond as calmly and wisely as my dad did.

As I reflect on that night and the words of my father, I find it amazing how closely this true story parallels a Christian's spiritual journey. When we are seeking to travel the road toward authentic Christian faith, if we aren't careful, we may find ourselves stuck in spiritual ditches—ditches that make further progress and maturity impossible. There are two spiritual ditches we must avoid: the ditch of legalism and the ditch of license.

At times in our Christian lives, we may find ourselves jumping into one of these ditches without much thought, much like I dove into the ditch in front of Ben's house that night years ago. Eventually, we wake up and think, *How did I get here? When did I decide to jump in a ditch?* Fortunately, we have a loving Father in heaven, who doesn't want us to remain stuck. He gives us directions in the Bible about how we can stay on the path. Much like my wise father did the night I ran away, God warns us that there are consequences if we continue to live in the ditches, but he also gives clear instructions about how we can get out.

The Ditch of Legalism

The first ditch to avoid is the ditch of legalism. Anytime we make strict adherence to the law the only thing we really care about, we're practicing legalism. In our Christian faith, legalism means that we try to earn God's love and acceptance by doing good things or by not doing bad things. Paul warns us of this ditch by writing, *Are you so foolish? After beginning by means of the Spirit, are you now trying to finish by means of the flesh?* The trouble with legalism is that we'll *always* screw up at some point, and so will those we love.

What would our world look like if it were a model of loveless, graceless legalism? People who made one mistake in their jobs would be fired. Everyone who failed once would be condemned. All prison sentences would be for life. I shudder to think what would have happened to me growing up if my parents had not shown the grace of God. Even more frightening: every sinner would be eternally separated from God. *For the wages of sin is death.*

In his book *Changes That Heal*, Henry Cloud writes,

> When Adam and Eve were in the Garden of Eden, they had grace and truth united in one God. When they sinned, they drove a wedge between themselves and God; they lost their grace-filled and truthful relationship with God.
>
> Without grace, Adam and Eve felt shame: when they heard God walking in the garden in the cool of the day, they hid from Him. God called out, 'Where are you?' Adam explained that he was hiding because he was afraid (Gen. 3:8–10). Shame and guilt had entered the world; human beings were no longer safe.[1]

Do you know what we often do when we don't feel safe? We try to construct elaborate systems of laws and requirements so that we know what to expect and so that we feel in control.

In Romans 2–7, Paul writes to the Romans about truth without grace and the things it does to us. This dramatic series of verses shows the necessity of staying out of the ditch of legalism on our Christian journey!

> *You, therefore, have no excuse, you who pass judgment on someone else, for at whatever point you judge another, you are condemning yourself, because you who pass judgment do the same things.* (Romans 2:1)

> *Now we know that whatever the law says, it says to those who are under the law, so that every mouth may be silenced and the whole world held accountable to God. Therefore no one will be declared righteous in God's sight by works of the law; rather, through the law, we become conscious of sin.* (Romans 3:19–20)

> *Law brings wrath.* (Romans 4:15)

> *The law was brought in so that the trespass might increase.* (Romans 5:20)

> *Once I was alive apart from the law; but when the commandment came, sin sprang to life and I died. I found that the very commandment that was intended to bring life actually brought death.* (Romans 7:9–10)

When I first became a believer in Christ, I was very legalistic in the way I viewed myself and the way I viewed others. I attended church every Sunday and tried to be a good person, and I looked down on others who didn't go to church or try as hard to be good. I knew the Ten Commandments and took pride in following them. I based my sense of self-worth, and even my very faith, on whether I could always follow all the rules. This legalistic attitude caused me to experience a lot of guilt. Because I thought I had to be extremely good to please God, I always felt I was falling short. How good was good enough?

Sadly, I didn't even realize I was in the ditch of legalism. When I read the Gospels and the stories of the legalistic Pharisees, I was quick to look down on them, even though I was acting like one of them! It wasn't until years later, through Bible study and through the gracious modeling of wiser Christian friends, that I learned the truths necessary to get out of the ditch of legalism and back on the road toward authentic Christian faith.

Avoid Legalism by Giving and Receiving Grace

Grace gets us out of the ditch of legalism every time. Grace is unmerited favor or unearned love, like what God showed to us when he sent his Son Jesus to live and die for us. If we give grace to someone else, it means that we give grace the same way God did for us. If truth is the knowledge of God, and legalism is an overemphasis on truth without concern for grace, how do we balance the importance of truth and grace in the Christian journey?

One answer is found in a word study of all the sentences in the New Testament that mention *grace* and *truth* in the same sentence. Interestingly, the word *grace* always comes before the word *truth*. We never read John, Paul, Peter, or Jesus encouraging us to be *"full of truth and grace."* Why is that? Could this mean that grace (unearned love) should come before truth in our thoughts, words, and actions? In my study of God's Word and in my experience in ministry, marriage, and parenthood, I've concluded that the answer to this question is "Yes!"

The Pharisees and Sadducees during Jesus's time on earth loved the truth! They spent most of their lives studying the laws and memorizing them. As if they didn't have enough laws already in God's Word, they made up some of their own. When Jesus arrived on the scene, they felt threatened and tried to publicly humiliate him. One of them, an expert in the law, tested him with this question: *"Teacher, which is the greatest commandment in the Law?"*

Jesus replied: *"'Love the Lord your God with all your heart and with all your soul and with all your mind.' This is the first and greatest commandment. And the second is like it: 'Love your neighbor as yourself.' All the Law and the Prophets hang on these two commandments. . . . No one could say a word in reply, and from that day on no one dared to ask him any more questions"* (Matthew 22:36–40, 46).

Hence, Jesus provides the way out of the ditch of legalism and so we can return to the road to authenticity. God knows our hearts, and only he can change our hearts. *This is love: not that we loved God, but that he loved us and sent his Son as an atoning sacrifice for our sins. Dear friends, since God so loved us, we also ought to love one another.*

There have been many times as a believer, especially early on, that I tried to earn God's love and acceptance. When I failed and gave into the temptation to sin, I beat myself up over it. One day when I was praying and confessing my sins, a thought came into my head. I believe this thought came from the Lord: "Chad, you can never do enough to earn my love and acceptance. Jesus has already paid the price for your sin. You are my child, my son, and I love you."

Paul anticipates the next question. *So what do we do? Keep on sinning so God can keep on forgiving? I should hope not! If we've left the country where sin is sovereign, how can we still live in our old house there? Or didn't you realize we packed up and left there for good?* (Romans 6:1–2 MSG). That's why, if we try to leap out of the ditch of legalism with our own strength, rather than in the power and purpose of God, we often go clear over the road and into the ditch on the other side!

The Ditch of License

The second ditch is the ditch of license. When we're stuck there, it means we're using our eternal security in Christ as a license to sin. My boys love watching the cartoon *Tom and Jerry*, and I recently saw an episode that illustrates the struggle taking place between our selfish desires and the desires of the Holy Spirit. The cartoon mouse Jerry had a little angel on one shoulder and a little devil on the other. The little angel told him he should be nice to Tom the cat, while the little devil told him to do something evil to aggravate Tom. Paul describes this situation in our spiritual lives: *For the flesh desires what is contrary to the Spirit, and the Spirit what is contrary to the flesh . . . so that you are not to do whatever you want.*

What would our world look like if we only loved people for who they are without speaking truth to them? Our workplaces would be completely inefficient. People would show up to work whenever they wanted and wouldn't get anything accomplished. Robbers would be allowed to pillage, and rapists would be allowed to roam free. Churches would become social clubs and would have no positive impact on society. Christians would never experience the heart change that Jesus can provide.

While truth without grace is deadly, grace without truth leads to danger as well. Just as Paul warns us about truth without grace, he also warns about the sin of license:

> It is absolutely clear that God has called you to live a free life. Just make sure that you don't use this freedom as an excuse to do whatever you want to do and destroy your freedom. (Galatians 5:13 MSG)

> The acts of the flesh are obvious: sexual immorality, impurity and debauchery; idolatry and witchcraft; hatred, discord, jealousy, fits of rage, selfish ambition, dissensions, factions and envy; drunkenness, orgies, and

the like. I warn you, as I did before, that those who live like this will not inherit the kingdom of God. (Galatians 5:19–21)

Put to death, therefore, whatever belongs to your earthly nature: sexual immorality, impurity, lust, evil desires and greed, which is idolatry. (Colossians 3:5)

When I've struggled with the sin of license, I've heard a voice in my head say something like this: I can just sin now and then repent and ask Jesus to forgive me later.

One example is the spiritual struggle I endured my freshman year in college. I remember several times getting drunk on Friday nights. Then on Saturday mornings, I felt so guilty that I would resolve to quit drinking. When Saturday evenings came and my friends wanted me to go out with them, I sensed the Holy Spirit telling me to stay at home while my subconscious told me to go with my friends.

When I decided to go with my friends, a part of me felt defeated. Even though I hadn't even gotten wasted yet, it was as if I had already lost the spiritual battle. I'll ask for forgiveness and quit drinking tomorrow, I thought to myself. Then I got drunk and started the whole process over again. Until I learned to avoid the ditch of license, my freshman year in college was probably the most frustrating time of my life.

Avoiding the Ditch of License

What is true freedom? Does freedom mean we can do anything we want to do? Hardly! There are some acts of so-called freedom that actually destroy freedom. For example, if you exercise your freedom by committing murder or armed robbery, you will go to jail and ultimately lose your freedom.

It's the same with sin. When we become followers of Christ, we are set free from the chains of the law. It's like being out of jail spiritually. However, if we abuse our freedom by doing things that we know break God's law, we choose to become slaves to sin and experience the consequences of that slavery again.

Paul writes, *What then? Shall we sin because we are not under the law but under grace? By no means! Don't you know that when you offer yourselves to someone as obedient slaves, you are slaves of the one you obey—whether you are slaves to sin, which leads to death, or to obedience, which leads to righteousness? But thanks be to God that, though you used to be slaves to sin, you have come to obey from your heart the pattern of teaching that has now claimed your allegiance. You have been set free from sin and have become slaves to righteousness* (Romans 6:15–18).

In Romans 6:8–14, Paul gives a great explanation of what it means to "die to self," and I believe that his instructions to the Romans are the very best instructions for getting out of the ditch of license and back onto the road toward maturity in Christ. Though the term "dying to self" sounds negative, Paul's words show how dying to your self-centered desires is the only way to experience abundant life in Christ.

The following verses are from the NIV and *The Message* translations of Romans 6:8–14. I've included both because I love the way each one puts it.

Romans 6:8–14 from the NIV:

> *Now if we died with Christ, we believe that we will also live with him. For we know that since Christ was raised from the dead, he cannot die again; death no longer has mastery over him. The death he died, he died to sin once for all; but the life he lives, he lives to God.*

In the same way, count yourselves dead to sin but alive to God in Christ Jesus. Therefore, do not let sin reign in your mortal body so that you obey its evil desires. Do not offer any part of yourself to sin as an instrument of wickedness, but rather offer yourselves to God as those who have been brought from death to life; and offer every part of yourself to him as an instrument of righteousness. For sin shall not be your master, because you are not under the law, but under grace.

Romans 6:8–14 from *The Message*:

If we get included in Christ's sin-conquering death, we also get included in his life-saving resurrection. We know that when Jesus was raised from the dead it was a signal of the end of death-as-the-end. Never again will death have the last word. When Jesus died, he took sin down with him, but alive he brings God down to us. From now on, think of it this way: Sin speaks a dead language that means nothing to you; God speaks your mother tongue, and you hang on every word. You are dead to sin and alive to God. That's what Jesus did.

That means you must not give sin a vote in the way you conduct your lives. Don't give it the time of day. Don't even run little errands that are connected with that old way of life. Throw yourselves wholeheartedly and full-time—remember, you've been raised from the dead!—into God's way of doing things. Sin can't tell you how to live. After all, you're not living under that old tyranny any longer. You're living in the freedom of God.

Ultimately, the way we get out of the ditch of license *and* avoid it is by confessing our sins and surrendering our lives to Christ. This is the Christ-directed and Spirit-filled life we discussed in chapter 3, "Striking It Rich!" Once again, I encourage you to read the end of that chapter and pray the prayer to give Christ control of your life.

One word of warning I'll give you is this: when you commit a sin you know is wrong (such as lust or drunkenness), part of you will immediately want to avoid talking to God about it. This is because sin causes guilt and shame. God still loves us, but we can't experience his love or enjoy intimacy with him when there is sin in our lives.

When this happens, I strongly encourage you to reject the temptation to put off talking to the Lord about your sin. Pray and confess your sin immediately so you can experience God's love and forgiveness. Even if you fall time and time again, confess your sin immediately. When I began to have a habit of confessing sin the moment I became aware of it, my faith grew stronger, and I found myself giving in to those temptations less and less. Experiencing forgiveness and love helps us to choose God the next time, rather than sin.

When we try to stay on the road by our own efforts, we often swerve from ditch to ditch, and our progress is slow. That's why we've emphasized the importance of being honest about who we are, our need to be filled with God's Spirit, and the value of true friends along the way.

When it comes down to it, and we're lying alone in the ditch, Jesus alone can help us out and get us back on the road toward authentic Christian faith!

CHAPTER 7 | Roadblocks

Sometimes we feel pretty good about avoiding the ditches of legalism and license. We're on the road toward Christian maturity, zipping along, listening to the radio, and watching the scenery flash by, when—*screech!*—a roadblock forces us to a complete stop. Without proper biblical training on how to navigate past these roadblocks, one could struggle for months or even years without advancing on the road toward authentic Christianity.

In the next few pages, we'll discover how to identify and then move past four major roadblocks: (1) lack of conflict resolution, (2) cynicism, (3) lack of boundaries, and (4) sexual immorality. Each of these roadblocks can completely rob us of our joy in the Lord and prohibit us from continuing our spiritual journey.

Roadblock #1: Lack of Conflict Resolution

Lack of conflict resolution, the first roadblock, not only affects us in our own personal journey with the Lord, but also can lead to major divisions within the body of Christ. It can ruin the godly friendships that are so vital to us. Based on my study of the Bible, church history, and my personal experience, I realize Christians have always struggled with this roadblock.

I grew up as a preacher's kid in a tiny little town in Alabama called Valley, "the place where people care and share" (according to the welcome sign seen when driving into town). I grew up thinking that it was permissible to talk bad about other people behind their backs. Of course, my Sunday school teachers taught gossip was wrong, but what I saw firsthand was that many churchgoing people did it nonetheless. I heard church members badmouth my dad (when he wasn't around) whenever they disagreed with his decisions. People talked negatively about the choir director, the youth leader, and even the sweet elderly woman who sat on the back pew of the church.

When I graduated from college and began working as a process engineer, I noticed a trend while I dealt with people in the paper industry. It seemed everyone talked badly about others! And since everyone else did it, I did it, too. At first, it made me feel better about myself to put down others. When I concentrated on their issues and weaknesses, I forgot about my own problems and shortfalls. Little did I know at the time my lack of confronting others and my talking behind their backs were causing me to miss out on the joy and peace that intimacy with God brings.

Then someone helped me to make a discovery that changed my life.

Let me introduce a topic I lovingly call "The Matthew 18 Principle" and share a story about how this principle transformed my life after I went into full-time ministry. I cannot emphasize enough how life changing and life giving this principle can be!

Matthew 18 in Action

Shortly after entering full-time ministry with Campus Crusade for Christ, I served as a mentor to six young college students on a summer mission project in Daytona Beach, Florida. One of my young guys was a sophomore from a college campus in

California, and from the minute "Jake" arrived on the mission project, he was trouble.

Within the first few days, the other five guys in my Bible study complained about Jake's behavior. One said Jake pushed him during a friendly basketball game and tried to pick a fight. A couple of the staff women approached me and informed me Jake made some of the female students on the project uncomfortable because of his comments and inappropriate physical contact.

I was ready to send this guy right back to California. I spoke with the project director, Earle Chute, about the situation with Jake.

Earle, a wise spiritual leader in our region of the country within Campus Crusade for Christ, sat me down and showed me something that forever changed my life. He opened up his Bible to Matthew 18:15–17 and read to me the "three-step process" Jesus laid out in those verses:

> *If your brother or sister sins, go and point out their fault, just between the two of you. If they listen to you, you have won them over. But if they will not listen, take one or two others along, so that 'every matter may be established by the testimony of two or three witnesses.' If they still refuse to listen, tell it to the church; and if they refuse to listen even to the church, treat them as you would a pagan or a tax collector.*

Wow! Those verses laid it out so clearly! If we sent Jake home, we would have taken step 3 before we ever tried step 1 or 2. Earle encouraged me to tell the students and staff members who spoke with me about Jake to follow Matthew 18:15 and go to him themselves.

Before I got a chance to talk to anyone about this "new revelation," a staff woman, Brandy, informed me Jake had just stormed out of an outreach team meeting she was leading and slammed the door in front of the whole group. She tried to confront him to find out why he left so violently (think step 1 above), and he responded by telling her she was the worst leader. He told her he had a lot he could teach her about leading a group!

Well, that was our opportunity to put step 2 into practice. Brandy and I sat down with Jake, and I explained to him how he had hurt Brandy when he left her meeting and insulted her leadership ability. We reviewed the prior conversation Brandy had with him, and we read Matthew 18:15–17 together with Jake. I then asked Jake whether he was softhearted and felt sorry for hurting Brandy or if he was hardhearted and didn't care about her feelings.

Jake responded by saying he just didn't care, but then he paused. He thought about it for a moment and said, "But I guess I can pray about it."

Brandy and I exchanged a look of surprise.

We all agreed to meet again the next day after Jake had an opportunity to pray. At this point, I still felt doubtful Jake would be allowed to continue being a part of the summer project.

The next day, Jake shocked us. He began to weep when we shared how the previous conversation hurt Brandy. Jake looked at Brandy and said he was sorry. He told her he was wrong for treating her that way, and Brandy expressed forgiveness.

When I told the other students and staff they should speak to Jake directly about the other problems he caused, I was pleasantly surprised to discover many had already talked to him. Even more surprisingly, I learned that Jake acted very humble in those conversations and that he had repented!

Many students' lives were transformed by the power of the Holy Spirit that summer in Daytona Beach, but I don't know if anyone changed more than Jake. Right before our eyes, he became more and more gentle and humble, and his love for the Lord and for other people grew.

Halfway through the summer, the staff went home while the students remained and took over the leadership of the summer project. I kept in touch with my six guys, and every time I talked to them I heard amazing stories about how God continued to transform Jake. He shared Christ with many others that summer, and he was even privileged to lead someone to Christ! Everyone was amazed at how God worked in Jake's life.

The story didn't end there. Three years later, tears of joy filled my eyes when I heard that Jake had become a full-time staff member with Campus Crusade for Christ! God is certainly amazing, and his truth transforms lives!

So we see that Matthew 18:15–17 is not just a friendly suggestion about how we should interact with other people. It's a *command* that's been given to us by the Creator himself! If we are to grow in our love for him and seek to live a life pleasing to him, we've got to master "The Matthew 18 Principle."

Conflict Resolution, Step by Step

The following is a paraphrased version of "The Matthew 18 Principle" with suggestions on how you can begin to apply this important principle to your life.

1. When a brother or sister in Christ does or says anything to hurt you or frustrate you, approach them and speak to them one-on-one about your concern or problem.

When you believe a person is a follower of Christ, then you *must* speak to him or her about a hurt or frustration. This principle can work in situations involving nonbelievers as well. It may even create an opportunity to share the gospel with them!

It's not a matter of *if* you're going to be hurt or frustrated by someone, but *when* you're hurt by someone. People are sinful, and we tend to make mistakes, especially when we're not walking in the Spirit.

On top of that, we also have differences in personality and preferences and differences in strengths and weaknesses. For example, some people thrive having structure and organization. They live scheduled lives and prefer timeliness and orderliness. Others are very spontaneous and prefer a flexible schedule and more freedom. While a schedule brings freedom to those loving structure, it can feel like bondage to those preferring flexibility.

We must understand others' preferences and appreciate how God created them. There may be times we just learn to bear with people and extend forgiveness if our conflict is a result of a difference in personality. However, we shouldn't keep our frustration to ourselves and let it build up. We still need to communicate our hurt to them in a loving way so they will know this is a potential source of frustration to us. They may respond by seeking to be sensitive to us and our needs.

For example, suppose you are leading a Bible study and want to get started on time. If someone in your Bible study is habitually fifteen minutes late, it's important to communicate your concerns. Gently explain how it makes you frustrated and how their tardiness is a distraction to the rest of the group. Who knows? You may find out important information that helps you understand why they're late (like they were praying with a friend or helping someone in need).

If you find that months go by without ever having to confront anyone about a problem or frustration, then you might ask yourself if you are allowing frustration to brew and bitterness to grow. We all have differences and disagreements; conflict is part of life. One sign of a healthy life is that we confront others in a godly way with some regularity; total lack of conflict means either that you're not being honest with yourself and others or that you live by yourself on an island!

2. If you confront someone and they are not repentant, then speak to them again with one or two others present.

Cultivating a healthy relationship with someone before speaking truth in love usually prevents the need for this second step of confrontation. However, it is necessary occasionally. God is a God of second chances, and sometimes time is needed for someone to turn away from his or her sin.

If you and a witness meet with someone to share a hurt or frustration, it's important that you don't make that person feel intimidated or ganged up on. Try to start out the conversation by being positive and affirming. Set the tone for constructive feedback by telling them something you appreciate about them.

Then each of you share your hurt or frustration and give the person you're confronting a chance to respond. In my experience, that person will most often have a repentant heart.

3. If the brother or sister in Christ is still not repentant over the sin, then take it to the church or to higher authorities in the body of Christ.

I've rarely had to take this third step with a brother or sister in Christ. People who have Christ in their lives have the Holy Spirit working to convict them of their sin, and a true believer would rarely be unresponsive to confrontation. However, it does happen. When it does, it's time to get higher authorities in the body of Christ involved.

This happened to me once a couple of years ago when "Mark" and "Luke" had a disagreement with one of our student leaders, "John." Mark and Luke wanted to be student leaders in our ministry, but they were too young spiritually and were also too socially immature to lead others. John cared a lot about these two guys, but they badmouthed him behind the scenes, telling others he was doing a poor job leading a freshman Bible study.

The incident began when a freshman in John's Bible study told Mark and Luke that he loved John and enjoyed hanging out with him, but he felt John was always preaching instead of giving the students a chance to discuss what they were learning. Instead of encouraging this freshman to talk to John about his concerns (think step 1), Mark and Luke told John that they would start their own freshman Bible study and that the freshmen in John's Bible study could just switch to theirs.

To make a long story short, John met with Mark and Luke individually (step 1) to share his hurt that they were talking behind his back with the guys in his Bible study. Both of the guys said they were sorry to John's face but continued to talk to the other freshmen about switching to their Bible study. Then John and I sat down with Mark and Luke together and asked them to stop badmouthing John (step 2), but they continued to cause problems. Finally, after they created a petition that they should be student leaders in our ministry and sent it around to students behind our backs, John and I had to sit down with them and ask them not to be involved in our ministry any longer. They were causing controversy and acting in a way that was manipulative.

Although I experienced this one example of Christians needing to agree to disagree and go their separate ways, I have hundreds of examples of students who reconciled their differences and healed their wounds by confronting each other just as the Bible instructs.

Matthew 18 has changed my life forever. I could share many more stories to demonstrate how that passage and other Scriptures have transformed and shaped my life, but don't take my word for it! If you haven't already, begin now to take time to read the Bible daily. Allow the life-giving words to transform your life. It gives not only explicit instructions on relating to people and dealing with confrontation, but also direction and wisdom that can be applied to all situations and decisions in life. The next time your road toward authentic Christianity is blocked by conflict, use these three steps to remove the barrier and continue your journey.

Roadblock #2: Cynicism

While speaking truth in love is required to resolve conflict, grace is required to avoid the roadblock of cynicism. It seems the older I become, the more I must be cautious to avoid the roadblock of cynicism. It's one of the great paradoxes of Christianity. We can have a lot of knowledge of the Bible, much like the Pharisees of Jesus's day, but if we don't have the love and grace of God to go with that knowledge, we may be tempted to think we are better than everyone else. Cynicism dissolves our compassion for others.

As I stated earlier, before I joined staff with Campus Crusade for Christ, I was a process engineer in a paper mill. Most of my friends and coworkers didn't have a personal relationship with God, and I'm embarrassed to say I often allowed some of their poor attitudes to rub off on me.

For example, a lot of the guys who worked in the paper mill had a poor attitude toward upper-level management. "They don't care about us," they would say. "They only want to make money. It's all about the bottom line." Instead of thinking the best of our managers, I would allow those words to ring in my head whenever something at work didn't go my way: "It's all about the bottom line." Slowly but surely, I grew cynical toward the company and some of my leaders.

Over time, this judgmental, critical attitude was notably taking its toll on my life. I lacked authentic joy, and I rarely felt contentment with my job. Because I was critical of other people, I lacked genuine concern for them. For example (and this is embarrassing), when a homeless person asked me for money, I was cynical toward him for not having a job instead of being compassionate. In general, during this period of my life, I was much more selfish than generous. I lacked a strong desire to spend time with the Lord daily.

Because this has been an issue in my life and has kept me from growing intimate in my relationship with Jesus time and time again, I've looked to the Bible for answers on how to conquer this issue of cynicism. I've discovered a great weapon to battle this issue is an attitude of thankfulness.

Whenever I find a word or phrase in the Bible that is repeated three times, I've made it a habit to highlight it. In Colossians 3, Paul uses a form of the word "thankful" three times to stress its importance. I call these verses the "Thankfulness Commandments":

> *Let the peace of Christ rule in your hearts, since as members of one body you were called to peace. And be* thankful. *Let the message of Christ dwell among you richly as you teach and admonish one another with all wisdom through psalms, hymns, and songs from the Spirit, singing to God with* gratitude *in your hearts. And whatever you do, whether in word or deed, do it all in the name of the Lord Jesus, giving* thanks *to God the Father through him.* (emphasis added)

I first discovered God's "Thankfulness Commandments" eight years ago while I was spending personal time with the Lord. At the time, I had just begun working in Spartanburg, South Carolina, with Campus Crusade for Christ. My director at the time, "Bill," was an amazing guy who was a great model of what a loving husband and father should be. However, his personality was the complete opposite from mine. He was spontaneous, while I was more structured. I was very grace oriented (naturally loving people the way they were), while he was more truth oriented (naturally loving people too much to let them stay the same).

I was struggling with cynicism toward Bill when I read these verses from Colossians 3, and it was clear to me the Lord was showing me I needed to be more thankful toward Bill. The next day, I saw Bill and thanked him for being my director. I also pointed out he was one of the most amazing fathers I knew, and I was glad the Lord put such a great model of a family man in my life. When I saw Bill a couple of days after that, I found something else to be thankful for. I thanked him again . . . and then again.

Within a couple of weeks, my whole outlook toward Bill had changed. He truly was the best boss I ever had, and I recognized that fact for the first time. From that time on, Bill became one of my closest friends, and he still is to this day.

Following the "Thankfulness Commandments" in Colossians has become a key strategy for winning the battle against cynicism in my life. Whenever I disagree with someone or struggle with a cynical attitude, I stop to pray. I thank God for placing him or her in my life as a tool to refine me and transform my heart. When I thank God, I begin to see that person in a totally different light. I remember God is sovereign and has orchestrated every circumstance in my life.

Is there a classmate, a friend, or a leader in your life toward whom you are critical? Is there a circumstance causing you to be cynical? I strongly encourage you to read Colossians 3:15–17 again and spend some time in prayer. Find things about that person or circumstance for which you can be thankful, and thank God for them.

You see, one of the keys to abundant joy can be found when we have a thankful heart toward God. Somehow, when we are thankful, the problems of life don't seem like problems at all but opportunities to experience joy and to grow more authentic in our relationship with Christ.

Roadblock #3: Lack of Boundaries

One of the most common roadblocks I see every day working with college students is a lack of boundaries, and it was a major roadblock for me when I was a college student. For example, as a student I struggled to set boundaries with my time. I was in a fraternity at Clemson and was also the student body vice president, as well as a student leader for Campus Crusade for Christ, among other things. I also loved to have fun with my friends. Between hanging out with my friends and being involved in so many organizations on campus, I rarely made time to study before midnight. My friends thought I was crazy for putting off studying until late each night, and my professors were frustrated with my inability to stay awake in my classes most days.

I also struggled with setting boundaries with my feelings. I stayed so busy that I rarely called my parents. I was the oldest child, and my poor mom struggled with the fact that her firstborn neglected to call and chat. In a disappointed and hurt voice, she left messages asking me to call every few days. Oh, how I felt guilty when I listened to those messages—and out of guilt, I would continue to put off calling her back! Clearly I had some boundary issues.

In his book *Changes That Heal*, Henry Cloud identifies the ability of setting healthy boundaries as a major ingredient needed for spiritual and personal growth. Cloud writes:

> Boundaries, in a broad sense, are lines or things that mark a limit, bound or border. In a psychological sense, boundaries are the realization of our own person apart from others. This sense of separateness

forms the basis of our personal identity. It says what we are and what we are not, what we will choose and what we will not choose, what we will endure and what we will not, what we feel and what we will not feel, what we like and what we do not like, and what we want and what we do not want. Boundaries, in short, define us. In the same way that a physical boundary defines where a property line begins and ends, a psychological and spiritual boundary defines who we are and who we are not.[1]

In the Bible, we see God exhibiting this over and over. He continually defines himself by saying who and what he is and what he is not, what he loves and what he does not love:

I am your shield. (Genesis 15:1)

I am God Almighty. (Genesis 17:1)

I, the LORD your God, am a jealous God. (Exodus 20:5)

I am compassionate. (Exodus 22:27)

I am holy. (Leviticus 11:44)

I am faithful. (Jeremiah 3:12)

God is love. (1 John 4:8)

Just as God defines who he is and who he is not, we must learn to define who we are and who we're not. Three areas in which I've grown the most by learning to set boundaries are my attitude, my feelings, and my time.

Attitude

Cloud writes, "Our attitudes are our opinions about or mental positions toward something. We are responsible for our own attitudes, for they exist inside our 'property lines.' They are within our hearts, not someone else's."[2] He compares it to having a house with a backyard fence. You have your own grass and bushes, and your neighbor has his own grass and bushes. You are only responsible for your own yard, not your neighbor's, and vice versa.

When we allow someone with a bad attitude to affect our own attitude, we are allowing that person inside our backyard to "cut our grass." We must not allow him or her to do that! To grow spiritually and emotionally, we must take responsibility for our own attitudes.

An example of this growth in my life involves the radio in my car. Before I went into full-time ministry many years ago, I used to go to lunch every day with my coworkers in the paper mill. One of our traditions each day was to listen to a popular political talk show on the radio, the host of which is not known for his positive attitude toward our government and the direction in which our country is headed.

Each day, I would listen to his show, and by doing so I allowed his negativity to rub off on me. Over time, my bad attitude toward the government really began to take away the joy of my spiritual journey with Christ.

Years later, I stopped listening to his radio show after I read Colossians 3 and began applying the "Thankfulness Commandments" discussed earlier in this chapter. I set a boundary by taking responsibility for my own attitude.

Do you find your attitudes affected by the attitudes of those around you? Is there a friend in your life who always seems to have a cynical attitude? If so, learn to draw healthy boundaries with your feelings by not allowing others' negative attitudes to rub off on you. If a close friend often has a critical attitude, consider talking to them about it and encouraging them to be more positive around you. Just tell them you're trying to become a more positive person with a better attitude. If they're a real friend, they'll respect your wishes, and perhaps their attitude will improve as well.

Feelings

During our newlywed years, Elizabeth and I lived far away from both sets of parents. As each Thanksgiving and Christmas holiday approached, our parents expressed their desire to spend the holidays with us at their homes. Elizabeth's parents and my parents lived in different states, so naturally one family always felt disappointment—or both when we chose to stay at our own house for the holidays.

For the first few years of our marriage, I let our parents' disappointments affect my feelings. Every time I thought about their disappointment because of our absence during a holiday, I felt depressed and guilty for letting down our loved ones. This often put a damper on my holidays!

Then one year, I sat down with both sets of parents and drew a boundary. I gently told my mom, "Mom, I love you with all of my heart. I love spending time with you during the holidays, but there will be some holidays we will not be able to come home. I would appreciate it if you could be supportive and understanding when we choose to spend holidays away from my family." I expressed the same sentiment to Elizabeth's parents. After I drew this boundary and recognized I was not responsible for our families' feelings, I enjoyed pressure-free holidays.

As you grow and mature, part of becoming an adult involves drawing healthy boundaries with your feelings. This may involve telling parents you are not visiting them during a holiday and asking them to understand like Elizabeth and I did, or it may involve something more serious. Oftentimes, people may try to manipulate us if we don't draw boundaries with our feelings.

A common thing I've seen among young couples who are dating is manipulation. For example, if a guy wants to have a physical relationship with a girl who wants to wait until she's married to have sex, he may act like his feelings are hurt in order to use his girlfriend's feelings against her.

Is there anyone in your life trying to manipulate you by using your feelings against you? We must draw boundaries by not letting others' feelings influence us to do something we don't want to do.

Time

Earlier, in chapter 2, I shared how I used to be incredibly busy with many church activities. Then I learned to add rest in the Lord to my life and draw healthy boundaries with time. I learned not to be involved in everything and to say no at times when people asked me to fill up my schedule with projects and tasks.

We only have twenty-four hours per day. A third of that time is used for sleep, and a third of that time is used for work. When it comes to that last third of our time, we need to learn to draw healthy boundaries to ensure we are cultivating our love for the Lord and our love for our family. Our hearts are more important than the activities in which we are involved!

A recent example of how Elizabeth and I have drawn boundaries with our time involves our local church. In some ways, I believe a lot is expected of us from the Lord. We've been blessed with amazing evangelism and discipleship training by our employer, and I know we need to bless others with this training. I also believe everyone should be involved in a local church.

However, we are also in full-time ministry and have a lot of responsibility in this role. With everything on our plates right now, we don't have the time to lead a church small group and spend the kind of quality time with our three small children (soon to be four) we desire. Therefore, we limited ourselves to a very small role of service in our church; we help with children's church on Sunday mornings.

How many activities are you involved in at church or school? How many leadership roles do you have? I always tell students that you can lead well in one activity or that you can lead poorly in two or three activities. It's best to prioritize quality time with the Lord first as we discussed in chapter 2 and then be involved in other activities if you have the extra time.

Roadblock #4: Sexual Immorality

The final roadblock is the pervasive problem of sexual immorality. Stephen Arterburn and Fred Stoeker ask the question: "What's your aim in life—authenticity or acceptance?"[3] To aim for acceptance is to live your life by the question: "How far can I go and still call myself a Christian?" You want to *seem* to be a Christian, but you are feeling pressured or want to give in to your lustful thoughts. Authenticity requires a different question, which can be stated like this: "How holy can I be?"[4]

"William" is alone in his room. His roommates are out playing football with a group of friends, but William sprained his ankle last week and can't play. His greatest spiritual struggle during his freshman year has been in the area of lust. This is the first time he's had his own computer without parental controls on it. A thought enters his mind: It's God's fault you can't play football. If he didn't want you to look at porn on the Internet, he shouldn't have let you get hurt.

"Sue" has been dating Tom for six months, and Tom has been pressuring her to have sex with him. She's in love with Tom and is convinced they'll get married as soon as they graduate from college. Her parents have met Tom, and this is the first guy she's dated whom her dad has ever liked. Tonight, Sue and Tom are going to be watching a movie together all alone in his room. She thinks to herself:

> I know Tom isn't a Christian, but I know he's the one. There aren't any decent Christian guys on this entire campus I'd want to date, and if God wanted me to date a Christian guy, he would have provided one. Tonight, Tom's going to try to make love to me. I'm not ready to go all the way yet, but I'm willing to go almost that far. I've already done so much physically with other guys anyway, and I don't even deserve a strong Christian guy.

Can you relate to either William or Sue? Do you know anyone like them? The statistics say you can, and you do!

While failing to resolve conflict, living cynically, and refusing to set boundaries are damaging, the roadblock that probably causes the most long-term damage in our relationships with God and others is sexual immorality. Paul writes, *Flee from sexual immorality. All other sins a person commits are outside the body, but whoever sins sexually, sins against their own body. Do you not know that your bodies are temples of the Holy Spirit, who is in you, whom you have received from God? You are not your own; you were bought at a price. Therefore honor God with your bodies.*

Former sex addict Michael Leahy travels around the country, sharing his story about his addiction and how God has set him free from it. In his book, *Porn Nation*, he shares some alarming statistics that show how "hyper-sexualized" our society is becoming. In 2008, studies showed the following results:[5]

1. The average age of first exposure to commercial pornography is somewhere between the ages of eleven and fourteen. Many young people reported that they were first exposed to pornography between the ages of four to five.

2. Over 80 percent of teens, ages fifteen to seventeen, have had multiple exposures to hard-core pornography, and

adolescents who watch television with high levels of sexual content are more likely to initiate sexual intercourse and also more likely to initiate other sexual activities.

3. One-third of teenage guys and one-fourth of teenage girls are feeling pressure to have sex. Twenty-seven percent of teens between the ages of thirteen and sixteen are now sexually active. Forty-two percent of guys and 33 percent of girls ages fifteen to seventeen have had intercourse.

Wow! These statistics make it seem like the fight for sexual purity is a fight we as Christians cannot win. However, the Bible tells us otherwise: *You, dear children, are from God and have overcome them, because the one who is in you is greater than the one who is in the world.* Paul tells us that *in all these things we are more than conquerors through him who loved us.*

God, who created us as sexual beings, has a very clear standard he wants us to follow. In Ephesians 5:3–4, Paul says, *Among you there must not be even a hint of sexual immorality, or of any kind of impurity, or of greed, because these are improper for God's holy people. Nor should there be obscenity, foolish talk or coarse joking, which are out of place.* Jesus said, *"But I tell you that anyone who looks at a woman lustfully has already committed adultery with her in his heart."*

There are many tactics Christians can use to practice sexual purity. For guys, accountability partners can help fight this battle well. Review the tips on finding an accountability partner in chapter 5, "An Epic Fireworks Battle." If you are a guy struggling with an addiction to Internet pornography, I'd strongly encourage you to visit xxxchurch.com for tips and tools on how to overcome that addiction, and I'd recommend getting accountability software such as Covenant Eyes on your computer.

Another tactic is to remove the things in life that would lead you to be tempted, such as using the Internet when you are alone. This tactic comes from Jesus in his Sermon on the Mount. *"If your right eye causes you to stumble, gouge it out and throw it away. It is better for you to lose one part of your body than for your whole body to be thrown into hell"* (Matthew 5:29). For a college student, having a computer for writing papers and completing class assignments is critical, certainly—but why not remove the web browser from your room computer and do your research in the library? What's more important in the long run: convenience or commitment to an authentic faith?

For girls, accountability is also necessary, especially if you're single but have a steady boyfriend. It's important for you to have healthy friendships with other women with whom you can be open and honest about your personal purity, but you also need to have some women in your life who are spiritually mature. A mature woman of faith cares enough about you that she is concerned about what type of guy you are dating. She will ask questions such as: Is he an authentic Christian? Is he leading you toward Christ or leading you away from Christ? Has he tried to pressure you into getting physical in the relationship? An authentic woman of faith won't let you settle for less than a mature Christian guy.

In any case, whatever your struggle with sexual purity, don't battle alone! The authentic friendships that God desires you to have and your deepening relationship with God are the best means to overcome temptation and sin in this area. There is hope, and it's time to get past the roadblock and start moving down the highway again!

While the ditches of legalism and license as well as the roadblocks discussed in this chapter can hinder us spiritually, there is one additional barrier that can keep us from loving God and others: the love of money. In the next chapter we'll discuss the dangers of making money a higher priority than relationships and list some ways we can fight this temptation.

CHAPTER 8 | Sometimes the Bedbugs Bite

I f you suffer from a fear of bugs, you might want to skip past this story. Every two years, Elizabeth and I travel to Colorado for a national staff conference with Campus Crusade for Christ. So far, every time we've returned home from this conference, we've faced some sort of major calamity within our house. One year, we returned to an entire house covered with green mold due to a problem in our crawl space. It took months to disinfect our house in Spartanburg, South Carolina, that year!

This summer, Elizabeth and I traveled home from our national conference to face an embarrassing problem within our house: bedbugs. We've all heard the saying "Good night, sleep tight. Don't let the bedbugs bite." Did you know those little bugs actually exist? And they are nowhere near as charming as that cutesy saying.

We became aware of our problem when my son Clark and I noticed huge welts on our torsos and arms. Elizabeth had been trying to determine for weeks what had been causing our daughter Evelyn's hives as she had been covered with smaller bumps all over her body, too. When we seriously investigated, we felt horrified and nauseated to find bedbugs under our mattresses.

We soon discovered that eliminating bedbugs is a major undertaking. Every article of clothing and fabric in the house was washed with hot water and bleach. Suitcases were tossed. Mattresses were encased in plastic coverings. We steam cleaned all carpet, hired a professional exterminator, and fumigated the house. We also were forced to throw away seemingly half of our material possessions.

The silver lining was that it was a great teaching opportunity for our children. As we threw away toys and stuffed animals that weren't salvageable, we explained things to our kids:

> "We're really sorry we have to throw away your toys, but Mommy and Daddy had to make sacrifices to get rid of these yucky bugs, too. We had to spend lots of money throwing away our couch and other furniture. We spent lots of money getting all our carpet steam cleaned, and we're spending a whole lot of money getting the bug man to come and help us get rid of them. You know what Mommy and Daddy are learning? We're learning we shouldn't love our money or our material possessions. They can be gone in a flash!"

We can see this same lesson in the stock market. During the dot-com bubble, everyone suddenly "became an expert" in the stock market because everything, especially in the technology sector of the economy, increased in value. I must admit I was one of those people. While I worked in the paper industry my last year before entering full-time ministry, I anticipated a period of no paychecks and financial struggle. I started saving extra money in preparation for this time. Instead of depositing the savings into a savings account where it would be safe, I purchased technology stocks that were expected to keep rising in value. Even "the real experts" predicted the Internet industry would continue growing at a fast pace. Word to the wise: when someone ordinary like me starts to make a hobby of buying individual stocks, it's probably a good time to sell your shares. The dot-com bubble burst, and many people's worldly possessions vanished almost overnight.

I don't need to rehearse the details of the subprime mortgage crisis—and the only certainty about our financial system is that there will be another crisis before too long! You've probably heard experts weigh in on what happened, why it happened, and how to prevent it. But I'm going to let you in on a secret: the cause of all our financial downfalls and crises can be explained in one word.

Greed.

And the church has tried to steer clear of that issue, denouncing the obviously unbiblical practices of a handful of greedy ministers who are clearly more interested in siphoning wealth than in saving souls. However, one way the church of the twenty-first century reacted was by launching a multitude of seminars, Bible studies, and sermons on how to eliminate debt and slowly build wealth. The idea is that we shouldn't try to "get rich quick"—greed, in other words—but should be careful stewards of the wealth we have. And if we get more wealth? Well, we can just use it to build God's kingdom. Radio talk shows and books on these topics have become extremely popular. As a result, many people changed lifestyles and reduced debt. Others started saving for retirement and for their children's college education at rapid rates.

While a lot of good has come out of this movement by the church, I'm concerned about the direction in which it is taking some people. It is important to pay off debt. I certainly wouldn't say otherwise. However, overcoming the greed in our lives requires more than just a change in lifestyle. Because greed is a symptom of a deeper problem found within our hearts, only a change of heart will help us conquer it. Jesus says it best in his famous Sermon on the Mount:

Do not store up for yourselves treasures on earth, where moths and vermin destroy, and where thieves break in and steal. But store up for yourselves treasures in heaven, where moths and vermin do not destroy, and where thieves do not break in and steal. For where your treasure is, there your heart will be also. (Matthew 6:19–21)

There are three subtexts of financial stewardship we may have regarding our money. In a novel or film, subtext is content underneath spoken dialogue. In other words, subtext is the unspoken thoughts and motives of characters—what they really believe. Since we are characters in this chapter, the subtexts of financial stewardship are what motivate us in the way we handle money.

The word *stewardship* implies that everything we own belongs to God and that we are just temporarily managing and taking care of *his* resources. We can be good stewards of the resources God has given us (by doing things like conserving electricity), or we can be poor stewards by being wasteful. *"But who am I, and who are my people, that we should be able to give as generously as this? Everything comes from you, and we have given you only what comes from your hand."*

There are three main subtexts of financial stewardship. In the first, we spend now on what we want, accumulate debt, and give little. In the second, as we try to correct the first, we save now, give a little now, and plan to give more later. The third subtext is radically different, however, because it says simply: "All of my money belongs to God." Each of these ways of relating to our money has to do with a deep heart issue. It is only when we begin to move toward authentic Christian faith by addressing the deep heart problem that the third subtext, "My money belongs to God," can begin to be true of us.

"Spend Now; Accumulate Debt; Give Little"

Whether or not we choose to admit it, we all operate with this subtext at times in our lives. It all began when we were little children and accompanied our parents to the grocery store. We saw that pack of bubblegum or candy we really wanted, and we said, "I want that right now!"

Growing up, I had an ongoing dream as I drifted off to sleep each night. In my dream, I earned a full-ride college scholarship for both football and baseball, becoming the greatest college athlete to play either sport. After college, I was a first-round draft pick in the National Football League and then naturally an obvious choice during the first round in the Major League Baseball draft. I dreamed I earned so much money I didn't know what to do with it all. Later, after I began having a more authentic relationship with God in college, I still often dreamed of bringing in a large salary, but one thing changed. I gave some of my money away—but not so much that I couldn't drive a nice sports car!

No matter how much money we have in life, we never feel like we have enough. The author of Ecclesiastes writes, *"Whoever loves money never has money enough; whoever loves wealth is never satisfied with their income. This too is meaningless."* We're never satisfied because as our income goes up, our "needs" go up as well, and what seemed like unattainable luxuries before are suddenly things we can't live without.

Anyone living in America or Europe, even in the lowest class of society, is living in the top 5 percent of the richest people in the world. In 2007, the World Bank reported that 21 percent of the world's population was living in severe poverty, which is defined as living on less than one dollar per day. More than 40 percent of the world's population—around 3 billion people—was living on less than two dollars per day. If these impoverished people were to visit us and see the things we possess, they would be amazed at our wealth.

Yet we keep consuming, and we continue to want more. When we live our lives with the subtext "spend now; accumulate debt; give little," we are headed for spiritual bankruptcy. Eventually, we are going to come to the end of our lives, and we can't take any earthly possessions into eternity.

Need scientific evidence that accumulating wealth or earthly possessions can't bring you happiness? Richard Easterlin, a professor of economics at the University of Southern California, has been studying happiness as it relates to wealth for over forty years. In the journal *Proceedings of the National Academy of Sciences of the United States of America*, he published his latest research findings that happiness in a population does not increase as the wealth increases, even in less-developed countries or transitional countries.

In the long run, Easterlin said, more wealth simply creates more want. "The higher your income goes up the more your aspiration goes up," he said. "Over time, the change in aspirations negates the effect of changing income."[1] Easterlin and his colleagues at USC are hoping his findings will encourage individuals and policymakers to focus on nonmonetary factors, like health and family concerns, rather than building wealth and economic growth.

If you are a college student reading this, there is probably a good chance you are living with this subtext. You may already have student loans in place to pay for college, and to some extent, you may be committed to building some school debt. If that applies to you, I still caution you to be careful not to build up too much debt. Being in full-time college ministry, I've seen many college students accumulate too much debt, hurt their financial well-being, and set themselves up to make loan payments for many, many years. After seeing so many of my younger friends make financial mistakes, I'd encourage you to do your best to reduce your education costs by applying for scholarships, or find a part-time job to help pay for college.

It's not enough, however, just to change our spending habits. If we change only our habits and not our hearts, we will find ourselves living with the second subtext.

"Save Now; Give a Little Now; Plan to Give More Later"

Money is not evil. It's the *love of* money, not money itself, that is *a root of all kinds of evil*, according to 1 Timothy 6:10. In fact, many people in the Bible who loved God the most were very wealthy, such as King David and Job. Therefore, some wisdom can be found in the subtext "save now; give a little now; plan to give more later." We can be tempted to think that if we save for retirement and our children's college education now by investing in the stock market, the investment will grow and even multiply through compounding interest. Then in the future, we will likely have much more wealth and be able to give more. Also, paying off debt is a great habit for financial stewardship. When we pay off a loan, we no longer have to pay interest on that loan, which gives us more money to give away.

There are at least three extreme cautions, however, with the subtext "save now; give a little now; plan to give more later." First and foremost, we are told, *Do not store up for yourselves treasures on earth*. Instead, we are told to *store up for yourselves treasures in heaven*. This means storing up riches on earth should not be our heart's desire, while storing up treasures in heaven should be.

We've heard it said that we can't take money or material possessions with us when we go to heaven—the only thing we can take with us is people. C. S. Lewis once said it another way:

"Everything that is not eternal is eternally useless." If these statements are true (and I believe they are), then any way we can invest our money toward helping people in need or helping people find a relationship with God is a wise investment of our money.

I've seen many students find creative ways to apply this principle. One example involves a recent graduate, Lacey, who is serving as a missionary overseas in Argentina. A group of students from her alma mater, the College of Charleston, has committed to supporting Lacey financially by making monthly contributions toward her ministry. Other students I know have volunteered on the weekends with two local churches that help provide for the needy.

The second extreme caution concerning this subtext is we don't know how long we'll live here on earth, and we need to be storing up treasures in heaven right now, even as we learn to develop good habits of financial stewardship. We don't want to be "bankrupt" when we get to heaven. This is why it's important to start investing while we're young so that our *eternal* investments have time to grow. We've recently heard stories from Lacey, our missionary friend in Argentina, and she has seen Argentine college students begin to have relationships with the Lord. If those students grow spiritually and lead others to Christ, the investment that the College of Charleston students are making into Lacey's ministry will grow long after Lacey returns to America.

The third caution is the focus of this subtext is not on God or his will. In the chapter entitled "A Conversation with the Creator," we discussed the importance of praying to God, *"Your kingdom come, your will be done, on earth as it is in heaven."* How can we pray this prayer if we are so focused on saving "our money" and paying off debt that we aren't willing to be generous with God's money each and every day? We've already budgeted every cent and are often inflexible.

By contrast, the Bible commands us to love God with all of our hearts, with all of our souls, and with all of our strength. Following this commandment will lead us to a lifestyle of extravagant worship of God.

In the Bible, God required his people to *"bring the best of the firstfruits of your soil to the house of the LORD your God."* No one was to appear before God empty-handed. God also required his people to offer burnt offerings to him from the very best of their flocks or herds. The priests would sprinkle the blood of the animal against the altar and then burn the entire animal, creating *"an aroma pleasing to the LORD."* One could argue this seemed to be a waste of good meat, but it's a great example of extravagant worship.

The concept of extravagant worship as it relates to spending money is also found in Matthew 26:6–11:

> *While Jesus was in Bethany in the home of Simon the Leper, a woman came to him with an alabaster jar of very expensive perfume, which she poured on his head as he was reclining at the table.*
>
> *When the disciples saw this, they were indignant. "Why this waste?" they asked. "This perfume could have been sold at a high price and the money given to the poor."*
>
> *Aware of this, Jesus said to them, "Why are you bothering this woman? She has done a beautiful thing to me. The poor you will always have with you, but you will not always have me."*

Yes, paying off debt and saving for college and retirement are important habits of financial stewardship. However, we need the Holy Spirit's guidance on a case-by-case basis. We need to daily check our hearts to see if we are doing what God wants us to do with our money. It is easy to slip into greed, which is subtle and creeps into our lives slowly. Keeping our hearts in tune to God as a lifestyle will help keep us focused on what God wants us to do with *his* money. We must pay attention to those in need around us. If our neighbor has an acute need, we may need to stop saving temporarily so we can reach out and help our neighbor.

After all, God will always provide what we need. We have the wonderful biblical promise that *God will meet all [our] needs according to the riches of his glory in Christ Jesus* (Philippians 4:19), so the only thing we're giving up is the control over "our" money—which isn't really ours in the first place!

Also, if the motivation behind our good habits of financial stewardship is to build wealth, our hearts are in the wrong place, and we are lacking a proper biblical view of what wealth really is. Real wealth, according to the Bible, is having a rich relationship with Jesus. I love reading 1 Timothy 6:6–10 from Eugene Peterson's *The Message*:

> *A devout life does bring wealth, but it's the rich simplicity of being yourself before God. Since we entered the world penniless and will leave it penniless, if we have bread on the table and shoes on our feet, that's enough.*
>
> *But if it's only money these leaders are after, they'll self-destruct in no time. Lust for money brings trouble and nothing but trouble. Going down that path, some lose their footing in the faith completely and live to regret it bitterly ever after.*

"My Money Belongs to God"

In C. S. Lewis's book, *Mere Christianity*,[2] he shares the story of a small child who wants to buy a present for his father, but must ask his father for the money first. The son then uses the father's sixpence—a small coin—to buy the father a gift. When the son presents the gift to his dad, the father is pleased, but monetarily he is "sixpence none the richer," since he had to pay for the gift in the first place.

This story illustrates how we store up treasures in heaven by being openhanded with the money God gives us. When we embrace and apply the truth that everything we possess belongs to God, our hearts become more focused on God and his will than on money and things of this earth. We begin to view ourselves as stewards of God's money, becoming more generous today as opposed to later.

For me, generosity isn't something that has come naturally, but it is an area in which I've grown and continue to grow. I've noticed that when I give financially toward someone or toward a certain cause, my heart goes there. *"For where your treasure is, there your heart will be also."*

For example, Elizabeth and I are members of a local church in a lower-income part of Charleston. A few years ago, we started giving clothes, food, and money toward the people in the community who have greater needs than we do, and we've spent time visiting people in the community and providing for needs that they have. The more we've given, the more we care about the less fortunate.

We've also seen the hearts of many of our ministry partners changed. Friends of our ministry have donated financially toward our ministry to help college students find a relationship with God and grow in their faith. At least once per week, we get letters and phone calls from ministry partners thanking us for what we do and for giving them a chance to give financially. Some of these ministry partners share that they pray for our ministry every single day! Again, they have given, and their love for college students has grown.

We should strive to live life with the attitude that "our money belongs to God," which will lead us to a more intimate relationship with him. Our faith in God and love for other people will grow as we are generous toward others.

Now, like the rich young ruler in Luke 18, we need to ask ourselves if we are ready to become generous Christians. What are the needs around you? Who are the people who may need your help? Are there others who are less fortunate? Are there missionaries you can help send to impact the world for Christ?

If you aren't generous immediately when God places a need on your heart, there is a chance you will forget about it and get caught up in your own needs and circumstances while forgetting others around you. You may be thinking you don't have much money to give, yet my encouragement to you is that God knows your circumstances and cares about your heart. If you have little, you can still give of what you *do* have, and your heart will still be transformed.

The rich young ruler in Luke 18 could not give up his control of his possessions, and he hung his head and walked away from Jesus. Jesus responded, *"Indeed, it is easier for a camel to go through the eye of a needle than for someone who is rich to enter the kingdom of God." Those who heard this asked, "Who then can be saved?" Jesus replied, "What is impossible with man is possible with God."*

Becoming a Generous Christian

As we close this chapter, reflecting on God's Word and the truth that your heart will be where your treasure is, let's focus on our hearts. If you are in a major financial bind or are in debt up to your eyeballs, there are many resources to help you, such as wise counsel from a mentor or a book by a financial planner who takes God's ownership of our money seriously. But changing our spending habits is only a Band-Aid to the deeper problem of our greed. The only real solution to this problem of our sin is a change of heart.

The following principles can help us become generous Christians as they help our hearts transform into the image of

Christ. When we travel the road toward authentic Christian faith with the understanding that our money belongs to God and that we need to be openhanded with *his* money, our hearts begin to reflect his heart, and our character begins to reflect his character. If we become generous Christians, then we are well on our way to becoming good stewards of God's money.

Eight Biblical Principles Regarding Generosity

1. ***God is generous.*** He paid the ultimate price to save our lives by sending his very own Son, Jesus Christ, to die on the cross as a payment for the penalty of our sins.

   For you know the grace of our Lord Jesus Christ, that though he was rich, yet for your sake he became poor, so that you through his poverty might become rich. (2 Corinthians 8:9)

2. ***We are commanded to be generous.*** Because God is generous, he expects us to follow his lead by being generous as well.

   Command those who are rich in this present world not to be arrogant nor to put their hope in wealth, which is so uncertain, but to put their hope in God, who richly provides us with everything for our enjoyment. Command them to do good, to be rich in good deeds, and to be generous and willing to share. In this way they will lay up treasure for themselves as a firm foundation for the coming age, so that they may take hold of the life that is truly life. (1 Timothy 6:17–19)

3. ***Our heart for God and others will develop as we become more generous.*** Our hearts will go wherever we place our treasure. If we place our treasure in worldly possessions, however good or necessary they seem, then our hearts will go there. On the flip side, if we place our treasures in eternal things, our hearts will go toward eternal things. Being

generous can actually help us pick up speed in our journey toward authentic Christian faith. As we are more generous toward God and others, our hearts for them grow, and we want to be even more generous.

For where your treasure is, there your heart will be also. (Matthew 6:21)

4. ***God is taking note of our generosity.*** Sometimes we forget that God is omniscient and is always watching us. He knows our hearts and everything about us. He is paying attention when we are or are not generous.

As Jesus looked up, he saw the rich putting their gifts into the temple treasury. He also saw a poor widow put in two very small copper coins. (Luke 21:1–2)

5. ***Do not wait until you have a lot of money to be generous. Be generous now.*** Some of us have made mistakes in how we have spent our money and have found ourselves with a substantial amount of debt. Yes, we do need to have a plan to methodically pay off our debt, but we should not wait until we are debt free to be generous. No matter what our financial situation is, we need to be generous so our hearts for God will grow.

"Truly I tell you," he said, "this poor widow has put in more than all the others. All these people gave their gifts out of their wealth; but she out of her poverty put in all she had to live on." (Luke 21:3–4)

6. ***There are eternal consequences for our generosity or lack thereof.*** My father is one of the most generous people I know. He said that before he became generous toward God, he had more problems and situations that robbed him of his money. When he began to be more generous, those

problems based on worldly choices seemed to take less and less from him.

In Luke 16, Jesus teaches two great parables of the importance of generosity and how it affects eternity. One of these parables is a story of a rich man whose money manager was wasting his possessions. Knowing the rich man was about to fire him, the money manager sat down with the people who owed the rich man money, and he reduced their debt in order to win their favor. When the rich man heard what happened, he commended the dishonest man for acting so shrewdly. After he finished telling this parable, Jesus said,

> *"For the people of this world are more shrewd in dealing with their own kind than are the people of the light. I tell you, use worldly wealth to gain friends for yourselves, so that when it is gone, you will be welcomed into eternal dwellings.*
>
> *"Whoever can be trusted with very little can also be trusted with much, and whoever is dishonest with very little will also be dishonest with much. So if you have not been trustworthy in handling worldly wealth, who will trust you with true riches? And if you have not been trustworthy with someone else's property, who will give you property of your own?"* (Luke 16:8–12)

7. ***We are to reflect God. Generosity is a reflection of him.*** We never know how much someone's life can be changed in a positive way by our generosity. In December 2004, a giant tsunami hit the coast of Indonesia. Several of the world's largest Christian organizations sent volunteers to help clean up, and hundreds of full-time staff and students involved with Campus Crusade for Christ traveled to Indonesia. The leader of this Muslim province sent a note

to one of the largest Muslim groups, asking for help. The response he received from the Muslim organization said, "God is punishing you. We will not help." The leader of this province then sent word to Campus Crusade for Christ and the other Christian organizations that he was opening his province (where it was once illegal to share the good news of Jesus) to Christian organizations that wanted to help, and they were free to share the good news of Jesus.

The wicked borrow and do not repay, but the righteous give generously. (Psalm 37:21)

8. ***Everything we have comes from the Lord. We can give only what is his already.*** When we have this proper perspective regarding our material possessions, it is easy to see how the Lord wants to use us to channel his money to those who need it. If we're going to make a mistake in how we spend our money, we should always err on the side of generosity.

But who am I, and who are my people, that we should be able to give as generously as this? Everything comes from you, and we have given you only what comes from your hand. (1 Chronicles 29:14)

As we travel on our road toward authentic Christian faith, we must view our money as God views it, not as the world views it. We cannot truly love God the way we were created to love him or love others the way he commands us to love them unless we are generous with our finances. *Where our treasures are, there are hearts will be also.*

PART 3 | The Great Commission
Make Disciples of All Nations

Then Jesus came to them and said, "All authority in heaven and on earth has been given to me. Therefore go and make disciples of all nations, baptizing them in the name of the Father and of the Son and of the Holy Spirit, and teaching them to obey everything I have commanded you. And surely I am with you always, to the very end of the age."

— the Gospel of Matthew

After we begin a relationship with Christ and follow the two Great Commandments by loving God and others, the Great Commission will become important to us. God has given each one of us different gifts and strengths, and he has different good work planned for each of us. However, every follower of Christ is to be a part of the Great Commission. In short, it involves putting the two Great Commandments into action by helping others find authentic Christian faith.

CHAPTER 9 | Dancing with a Black Bear

The summer before my tenth-grade year, my daring youth pastor, "Mr. Tony," led our youth group on a camping trip to Cherokee National Forest in eastern Tennessee. One afternoon during the trip, we visited a mountaintop rest area in the Great Smoky Mountains.

As the church van pulled into the rest area, we noticed a crowd of tourists gathered at the base of a steep hill. Everyone looked and pointed upward, and many took pictures. Eager to see what all the fuss was about, I jumped out of the van and joined the crowd. About fifty yards up a huge embankment, directly above the crowd, a three-hundred-pound black bear sat next to a large tree. Judging by its medium size (for a bear), I figured it was probably a "teenager" like me.

One of the girls from my youth group quipped, "Chad, I dare you to go up and get a close-up. You're so crazy! You'd probably do it!" Several other teens laughed in agreement.

Now, this was a period in my life when I felt indestructible and had quite a wild and carefree reputation. Being a showoff, I wasn't about to miss this opportunity. I responded, "As a matter of fact, I *would* like to get a close-up. A picture of that bear would look nice in my bedroom." The laughter quieted, and a couple of my closest friends coaxed me to stay with the group.

Filled with determination and with a camera in my hand, I jogged about forty yards and climbed the embankment. I slowly approached the bear, using the tree to shield me from the bear's sight.

As I neared the tree, I heard the stern voice of Mr. Tony yelling my name. "Chad! Chad, you get down here right now!"

Normally, I would have obeyed my leader, but I was determined. I arrived at the tree, and the bear stood on the other side. It was questionable what would happen if I ran down the embankment. Not only would I fall and break my neck, but the bear could possibly chase me and eat me for lunch.

Mr. Tony continued to call, and I heard his clear direction: "Chad, listen to me. If you turn around and just go back quickly the way you came, you'll be okay. The bear hasn't seen you, and you can get away safely if you move quickly right now."

I looked at Mr. Tony and nodded, but then foolishly thought I didn't want to run away empty-handed. I planned to quickly reach the camera around the tree, snap a picture, and run for safety. With the camera to my face, I glanced around the tree but didn't see the bear. I took another glance. Again, no bear!

Apparently, while I approached the tree, the bear heard the rustling of the leaves. While I was peeking to the right, the bear, curious, walked around the opposite side of the tree to investigate.

Screams came from the crowd below, and once again Mr. Tony's voice called out clear directions: "Run, Chad! Run!"

Foolishly ignoring his direction once again, I turned around and came face to face with the bear. At first, it looked surprised. It must have been shocked by the up-close human encounter. Quickly, its look of surprise turned into a look of anger, and a deep growl came from the back of its throat. Think big teeth!

In hindsight, I'm sure the bear attempted to frighten me away when it jerked forward, but I thought it was preparing to eat me! I lost my footing and fell backward. Unfortunately, the bear also fell—right on top of me!

The bear and I tumbled down the hill together. Sometimes I was on top; other times I felt my back crack as it rolled on top of me. Near the bottom of the embankment, the bear finally stopped rolling, found its footing, and dashed back up and over the embankment. I never stopped moving. When I rolled to the bottom of the hill, my feet met the ground and quickly carried me far away from the bear!

The terrifying experience left me wiser. Our Father in heaven is a lot like Mr. Tony. God has a good plan for our lives, a plan for adventure and safety found with him. However, we often turn away from him and go our own way—and that usually gets us into big trouble!

A lot of times, sin is like that medium-sized bear. From a distance, I thought the bear was harmless and picture perfect; it seemed like something I could safely approach. When we get dangerously close to sin, it has the power to destroy everything: our friendships, marriages, careers, and, even worse, our enjoyment of God's grace.

We need to find God's voice and learn to listen closely. Just as Mr. Tony called out to me with clear directions, God is constantly calling to us: *"Hear I am. I stand at the door and knock. If anyone hears my voice and opens the door, I will come in and eat with that person, and they with me"* (Revelation 3:20). When we hear his voice, we must stop and open the door of our hearts to him. Christ is the only true navigator on the road to authentic Christian faith, so it's always in our best interest to determine God's will for our lives.

God's GPS System

It seems like everyone but Elizabeth and I own a GPS navigation device for his or her car. My dad drives with one, but that's to be expected because of his love for electronic devices. The real signal we were behind the times came when Elizabeth's dad received a GPS for his birthday. Although my father-in-law is extremely skilled at home repairs and building anything wooden, he has never been comfortable using modern electronics. When it turned out he could use one, we knew we were way behind the times.

The GPS we bought speaks instructions to us: "Turn right in one quarter mile onto Lawrence Avenue." Wouldn't it be something if it were that easy to discern God's direction for our lives? Or what if God wrote his plan for my life in the sky during high school: "I want you to attend Clemson University. My plan is for you to marry Elizabeth Koches from Charleston, South Carolina, in 6.1 years. My will is for you to work in the paper industry for 5.9 years and then transition onto full-time staff with Campus Crusade for Christ." He might have to stretch the full message out across several sunny days, but you can bet we'd hang on every word!

But God doesn't work that way. With God, most of what we do requires faith, believing in something we can't see, touch, or hear. *We live by faith, not by sight.* When we live by faith, we bring glory to God.

Although God doesn't blurt out his intentions for our lives in an audible voice, he does possess a plan and desires us to know his will. Much of his plan is clearly spelled out in the pages of the Bible already. The trouble is that we expect something "unique" for us, rather than the general instructions that apply to all people in every time and place. Biblical principles serve as a navigation system for us in our lives. The following are some of the principles of God's desire for our lives:

- God desires (Ephesians 1:15–17) and requires (Romans 12:1) we know and experience his will for our lives.
- God's plan is the very best for us.
  - It's good, pleasing, and perfect (Romans 12:2).
  - It reflects his deep love for us (Jeremiah 29:11; Romans 8:28).
  - It results in a life of fruitfulness, joy, and glory to God (John 15: 5).
- It is not unusual for God's direction to be in line with our desires, if we are walking in the Spirit (Philippians 2:13; Psalm 27:4).
- If we are walking in the Spirit, sincerely desiring to do God's will, we have assurance that God will always lead us according to his perfect plan (Psalm 25:12; 37:5, 22, 23).
- God's primary desire for us is a relationship with him, rather than a place, activity, or job (John 17:3; 15:14–15; Colossians 3:23).

These principles, read in order because they build on each other, should come as very good news to those of us who obsess about details and struggle with doubt. And this last principle is of critical importance. *The most important part of God's will for our lives is that we know him and love him.* This is the Great Commandment. Every decision we make in life is minuscule compared to the important decision we make every day to know God and love him.

This past January, one of the women on our staff team in Charleston, "J-Lynn," considered resigning from her position with Campus Crusade for Christ to pursue a career in counseling. She loved our staff team and her job, but being a counselor was something she always wanted to pursue. She let me know she wasn't 100 percent sure God wanted her to go to graduate school and asked me to pray for her decision.

A few months later, I asked J-Lynn if she had made up her mind. I told her she was a key part of our staff team. I assured her our team loved her and wanted her to stay, unless she had a peace about going to graduate school.

She responded by saying, "Chad, I really am unsure. I can't say I have a peace about going back to school, but there is one thing I feel the Lord has given me a peace about. I believe the Lord has laid on my heart that even if I am making the wrong decision, he will always be with me and love me the same no matter what I do."

How right J-Lynn was! Because God's desire for us to have an intimate relationship with him is so much greater than any other decision we will ever make, we can't go wrong when we choose to love and know him! Of course, we still want to make wise choices and seek God's will regarding every decision we make. That's why it's important to know what sources he's provided to help us make good decisions.

The Parts of God's GPS

In my junior year of high school, my church youth group took a trip to Disney World's Epcot theme park. Excited about this trip, I invited a few good friends to come along, and we planned on having the time of our lives!

Standing in a line for our first Epcot ride, I realized I needed to visit the restroom. I told my youth pastor, who stood next to me in line, I'd be back in five minutes.

Immediately after I left the group, someone announced the group would split up and meet back together at the end of the day. My youth pastor took a group and headed toward a show, and a group of girls headed toward another ride, leaving my friends by themselves in line.

When everyone walked off, my friends realized I was missing but thought I left with a different group. They couldn't understand why I didn't want to spend the day with them, but they went ahead and boarded the ride.

I returned from the restroom and couldn't find anyone. I felt so confused and hurt that everyone had left me. Even my friends had disappeared. I waited for thirty minutes, but no one came back.

For the next seven hours, I searched the park, looking for my friends or anyone else in the youth group (this took place before everyone carried cell phones). At one point, I sat at the lost-and-found booth, but no one knew I was missing. Everyone thought I was hanging out with someone else.

Around dinnertime, I finally ran into my sister and one of her friends. I ate dinner with them, and then we went to meet everyone else to leave the park and go back to our hotel.

I missed the entire day with my friends and didn't ride any rides. My day at Epcot was a complete disaster! So consider how much better my day would have been if I had known exactly where to find my friends. I would have enjoyed a wonderful adventure at Disney World.

The journey of life with Jesus is even more exciting than a day at Epcot. He has a plan for our lives, and life can be a great adventure if we can discern and follow God's will. Fortunately, God's navigation system helps us in our journey when we discover it and determine how to use it properly. I'd like to share some of the sources for determining God's will for our lives. Think of them as the parts of God's GPS:

- The Bible: Seeking his revealed will (Psalm 119:104; 2 Timothy 3:16–17)

- Prayer: Seeking his wisdom (James 1:5–6; Philippians 4:6–7)
- The Holy Spirit: Submitting to his direction (Philippians 2:13; Acts 16:6–8)
- Spirit-filled Christians: Weighing their counsel (Proverbs 19:20; 27:17)
- Providential circumstances: Seeing God at work (2 Corinthians 2:12). However, one of the greatest pitfalls of discerning God's will is placing too much emphasis on our circumstances or always looking for a sign from God. *Has God "opened the door" by allowing me to get accepted into medical school? Has God "closed the door" by causing me to be rejected from the medical school I wanted to attend?* Yes, God does *sometimes* use our circumstances to guide us, but not always, and we must never demand a sign from God (Matthew 16:1–4). Relying on the Holy Spirit through prayer and God's Word should be our most important GPS components.
- Our desires: Evaluated under his lordship (Romans 1:9–11)

An example of how the Lord used these sources to show me his will was when I resigned from my position at a paper company and went into full-time ministry with Campus Crusade for Christ.

My desire to work with college students as a campus minister began my junior year in college, but I didn't believe I was mature enough spiritually for full-time ministry when I graduated from college. During the next several years, as I worked for two different paper companies in Ohio and Georgia, my relationship with God grew.

It seemed nearly every time I read the Bible, the passage of Scripture I read confirmed the Holy Spirit was leading me into full-time ministry. I constantly thought about 2 Timothy 4:7, where Paul said at the end of his life: *I have fought the good fight, I have finished the race, I have kept the faith.* I wanted to be able to say that at the end of my life.

Elizabeth and I prayed daily for God's direction. One day I told Elizabeth, "I believe God is leading me into full-time ministry, but one factor that confuses me is my love for my job. If I love my job so much, why should I quit?"

Elizabeth responded, "Well, let's pray if God really wants you to quit your job, he would confirm it by changing your heart so you don't like your job so much."

That sounded a bit odd, but we prayed, and God answered! Before long, some circumstances changed at work, and my boss, who was a close friend, changed departments. I won't go into the details, but I became miserable at work. That seemed like a clear answer to prayer!

Finally, we began to talk to our pastor and friends at our church in Macon, Georgia. Nearly everyone we told we were considering full-time college ministry responded by saying, "We knew you'd be in full-time ministry working with young people one day! That's a natural fit!"

We used God's navigation system to make the decision to enter into full-time ministry. Of course, as with all complicated navigation devices, an instruction manual is essential! Be sure to keep your Bible close and read it as you navigate your decisions and your life.

What decisions are you in the process of trying to make? What are your goals? Are they only *your* goals, or have you asked God what *he* wants you to do? What fears about your future are you holding on to? Try using the navigation system God has provided to help us determine his will.

How to Use God's GPS

In 2 Timothy 1:7, Paul writes, *For the Spirit God gave us does not make us timid, but gives us power, love and self-discipline.* Self-discipline can also mean "sound mind," and those with a sound mind possess the mind of Christ as a result of God's transforming and renewing work. They are under the direction of the Holy Spirit by faith and thus receive wisdom and guidance from God. By contrast, dependence upon human wisdom may lead us away from God's best for us because it's based upon self-interest and an undue emphasis on emotions and chance circumstances. Think of it as the light of God versus a darkened world. Trusting God's wisdom is like following a light that always leads us to the place we are supposed to be—and God will always be there with us.

So what should you do if you need to make a life decision? I'm going to walk with you through a process that will help you clarify things. While not every step will be the same for every person, these are biblical principles that can help us discover the will of God for our lives.

1. *Pray for wisdom.* James says, *If any of you lacks wisdom, you should ask God, who gives generously to all without finding fault, and it will be given to you.* God doesn't give us everything we ask of him, but he does promise to give us wisdom when we ask for it. He may not give it to us immediately, but he will give it to us if we wait on him.

2. *Be sure you are walking in the Spirit.* We talked about the importance of being filled with the Spirit in chapter 3, "Striking It Rich!"

3. *Determine the options in the decision.* It's helpful to get a piece of paper and actually write down all of the options so you can get a visual picture of all possibilities.

4. *Search the Bible for any relevant principles and commands.*
    More often than not, the Bible helps provide clear direction
    on determining God's will.
5. *Collect all available information and the counsel of mature
    believers on each option.* It's important that the believers who
    counsel you are walking in the Spirit. A question you might
    ask yourself is whether or not the fruit of the Holy Spirit
    is evident in their lives. *But the fruit of the Spirit is love, joy,
    peace, [patience], kindness, goodness, faithfulness, gentleness
    and self-control* (Galatians 5:22–23). It's critical to have God
    involved in every aspect of the decision-making process. You
    don't want to risk making the wrong decision by getting
    poor counsel.
6. Review the following key questions:
    a. Why did Jesus come? *"For the Son of Man came to seek
        and to save the lost"* (Luke 19:10).
    b. What is the most important thing you can do for
        others?
    c. In light of the above, which option in this decision
        will best maximize my ability to help fulfill the Great
        Commission?
7. *Go back to your list of options, and list the pros and cons of
    each.* Pay particular attention to the pros and cons that have
    to do with helping to fulfill the Great Commission.
8. *Trust God for his wisdom, evaluate the options, and make a
    decision according to his promises in Psalm 37:23–24 and
    Proverbs 3:5–6.*
9. *Be careful not to depend too heavily on your feelings.* Sometimes
    God may use our emotions to help us make a decision, but
    there are times our emotions can lead us astray as well,
    especially if fear is involved. God promises wisdom, not
    always the feeling of wisdom.

10. *Move forward in faith, and do what God has called you to do.*
This is what authentic faith is all about! It's trusting God to
lead us and guide us, and being patient to wait for God's
timing and not ours. Then when we know God has shown
us what decision we should make, we continue on our
spiritual journey with confidence that he is right beside us!

Being Faithful during Times of Transition

One of the things God has been teaching me is to be faithful during times of transition. I recently read the story of a man named
Simeon in Luke 2 while I was spending time with the Lord, and
the teaching pastor at my church, Geoff Saratt, taught the next day
using the exact same story.

To give you some background, Simeon was a devout man of
prayer. The Holy Spirit had revealed to him that he would see the
promised Messiah before he died, but he had been waiting a long
time and was getting to be very old. Moved by the Holy Spirit, he
went into the temple courts:

> *When the parents brought in the child Jesus to do for him
> what the custom of the Law required, Simeon took him
> in his arms and praised God, saying, "Sovereign Lord,
> as you have promised, you may now dismiss your servant
> in peace. For my eyes have seen your salvation, which
> you have prepared in the sight of all nations: a light for
> revelation to the Gentiles, and the glory of your people
> Israel."*

Many of us are in a transitional stage of life during which we
are waiting to see what God has in store for us next. *What is my
future career going to be? Who am I supposed to marry? What is God
leading me to do next?* I would imagine Simeon was tempted to lose
his faith that he would live to see the promised Savior. He must

have been near the end of his life if he said, *"You may now dismiss your servant in peace."* Yet he continued to trust in the Lord, and he was ready when the Holy Spirit told him to go to the temple courts. My guess is he passed away right after that because we never hear anything else in the Bible about Simeon.

The faithfulness of Simeon suggests at least three principles as we go through transition and seek God's direction: (1) be faithful, (2) stay focused, and (3) trust in the Lord.

Simeon remained faithful, doing the tasks that were set before him, until he saw Jesus. Another story this reminds me of is the story of David in 1 Samuel 16. David was very young, almost a boy, when he was anointed by Samuel as the king of Israel. However, he had to wait many years before Saul died and he officially became king. David continued to be a faithful son and shepherd, and we must also be faithful to complete the tasks we are currently undertaking as we're in this time of transition. If we're students, that means that we do well in school, even as we wait to find out what our career will be.

We must also stay focused and alert. Simeon did not take his eyes off the Lord. He continued to be focused on God in prayer throughout his life. David is also a good example of this as he waited to officially become the king of Israel. Saul had been trying to murder him when David found Saul asleep one evening (1 Samuel 26). Abishai, one of the men with David, said, *"Today God has delivered your enemy into your hands. Now let me pin him to the ground with one thrust of my spear; I won't strike him twice."* But David said to Abishai, *"Don't destroy him! Who can lay a hand on the LORD's anointed and be guiltless?"* David stayed focused on God's timing, and he didn't sin by being disobedient to God and taking matters into his own hands.

The story of Simeon also reminds me to trust in the Lord as I'm waiting on his direction. God loves us perfectly, and his plans for our lives are good. *"For I know the plans I have for you,"* declares the LORD, *"plans to prosper you and not to harm you, plans to give you hope and a future."* God is always good, and he can always be trusted.

What decisions are you currently facing? How does this story of Simeon speak to you? Spend time praying for wisdom in your decisions, and ask God to give you faith and patience like Simeon and David had. Surrender your heart to the Lord, and trust him to lead you well.

Remember, no matter what shape your life takes, it is *always* God's will for us to be involved in helping to fulfill the Great Commission of Matthew 28 to *"go and make disciples of all nations."* However, I know many of us are not confidant or comfortable sharing our faith with others. Some of us would rather go "dancing with a black bear" like I did as a teenager in the earlier story than *"go and make disciples."*

My own perspective is that if I knew the cure for cancer, it would be cruel to keep that information to myself. In the same way, Christ has conquered death and can take away all sorrow and suffering, so it would be cruel for me not to share that information with those who need it! No matter who you are, or how you share (or don't share) your faith, God loves you, loves the world, and wants everyone to know it. So grab a friend, and get ready to dig into the next chapter, where we'll learn several nonpushy ways of sharing our faith with others.

CHAPTER 10 | Just Talkin' about Jesus

Several years ago, I had the privilege of getting to know an amazing young man. Two of the Campus Crusade staff members on our team, Kurt and Morgan, were conducting spiritual interest surveys at Trident Technical College when a student named Hunter walked up. Hunter, a tan young guy with sun-bleached, shaggy hair, spoke slowly with a southern drawl.

Hunter said, "Hey, y'all, I just became a Christian a few months ago, and I'm really excited about Jesus. Who are you?"

Kurt explained a little bit about Campus Crusade for Christ and asked Hunter to fill out a survey. A few days later, Kurt gave Hunter a call to get together with him.

As Kurt stepped inside Hunter's house, Hunter told him, "Well, I took some classmates down to the beach today to go surfing. And while we were there hanging out, I told them all about Jesus." He went on to explain to Kurt the most amazing story of how God had changed his life from one of endless parties, alcohol, and damaging relationships to one of obedience and love for the Jesus who saved him.

Then, in the most humble way possible, almost as if he didn't understand why it would be a big deal, Hunter said that since he had become a Christian, he had led twenty-five of his friends to the Lord! That was one or two people a week!

As Hunter started to come to some of our weekly meetings on campus, I got to know him personally, and his humility and boldness to share his faith challenged me. He went home for the Christmas holidays, and when he returned for classes, I asked him one day how his Christmas break went.

Hunter said, "Well, I read Revelation 3:20 one day while I was home and realized Jesus isn't just saying he's knocking on the doors of hearts of people who don't know him. Jesus is knocking on the doors of everyone's hearts and constantly pursuing a relationship with each of us. I was so excited about this discovery I ordered some pizza and invited my best friend, who wasn't a Christian, to come over and talk about it. We talked about Revelation 3:20 all night that Friday. He said he wanted to do it again the next night, and we invited some more of our friends who weren't Christians to come over, eat pizza, and talk about it. We talked about Revelation 3:20 every night over Christmas break, and several of my wildest friends decided to give their lives to Jesus."

Wow! While most of the students involved with our ministry were at home, hanging out with family, watching football, and trying to recover from a busy semester, this believer of just four months was talking about Jesus with his surfing friends!

When asked if he used a specific method to share his faith, he said, "Naw, man, God has done so much in my life! I was sitting on my surfboard about a month after I first trusted Christ, and I got to thinking, *Jesus did this for me. He completely changed my life, and I love him! The least I can do is share Jesus with everyone around me.* So that's what I do now. Everywhere I go, I just get people to come along with me, and I tell them about Jesus."

That's what a spiritual movement of God entails! Hunter felt so excited about what God was doing in his life that he was compelled to share it. At the end of that semester, Hunter transferred to a college in Florida to complete his studies. I'm not sure where Hunter is now, but I imagine he's still surfing and encouraging others, saying, "Come along, and I'll tell you about the most amazing person."

Hunter found his own individual and effective way of sharing Jesus with others, and that is the heart of evangelism. It's simply sharing the *good news* that has *already changed* our lives. The hesitation we often feel when we think about sharing our faith can be because we don't have anything really special to offer other people. If we aren't living an authentic relationship with God, we may be at a loss to explain what's so "good" about following him.

Good News

When many people think of the term "evangelism," they imagine someone handing out cheesy tracts in an airport or a young man in a white shirt and tie, riding on a bicycle and knocking on doors. However, in the Bible, the term "good news" shares the same root word in the Greek language as that which is translated "gospel." That root word, *euagellion* (from *eu*, meaning "good" or "well," and *aggelos*, meaning "to proclaim"), is the source of our transliterated English term "evangelize."

Think about that—evangelism isn't a religious obligation to twist people's arms and offend them with pushy or demeaning attitudes. It's not a duty, but a privilege—the opportunity to tell the good news of your story. The number one evangelism strategy that I use every day on campus isn't to knock on doors or pass out tracts—I personally wouldn't pass out a tract anyway if I didn't care enough about someone to have a conversation with him or her. Instead, my number one tool is my story! I simply share my personal story of finding authentic faith in Jesus with everyone I know. That's good news, and I find it's the kind of news people are interested in hearing.

In today's society, we don't hear enough good news. Pick up a newspaper or visit any news site on the Internet, and you will be overwhelmed by bad news. "Today the stock market plunged eight hundred points. Unemployment rose to the highest levels in decades. A girl was apparently strangled by her pet python." (That last one was a real headline in yesterday's news!) All of that bad news can be depressing!

The good news of Jesus is the polar opposite. It's the cure to all of our problems! When we receive Christ as our Lord and Savior, we receive eternal life. This literally means that at the end of time we will live with God and others for all of eternity! *For God so loved the world that he gave his one and only Son, that whoever believes in him shall not perish but have eternal life.*

If someone invented a pill to completely cure cancer in just twenty-four hours, wouldn't that be great news? If that happens, it will make the headlines of every newspaper and every Internet site in the world: "Millions saved! Cancer cured!" Everyone with a family member or friend suffering from cancer will be rejoicing! *Like cold water to a weary soul is good news from a distant land.* The cure to cancer would be the closest good news on this side of heaven that could compare to the good news of Jesus. Yet even a cure to cancer pales in comparison to the good news of perfect life that never ends.

According to author Eddie Rasnake, "Evangelism is like one person showing another a safe way of escape from a burning building, or as one beggar telling another beggar where to find bread. Yet it's more than that—it's a message to a person under the table begging for crumbs, telling him the location of a bakery with free entry." So if evangelism is so great, why aren't people excited about the good news of Jesus? Perhaps many in our world today have become so accustomed to a diet of stale, dry bread crumbs that they can't imagine anything else. They don't even realize there is much more out there to eat than just stale bread crumbs! Rasnake states, "God must first make them dissatisfied with what they have; when He does, they'll be ready for the good news."[1]

Yet David Kinnaman and the research from the Barna Group tell us it's more than that. According to their studies, Christians are primarily perceived for what we stand against rather than the good news we bring. Kinnaman says, "We have become famous for what we oppose, rather than who we are for."[2]

As I shared in the introduction, the recent studies by the Barna Group indicate 97 percent of all Americans between the ages of sixteen and twenty-nine have an unfavorable view toward evangelical Christianity. They're running away from Christianity! That means there is something about the *way* Christians have been communicating the good news of Jesus that is turning the younger generation off from Christianity. In other words, the news isn't sounding so good to them.

The teenagers and young adults in their studies even gave their reasons why they are turned off from Christianity: "Christians are hypocritical." "Christians are too focused on converts and don't really care about getting into the grit and grime of people's lives." "Christians are antihomosexual." "Christians are too conservative politically."

As Christians, we need to do a "gut check" and find out where we are going wrong. We all know we are supposed to share the good news of Jesus, but in reality what message are we communicating? If we can learn to correct our mistakes and just focus on talking about Jesus the way Hunter does with his friends, maybe more people around us will hear and believe our good news.

Before we talk about becoming more effective at sharing Christ with others, it's important to know what evangelism is not. There is one huge hindrance that can completely destroy evangelism: Christian cliques.

What Evangelism Is Not

The church was never meant to be sheltered from society. In John 17, Jesus prayed that the church in and among the world would be protected, not that we would be taken out of the world. He said to the Father, *"My prayer is not that you take them out of the world but that you protect them from the evil one. They are not of the world, even as I am not of it. Sanctify them by the truth; your word is truth. As you sent me into the world, I have sent them into the world."*

There is something good and healthy going on behind the scenes between Christians that leads to the formation of cliques. It's called bonding (and was discussed in chapter 5, "An Epic Fireworks Battle"). Bonding is an important element in spiritual growth, and yet if it is taken to the extremes, it can prohibit others from coming along with us on our spiritual journeys.

A few years ago, when Elizabeth and I moved to Charleston, we noticed many of the Christian upperclassmen at the College of Charleston lived away from the dorms in two houses on Bull Street. The guys lived in one house, and the girls lived in another.

One evening during our first semester on campus, a freshman young woman was struggling and looking for someone to talk to about spiritual things. She knew some Christian girls lived in the house on Bull Street, and she walked across campus to see if she could find someone there to talk to her. As she approached the house, she saw a group of girls out on the balcony singing a song. She was shocked when she heard the words to the song the girls were singing: "Liars go to hell. Liars go to hell. Burn, burn, burn. Burn, burn, burn."

It hurts to think how that young woman must have felt as she heard the words to that song. Needless to say, she turned around and never approached that house again, and we heard about it from someone else on campus. Were those Christian women so involved in their own Christian friendships that they lost the ability to welcome others and share the good news?

As we look at the life of Jesus, we see that he connected with those who were considered the worst people of society, and the leaders of his time mocked him for it. They asked his disciples, *"Why does your teacher eat with tax collectors and sinners?"* To this Jesus responded, *"It is not the healthy who need a doctor, but the sick."*

In Jesus's famous Sermon on the Mount, which begins in Matthew 5, he talked about how we shouldn't spend all of our time hanging out with other Christians; rather, we should build relationships with people who don't know him:

> *"You are the salt of the earth. But if the salt loses its saltiness, how can it be made salty again? It is no longer good for anything, except to be thrown out and trampled underfoot.*
>
> *"You are the light of the world. A city on a hill cannot be hidden. Neither do people light a lamp and put it under a bowl. Instead they put it on its stand, and it gives light to everyone in the house. In the same way, let your light shine before others, that they may see your good deeds and glorify your Father in heaven."*

Clearly, then, people who know Jesus should have authentic relationships with people who don't have a relationship with Christ. How else could they possibly see that our faith in Jesus is authentic? How could they ever believe that Jesus is real and is not just a myth? How else could they understand that Christianity is not about what we stand against, but that it's simply about a life-changing relationship with God?

Now that we know what evangelism is not, let's look at how relational and conversational evangelism can be very effective.

I Want to Know You

Jesus didn't just tell his followers to let their light shine before all people—he lived that. Jesus spent time with sinners. *"Why does your teacher eat with tax collectors and sinners?" "If this man were a prophet, he would know who is touching him and what kind of woman she is—that she is a sinner."*

In Luke 19:10, Jesus said his purpose was to seek and save the lost. He said people who didn't have a relationship with God were lost, like sheep without a shepherd, and he actually spent time with them! He spent time with a Samaritan woman at the well, a prostitute with seven demons, and he even took time to share his good news with a thief while hanging on the cross. Imagine that!

By studying the life of Jesus and learning about the things important to his heart, we can only conclude the road toward authentic Christian faith is a road that leads us alongside people who don't know Jesus.

There is an old saying that goes like this: "People won't care what you know until they know that you care." In my experience, this saying is true. Gone are the days when Christians could just pass out tracts and expect results—if those days ever existed—and gone are the days when churches could simply open their doors and expect people to come in. People of today's culture are tired of hearing Christians preach at them, and a popular bumper sticker summarizes their response: "God, protect us from your followers!"

So how do we connect with people in our communities, on our campuses, or at work who don't know Jesus? Let me tell you some stories.

Many Christian students at Charleston Southern University have connected with others by living on campus in the residence halls. "Amy," a junior at Charleston Southern, was deeply impacted by Christ her freshman year in college, and she decided she wanted to help other students to find the joy she found in Jesus. She accepted a position as a residence life assistant (RA for short) and lived on campus her sophomore year as an RA in a residence hall. All of the female freshman athletes (the Lady Bucs) were assigned to live on her hall. She went to all of their games and earned the respect of the girls because her love for them was so genuine.

This year, Amy was once again the RA for the freshman Lady Bucs, and now just about every girl playing every sport knows her. By hanging out with the girls, Amy has found ways to have spiritual conversations, and God has used her to have an eternal impact. This fall, two freshman women on the women's basketball team prayed with Amy and asked Jesus to be their Lord and Savior!

In our college ministry, we encourage the freshmen to continue living on campus in the dorms like Amy, or at least to get involved with other organizations besides our ministry. We also love when they become RAs in order to have an influence in the residence halls. We often wonder if many college campuses are known as "party schools" with few Christians because the Christians who *are* there have moved off campus to get away from the culture!

A second example of how we can connect with people in our communities involves my wife, Elizabeth. She is a mother with three young children, and because of the ages of our children, she is unable to be on campus as much as the rest of our staff team. Instead, she has found other ways to build relationships with people who don't know Jesus. She joined a local MOPS (Mothers of Preschoolers) group in our community, and she volunteered to host a table for the group.

During their MOPS meetings, the content is usually centered on being a good mother and having a healthy family. The group always provides childcare, and many women usually come just to have baby-sitting and adult conversations with other women. Many military wives have joined the group, and Elizabeth has built some great friendships with them. As she gets to know the women and earns their trust and respect by caring for them, she looks for opportunities to share Christ in a genuine way, based on her previous relationship.

How can we shine the light of God's good news into a dark world if we're all huddled together, hiding? How can we travel on the road that leads toward authentic Christian faith while avoiding authentic relationships with the lost? Jesus didn't do this, and we must not either.

I Want to Listen to You

Once we establish a relationship with someone who doesn't believe in Jesus, we must learn to have wisdom and tact when it comes to finding the right time to share the good news of Jesus. I'm not saying to avoid sharing the gospel if someone asks you to tell them about yourself. I'm just saying we need to be wise.

In his book *Questioning Evangelism*, Randy Newman states there are three skills absolutely necessary in conversational evangelism:[3]

1. *Declaring the gospel*—including the ability to clearly and concisely articulate the message of salvation. Learning to use a gospel tract or share your personal testimony can help you master this skill.

2. *Defending the gospel*—anticipating common questions and always being *prepared to give an answer* (1 Peter 3:15).

3. *Dialoguing the gospel*—the skill of giving and taking, bouncing ideas back and forth, and most importantly, listening.

While a lot of books have been written on declaring the gospel and defending the gospel, the art of asking good questions and dialoguing the gospel are often neglected and difficult to master. It takes time to cultivate love, caring, and trust, which lead to deeper conversations. The best place to learn how to have an evangelistic conversation is to study the conversations Jesus had in the four Gospels. In the NIV New Testament, Jesus asks 252 questions in eighty-five chapters—that's almost three questions per chapter!

One of the most powerful pictures of Jesus using conversational evangelism is in Luke 24, right after his still-secret resurrection. At this point in time, the good news of Jesus didn't seem too good to his followers. Their leader had been crucified, and they had been scattered.

On the day of the resurrection, two of them were walking along a road toward a village called Emmaus, about seven miles from Jerusalem. They were having a conversation about everything that had happened to Jesus. As they were walking and talking, Jesus himself came up and walked along with them, but they were kept from recognizing him.

Jesus asked them, *"What are you discussing together as you walk along?"*

They stopped and looked at him sadly. One of them asked him, *"Are you only a visitor to Jerusalem and do not know the things which have happened there in these days?"*

Jesus asked, *"What things?"*

They then told Jesus about all of the things that had happened and that the tomb was empty earlier that morning. Jesus continued to walk and talk with them, and they invited him to stay with them for the night and have dinner. Jesus accepted the invitation, and at dinnertime their eyes were opened so they could recognize who he was. He then immediately vanished from their sight.

They got up and returned at once to Jerusalem. There they found the Eleven and those with them, assembled together and saying, "It is true! The Lord has risen and has appeared to Simon." Then the two told what had happened on the way, and how Jesus was recognized by them when he broke the bread.

Do you see from that passage how Jesus used relational evangelism and conversational evangelism together? As the two men were walking on a road during their spiritual journey, Jesus joined them and traveled alongside them. He connected with them so deeply they urged him to stay, and then he shared his good news.

Recently, I experienced a successful evangelistic conversation by asking questions and taking the time to listen. While I was having lunch in a college cafeteria, I noticed a young man sitting by himself and sat down next to him. He looked like he was an older student from somewhere in the Middle East.

I asked, "Are you in grad school here? Where are you from?"

The young man told me he was from Iran and moved to the United States to get his master's degree.

I responded, "Really? I've traveled to a couple of countries in that part of the world and am trying to learn more about their religions. Are you religious?"

This simple question opened the door for a three-hour conversation. I did little of the talking and mainly just asked questions and listened intently. This young man was a devout Muslim and was very knowledgeable about his religion, and I learned a lot about his culture and beliefs from this conversation.

During the next couple of hours, he told me just about his entire life story. He then turned the conversation by saying, "So you know all about my life now. What about you? What's your story, and what do you believe about God?"

This was my opportunity, and I then had the privilege of sharing the good news of Jesus with him.

When he finally had to leave to go to class, he stood up and put his hand over his heart. "Thank you for spending time with me today. I will always treasure this conversation in my heart."

Even though this young man didn't make the decision to follow Christ at that time, this conversation was important for me on my own spiritual journey. I was paying attention that afternoon and took the time to slow down and take notice of him. Because I genuinely cared for him, I was a good listener and showed I loved him right where he was on his spiritual journey. Finally, I encouraged him to join me on my spiritual journey by leaving the door open for further conversation. A fast speed is never the best way to approach conversational evangelism.

From a biblical standpoint, evangelism is not so much a person, place, group, or strategy. Instead, it's more of a natural response from someone who has had a personal life-changing encounter with Jesus! When I understood just how much Jesus loved me and what he sacrificed for me, I wanted all of my friends and everyone else to join me on that joyful road. All Christians have special stories about how Jesus has changed them, so be willing to share your story with others!

On the road toward authentic Christian faith, I continue to grow in the areas of relational evangelism and conversational evangelism. In the next chapter, I'll share the importance of mentors in helping me learn to share my faith. I'm excited for you to discover the wisdom and life-changing power of having a mentor, but even before you read the next chapter, I want you to know something: if you love Jesus, and love other people, you can share the good news of your faith with grace and sensitivity—starting now!

CHAPTER 11 | Please Help Me!

As I mentioned earlier, my freshman year in college was marked by frustration as I struggled with Christian hypocrisy. I said I believed one thing, but my lifestyle didn't reflect those beliefs. Then one night, after a friend pointed out my hypocritical lifestyle, I reached a point of utter brokenness. Alone in my room, I prayed to God a simple prayer over and over again: "Lord, please help me!"

Within a couple of weeks after I prayed that prayer, God answered when I met an older brother in Christ named James Stecker, who cared about me and wanted to help me out. I opened up to him and shared my struggles, and God used him as a spiritual guide in my life for the next three years as he mentored me. I honestly believe I would not be in full-time ministry today if I hadn't met James or if he hadn't taken the time to help me grow.

When Elizabeth and I moved to Charleston, South Carolina, to lead the ministry of Campus Crusade for Christ here, one of the first students I met at the College of Charleston was a freshman named Aaron Tripp. Aaron, a recent graduate now serving full-time on our staff team, recently received acceptance into a great seminary program to pursue a career as a pastor. I asked Aaron to share his personal story, and these are his words:

Have you ever had that overwhelming feeling that something was missing? Maybe you've seen it as a need to perform in order to stand out, or maybe it is a loneliness that clouds your thoughts and actions. I've experienced both of those emotions, and neither one was going away on its own.

My freshman year I was consumed by the need to get straight As and be the most popular party guy on campus. Yet I was still lonely and unfulfilled. I had obtained the life I dreamt of at the beginning of that year, but I was still empty.

I grew up in a Christian household, going to church twice weekly. I knew there was a God who loved me. I believed he sent Jesus to die on the cross to pay the penalty for my wrongdoings, but unfortunately I lived most of my life without that at the forefront of my mind. I was homeschooled until my junior year of high school, but then I attended a boarding school, where I majored in academic achievement and minored in sexual freedom.

My time at Governor's school was marked by allowing myself to be ruled by the flesh from which Christ had set me free. These indulgences mainly centered on physical relationships that only left me scarred and empty, but the move to the College of Charleston did not help. The Christian community when I enrolled at my school was practically non-existent. My coping mechanism for dealing with all of the hurt from high school, which was to build a wall around my heart, did not help with forming relationships with any Christians on campus. I was miserable. I turned to alcohol, which only deepened my depression as I ignored the Holy Spirit and the conviction he brings.

One day on campus, a guy offered me a water bottle and invited me to a Campus Crusade for Christ meeting. My heart was crying out for the healing I knew this could offer. At the end of the meeting, in the middle of around two hundred students, Chad, the man who had given me the water bottle, found me and asked me to meet him for lunch. That next day would change my life forever. Christ used Chad to mentor me and lead me to realize I had turned into a carnal Christian. From then on, I continued to grow in my faith throughout college. I went on mission trips to New York and La Plata, Argentina, and I fell more and more in love with God.

The broken relationships I see around me, and the things people use to try to fill the hole in their lives that only God can fill, have solidified my decision to go into ministry. I want to reach young men and women and teach them how to fall in love with God so they don't go through what I went through— so they will lead. As Christians, it is our responsibility to raise godly men and women and teach them how to lead by faith. I want to help reach the world with the message of Jesus Christ. God has offered us such a wonderful gift, and by sharing our faith and mentoring young believers, we can reach every nation!

Yes, God transforms lives! In my personal experience, I've learned God changes lives by using mature believers to build up younger believers. Both my story and Aaron's story demonstrate the need for spiritual mentorship.

Recently, I spoke to the women's basketball team at Charleston Southern University and explained the need for a spiritual mentor. I emphasized that as a campus minister, my heart yearned to see them develop and become a "total athlete."

"There are three components of an athlete: the body, the mind, and the spirit," I explained. "A total athlete is one who has been developed in all three areas. Your coaches help you develop your body by making you run and lift weights, but a personal trainer can help you develop your body faster. You go to college to develop your mind, which also makes you a better player. Having a personal tutor can help you achieve better grades. My desire is that you would grow spiritually to be the best athlete you can be. Just as a personal trainer can make you stronger and faster and a tutor can help you become smarter, a spiritual mentor can help you grow."

Have you ever had a tutor or spent personal time learning from a professor? When I was in graduate school, I took some very challenging chemical engineering classes that I could not have passed on my own. One particular course I might have failed was kinetics. I could never understand the advanced homework assignments in that class on my own, and I visited my professor nearly every day to ask him questions. Not only did he answer my questions, but he took the time to explain the concepts I couldn't understand on my own or during his lectures. Because of this professor, I not only passed the class, but also received an A as my final grade.

Mentorship is similar to tutoring in a spiritual sense. When we are struggling spiritually, sometimes the only way to overcome our obstacles is by having someone coach us and teach us how to grow. If someone takes the time to help us fall in love with God and become authentic in our faith, we will do more than just "get by"—we'll experience true life the way God intended. *"I have come that they may have life, and have it to the full."*

The Lost Art of Mentorship

As Elizabeth and I travel around the country, speaking at churches and sharing our ministry, we notice that few young Christians are being mentored by more mature believers in Christ. Many young believers are involved in Bible studies, Sunday school programs, and youth programs, but *not* with in-depth, one-on-one teaching. Surprisingly, we've also found relatively little has been written on the topic of one-on-one mentorship. Mentoring young believers to grow and develop isn't often presented as a requirement, or even an option.

As we explore the idea of spiritual mentorship and what it means to be mentored, you may be thinking, I don't need to be mentored. I know how to read my Bible and pray, and I can just get everything I need from others by being in a Bible study or going to church. I don't even have time to find a mentor, much less be mentored.

If you can relate to this thinking, I assure you that you're not alone. We're living in a society where independence is celebrated and following authority is not in style. However, it's more than worth your time and effort to find a mentor and learn from him or her. Actually, I feel confident the Lord will use it to change your life forever! Still have doubts? Let's address some of the concerns you may be feeling.

How Exactly Can a Mentor Help Me?

When Jesus preached his famous Sermon on the Mount in Matthew 5–7, he completed it by saying,

> *Therefore everyone who hears these words of mine and puts them into practice is like a wise man who built his house on the rock. The rain came down, the streams rose, and the winds blew and beat against the house; yet it did not fall, because it had its foundation on the rock. But everyone who hears these words of mine and does not put them into practice is like a foolish man who built his house on sand. The rain came down, the streams rose, and the winds blew and beat against that house, and it fell with a great crash.*

You see, we all have areas in our lives that we have built upon the sand rather than upon the rock of Christ Jesus. For some of us, one of those areas may be sexual purity. For others of us, it may involve our use of time. We may spend little time developing a deep relationship with Christ while we spend most of our time living to please ourselves. Many of us have built our entire lives on a foundation of pride. We're too prideful to admit we don't have it all together or that we need help in our spiritual lives. Most of us have built our house on a foundation of selfishness. Our lives are all about us. We don't live to please God or help others. The one common element in all of these areas is that we can *never* solve them on our own. For lasting transformation, we need the ongoing wisdom and honesty of a mentor.

What we look for in a mentor is someone who can help identify the areas in which we've built our house upon the sand—someone who can help us replace those areas of sand with a solid foundation built upon Christ. Being in a small group or attending church may or may not be able to help us with that. In a small-group environment, no one is likely to ask you how you're doing in the area of sexual purity. A pastor of a church may spend many months preaching on different topics that are not related to the areas of "sand" in your life. It may take months or years for your pastor to address the issue that is keeping you from growing the most—and even when the issue is addressed, what guarantees that you'll follow through with changing it?

A good mentor can ask the right questions to get right to the heart of what you're dealing with. They can ask questions such as: How are you doing? What's the area in which you want to grow the most this year? What is your greatest struggle? What are your hopes and dreams? What is keeping you from being the man or woman God is calling you to be? And since they know you, they can keep you accountable to those answers.

How Do I Know If I Need a Mentor?

We could all use mentors. Just as I told the CSU women's basketball team, a good personal trainer assists athletes to become stronger, healthier, and faster by teaching good technique and pushing them to be the best they can be. Every student would benefit from a personal tutor in school or a teacher who gives one-on-one counsel. That student can get all of his or her questions answered and can fill in the gaps of knowledge required to do well in class.

Similarly, with spiritual mentorship, every young believer benefits from meeting with a mature believer. This mature Christian may detect and point out blind spots or areas in which we need to grow. It often helps to have someone else's perspective, as we're not always the best judge of how we're really doing. Personal time with a more mature believer can lead to rapid spiritual growth.

In short, we all need a mentor!

This is a biblical concept, found in Acts as well as 1 and 2 Timothy. The apostle Paul led Timothy to Christ during his ministry in Lystra on his first missionary journey. When he revisited Lystra on his second missionary journey, Paul chose Timothy to accompany him. Timothy was Paul's disciple (or pupil), friend, and co-laborer for the rest of the apostle's life. In his last letter to Timothy, Paul charged Timothy to mentor others: *And the things you have heard me say in the presence of many witnesses entrust to reliable people who will also be qualified to teach others.*

What Should I Look For, and What If I Don't Feel Comfortable Opening Up?

As we look for someone to lead us spiritually, the fruit of the Holy Spirit found in Galatians 5:22 should be our guide. If a Christian isn't full of *love, joy, peace, forbearance, kindness, goodness, faithfulness, gentleness, and self-control,* then that person may not be living the Spirit-filled or Christ-directed life we discussed in chapter 3.

We want to be sure our spiritual leaders are leading us toward Christ, so it's imperative to have mentors who are living Christ-centered lives. The most common pitfall in the mentorship process is to have an older mentor who is mature in many ways, but who isn't really in love with Christ. The way to avoid this pitfall is to ask the following two questions: Is this person truly in love with Jesus? How often do they talk about Jesus? Just as an engaged woman in love can't help but talk about her fiancé, someone in love with Jesus can't help but think and talk about him.

When we're looking for someone to mentor us, it's also important to find someone who is approachable and understanding when we fail. We are all sinful, and we all make mistakes. We want the person mentoring us to be encouraging and forgiving. That way we won't be too insecure to be honest and authentic when we open up and share our struggles.

Most of us struggle with insecurity from time to time. I know one of my biggest struggles in the past was worrying about what others thought of me. In the first chapter of this book, I stressed the importance of being honest with ourselves about where we are spiritually. This is the first step in finding authentic faith.

In order to grow spiritually, we must also learn to be honest and transparent with others about where we are spiritually. That doesn't mean you should spill your guts and open up completely the first time you spend time with a mentor. Take your time getting to know the person mentoring you, and open up and share as you build a relationship with mutual trust and respect. You and your mentor should also agree that whatever is shared is kept confidential.

What Will the Mentoring Process Look Like?

The short answer is: different every time! It's largely dependent on your personality and the personality of your mentor. For example, if both of you like to live structured lives, you may meet once per week over some coffee or lunch to discuss areas of your life in which you need to grow. The mentor may pull out his or her Bible to sharpen you in areas that need to be sharpened. On the flip side, if both of you are spontaneous and hate structure, you may find an activity you both enjoy and do it together while you talk. I've known mentors who work out in a gym or go running with people they're mentoring. As they're exercising together, they talk about areas in which the younger believer needs to grow.

Whatever shape the relationship takes, there are three key components that must be present: the relationship (you need to know the mentor cares about you as a person), the Word of God (he or she must use truth found in Scripture to sharpen you), and doing ministry together (you need someone to model ministry to you as well as observe you doing ministry). If all you ever do is talk about things such as the importance of praying or sharing Christ with others without doing them, you will miss the opportunity to grow and develop in your faith.

As you grow and mature as a believer, no doubt you will have the desire to "pay it forward" by mentoring others and passing along the things you've been taught, especially when you see how quickly you can grow through biblical mentorship. Some of you reading this book may already be in a place where you are ready to mentor others. If and when you are ready, visit www.findingauthenticchristianity.com to learn how to find some-one to mentor and how to mentor them.

In a nutshell, mentorship is simply a way to grow spiritually. It's like having a general practitioner versus a specialist as a doctor. If you go to church and attend a small-group Bible study each week, you receive the Word of God as if it were a physical or checkup at the general practitioner's office. You may or may not find out what your weaknesses or struggles are depending on what topic you happen to be studying. For example, if you are in a Bible study that is studying pride, you may never discuss your biggest struggle if you are struggling with sexual purity.

However, if someone is mentoring you and asks the right kinds of questions, he or she can find out exactly where you are spiritually and determine your greatest needs for growth, like a specialist. I've had eight major knee surgeries, and when I'm having knee pain, I won't visit my general practitioner to determine the problem. Instead, I'll go and see my orthopedic doctor, who will specifically address my knee. If we're to overcome our roadblocks on our road toward authentic faith, we need a mentor who will take the time to help us move past them.

As we close our discussion of the benefits of mentoring, I want to emphasize that this does not mean you shouldn't find a healthy local church or participate in a small-group Bible study. On the contrary, every believer needs the fellowship and community that can be found only in a local church, and small groups are wonderful places of fellowship and growth.

The Bible says the body of Christ is made up of many parts. Every believer has different gifts and different strengths. When we join together in a local church with Christ as the head, we can change the world in ways that we can't as individuals. Finding the right church or small group sometimes takes a little time, but it's well worth the effort, as we'll see in the next chapter.

CHAPTER 12 | The Right Pit Crew

Last year, my son Wyatt and I attended our first NASCAR race at Daytona Speedway. We were on a summer mission trip with Campus Crusade for Christ, and we spent one of our free evenings at the races. Along with college students from all over the country who were a part of the mission project, Wyatt and I shopped at thrift stores around Daytona and found the perfect Harley-Davidson T-shirts and do-rags for the event. Posing as biker dudes, we took a lot of fun "tough guy" pictures with the college students.

During the Pepsi 400 race, we watched as race cars stopped in the pits to switch drivers or for refueling, new tires, repairs, and adjustments. While a pit crew of fifteen to twenty mechanics worked, the driver waited in the vehicle or allowed another driver to take his spot.

Much like baseball or football, motorsports is a team sport. The entire racing team works together for a common goal: to win the race. The team as a whole is more important than any individual part. Each member of the team is essential to the team's performance, and ultimately, each member affects the results of the race. Races are often won by seconds or less, and every tenth of a second spent changing a tire can make the difference to a team winning or losing a race.

I find it fascinating God designed his church to function in a similar way. Paul writes, *Do not think of yourself more highly than you ought, but rather think of yourself with sober judgment, in accordance with the faith God has distributed to each of you. Just as each of us has one body with many members, and these members do not all have the same function, so in Christ we, though many, form one body, and each member belongs to all the others.*

Christ designed us to play specific roles within the church, and only by getting involved can we fully understand our role and determine our purpose. Just as each pit crew member is essential to the overall success of the racing team, each member of the body of Christ is essential to the effectiveness of the body. It's the responsibility of each believer to find the right church and get involved.

There are churches everywhere in our country, but "the church" is made up of all those who are truly following Christ all over the world. Paul says, *Christ loved the church and gave himself up for her.* The church is invisible, yet visible. In reality, we don't know who belongs to God and who doesn't; only God knows. *"I am the good shepherd; I know my sheep and my sheep know me—just as the Father knows me and I know the Father—and I lay down my life for the sheep."*

This is one of the reasons so much hypocrisy exists in American Christianity—since there are so many churches, we know that not everyone in every church is an authentic follower of God, yet from the outside churches are viewed as pretty much the same. So if a church is unhealthy, or many of the people who attend it act in unhealthy ways, some see that as demonstrating that Christianity itself—or even Christ—is unhealthy. That's why it's so important for every believer to be involved in a healthy church or to help unhealthy churches become stronger, so that the public witness of the church is a shining city on a hill.

What characterizes a healthy church? While there are no churches without faults, there are certainly healthy attributes to look for when selecting a church where you can worship God in the Spirit and in truth.

Elizabeth and I moved to five different cities during our first twelve years of marriage, and we understand well the difficult task of finding the right church. There is no perfect church. Every church is made of people, and no person is perfect!

That isn't to say that all churches are equal. When we look at Philippians or 1 Thessalonians, we easily see Paul's great joy in churches with a relative absence of major moral problems or doctrinal flaws. On the other hand, serious doctrinal and moral problems were festering in the churches of Galatia and Corinth.

Say you're getting ready to find a church your first weekend in college—what should you look for? Well, first of all, Christians should not necessarily seek the purest church and stay there until a purer church comes along. Rather, we should find a church in which we can grow personally and spiritually as well as become a contributing member of effective ministry. We should seek to add purity to the local church family in which we are a part.

I have a lot of experience in choosing a church because I've lived in several cities, and it isn't always easy! Recently, an excellent book by Wayne Grudem[1] helped me put into words the many characteristics we should look for when finding the right church. I'd like to share some of those characteristics to look for, and I hope you can imagine yourself choosing along with me.

Hypothetically, if I were visiting churches right now and looking for the right fit, the first thing I would look for would be the authentic love for Christ and the exaltation of him. When people leave a church service, Sunday school class, or Bible study, what are they thinking? Are they thinking, "Wow, isn't that preacher or leader great?" Or are they focused on Christ?

In Genesis 11, the world had one language. The people said, *"Come, let us build ourselves a city, with a tower that reaches to the heavens, so that we may make a name for ourselves."* But the LORD came down to see the city and the tower the men were building. The LORD said, *"If as one people speaking the same language they have begun to do this, then nothing they plan to do will be impossible for them. Come, let us go down and confuse their language so they will not understand each other."* A church that is more dependent on the leaders than it is on God himself is in trouble.

Pastor and teacher Tim Keller has said he hopes people leave church worship services, Bible studies, and other church events thinking, "Wow! Isn't God great?!" Only when Christ is exalted will we see how wonderful he is and how badly we need him as Lord and Savior in our lives. When a church exalts Jesus, lives are changed, and people begin to travel on the road toward authentic Christianity.

The second characteristic I would look for in a healthy church would be effective prayer. I've been in full-time ministry long enough to know that the body of Christ can't do anything without complete dependence on God, and the number one way we depend on God is through prayer.

Two years ago, I felt convicted for depending on myself too much and for not depending enough on the Lord to change students' lives on one of our college campuses, Charleston Southern University. I spoke with a couple of the student leaders of our ministry, and we spent the next couple of months praying and asking the Lord to give us direction on how to become more dependent on him.

The answer became clear: the more we prayed, the more we realized we needed to make prayer the central focus of our ministry!

We faced a crossroads. At the time, our meeting looked somewhat like a Sunday morning worship service. We had praise and worship, and then a speaker taught from God's Word. It was clear to us that the Lord was leading us to change this main meeting to a prayer meeting, but we knew we risked losing students who didn't like change or didn't want to attend a prayer meeting.

Because we felt strongly that the Lord was leading us to be more prayer focused, we obediently changed the format of our weekly meeting. We still had praise and worship, but we blended it together with prayer. During that time, students were led to confess any sin the Holy Spirit revealed to get their hearts right before the God, and then we prayed for students on campus who didn't have a relationship with Christ.

During the first year after we made the change, we didn't see a huge increase in the number of students involved in our ministry. In fact, the number of involved students may have declined because some students didn't like the change. However, while the quantity of involved students didn't change, the quality of our worship did. By the end of the year, we all felt we had grown in our love for the Lord and for others. We had become an authentic Christian community.

The second year was when we really began to see a change at Charleston Southern. We learned that if you pray long enough for students who don't have a relationship with Christ, then sooner or later your heart will go there. *"For where your treasure it, there your heart will be also."*

This past semester, we saw more than thirty students accept Christ as their Lord and Savior as students shared Jesus with their friends. The administration at Charleston Southern has also taken notice. Dr. Rick Brewer, a dear friend of mine who is the vice president of Student Affairs and Athletics, recently stated in an interview, "I've seen God moving on campus this year, and I've seen student-led prayer increase. If I called any student involved with Campus Crusade for Christ right now with a prayer request, I know for a fact they would pray for it."

Yes, we've seen God transform many lives this year at Charleston Southern, and we're convinced more than ever that God moves when we pray. He loves us too much to let us think we can do great things without his help. He's just waiting on us to trust in him!

A third characteristic I'd look for in a healthy church would be effective evangelism. In chapter 10, I discussed how the church was never meant to be sheltered from society. In John 17, Jesus prayed that the church in and among the world would be protected, not that we would be taken out of the world. He said to the Father, *"My prayer is not that you take them out of the world but that you protect them from the evil one. They are not of the world, even as I am not of it. Sanctify them by the truth; your word is truth. As you sent me into the world, I have sent them into the world."*

Elizabeth and I are members of a church in North Charleston, South Carolina, called the Dream Center. The church was planted a couple of years ago by a large church called Seacoast. What first attracted us to the church when we moved to the area was its commitment to evangelism. Seeing the need for Christ in North Charleston, a town with one of the highest crime rates in the country per capita, Seacoast planted the Dream Center right in the middle of a lower-income area. The church provides free food and clothing for the needy in the community with no strings attached, and many people have come to know the Lord as their Savior in this part of town. We just heard recently that the crime rate in the part of town where the Dream Center is located has dropped 30 percent in the past three years!

The next characteristic I would look for in a healthy church would be genuine spiritual growth fueled by teaching from

God's Word and a simple discipleship process. As we discussed in chapter 9, "Dancing with a Black Bear," the Bible is God's primary way of communicating to his people, and a healthy church is a church where the preaching and teaching come straight from the Bible. This ensures that God is ultimately doing the teaching, not the pastor or teacher. When Elizabeth and I first went into full-time ministry with Campus Crusade for Christ, we were placed in Spartanburg to help plant and grow ministries on twenty-five college campuses in upstate South Carolina. We felt led to join a church called Anderson Mill Road Baptist Church, and the pastor, DJ Horton, was an expository preacher who taught straight from the Bible verse by verse. We learned so much about God from his sermons each week and grew in the knowledge of the Bible, too!

It's also important that a church has a simple process for making disciples. Thom Rainer and Eric Geiger, in their book *Simple Church*[2], published their findings that the main difference between growing and declining churches is the existence of a simple process for making disciples. Churches that aren't growing or are spiritually stagnant usually have a lot of programs taking up everyone's time, but there is a lack of focus on helping young believers to mature in their faith. Because we all have different barriers to overcome in our journey with Christ in order to become mature, mentoring is the most effective method of discipleship, as we discussed in chapter 11.

There are other components of a healthy church as well, such as community among the believers, genuine worship, care for the widows and poor, biblical confrontation (chapter 7), spiritual power in ministry (chapter 3), and personal holiness among the church members. Questions I would ask myself would be: Do the members of this congregation seem to genuinely love God and each other? Are they authentic? Are they trusting and relying on the power of the Holy Spirit rather than on their own strength?

Do they genuinely love the people in the community who don't go to church?

The church was, and still is, Jesus's plan for reaching the world with the gospel. He spoke of no other plan. Finding the right "pit crew" or church is essential for every believer.

Elizabeth and I have been blessed to be a part of five healthy churches in the five cities in which we have lived during our marriage so far. We have fond memories of the times we spent building deep friendships with other believers as our lives were transformed by Christ. We have also seen many people come to know the Lord and have their lives changed as a result of the love showed by the church. Our prayer is that every believer would find a healthy church where they can get involved in what the Lord is doing around them! Don't miss out!

Even if you are in a transient stage of your life where you are only living somewhere for a few years (such as college or the military), it's important to find a church and get plugged in. It's worth it in the moment, and it will pay dividends later. Who knows what God may teach you through the pastor's sermons? Who knows how many people you will impact by being involved in a local church or how much you'll be impacted by others? You may meet people in church who end up being lifelong, eternal friends! We must live in the moment and get involved in a church.

The church is both local and universal. Every Christian in the world is a part of the same church, the same body of Christ. In the next chapter, we will explore how common, ordinary people can be a part of expanding Christ's church throughout the whole world.

CHAPTER 13 | A Trip around the World

S everal years ago, I visited a central Asian country and shared an evening with a small gathering of Christians. Half of the group consisted of young American missionaries, fresh out of college, and the others were young Middle Eastern believers. We circled together in a small, modest living room, taking turns sharing our stories.

The Americans shared stories of their spiritual journeys first, me included. After several of us shared, I noticed a trend in our spiritual journeys. The Lord had placed someone in each our lives to share the good news of Jesus. For some, our parents introduced us to church and planted seeds of the gospel. For others, a college friend was the first to share the good news of Jesus.

When I realized each American's story followed this trend, my curiosity began to grow in anticipation of hearing the stories of the young believers from this central Asian country. In a part of the world with only one missionary for every 2 million people, how had these young college students heard about Jesus?

Finally, the time came for the first Asian young woman to share. We'll call her "Annie" to protect her identity because she lives in a country where Christians are persecuted. In a soft voice with a strong Middle Eastern accent, Annie shared her personal testimony of how she met Jesus:

> I had never heard the name of Jesus or even knew he existed. My family is a strong Muslim family, and we never heard anything about other religions in school. Everyone I knew was simply born a Muslim. Then one night I had this dream. There was a man in a robe with outstretched hands, and he said to me, "Come to me, Annie. I am the Way, the Truth, and the Life. Come to me." I do not know how I knew his name, but somehow when I woke up the next morning, I knew this man's name was Jesus. Several months passed by, and over time I forgot about this dream.
>
> Then last year during harvest season, I left college to go home and help my family with the harvest. I was out in the field with my friends, and suddenly two bad men appeared and started chasing my friends and me. After a few minutes, I tripped on something and fell to the ground. The two men started kicking me and hitting me, and then one of them got on top of me to rape me.
>
> As the man started to rip my clothes off, I closed my eyes and began to cry out to Jesus. I began praying to him, asking him to help me and vowing to follow him if he saved me. A moment later, I opened my eyes, and the men had disappeared. That day, I became a believer of Jesus. I have been following him ever since, and I was so excited a few months ago to meet a few more Christians. I thought I was the only one in my country.

One by one, the other central Asian college students shared their stories, and most of them were very similar to Annie's. None of them had ever heard of Jesus growing up, but most of them met him in a vision or a dream.

During that trip to central Asia, I began to understand the gospel in a fresh, new way. Although there existed few Christians to share the good news of Jesus in this country, God still provided a way for people to meet him. A familiar verse in the Bible became more real to me that week: *For God so loved the world that he gave his one and only Son, that whoever believes in him shall not perish but have eternal life* (John 3:16). In other words, he loved the world so much that he was willing to pay an infinite price—the life of his own beloved Son.

In the beginning, God created humans and loved us. However, we chose to go our own way. The Bible says that when we turned away from God to live independently, his heart was broken. God didn't give up on us, though. Because he *so loved* us, he sent his one and only Son to bring us back into a relationship with him.

Remember identifying the main idea of stories in elementary school? Well, this is the main idea of the Bible—a perfect, loving God has a rescue plan for the world!

If we are to become authentic Christians who love God, we must develop compassionate hearts for the things God loves. God *so* loves the world, and as we become more authentic followers of Christ, we will love the world, too!

After Jesus was crucified for our sins and was resurrected, he issued the Great Commission to each and every believer to be a part of what God is doing to restore his relationship with people all over the world:

> *"All authority in heaven and on earth has been given to me. Therefore go and make disciples of all nations, baptizing them in the name of the Father and of the Son and of the Holy Spirit, and teaching them to obey everything I have commanded you. And surely I am*

with you always, to the very end of the age." (Matthew 28:18–20)

When I was in graduate school, I felt convicted because I had never embraced Jesus's Great Commission, and I jumped at an opportunity to go on an overseas trip to Slovakia with Campus Crusade for Christ. It was there I realized many people in other countries have not been blessed with the opportunities to learn about Jesus that you and I take for granted.

That summer, Elizabeth and I spent six weeks teaching English to college students at weeklong "English Camps." We used the Bible as our textbook to teach the Slovak students English, and naturally we were able to strike up spiritual conversations and share the good news of Jesus. Through group lessons, one-on-one dialogue, and simply bonding with each other, more than twenty Slovak students trusted Christ as their Savior.

How can a college student help to fulfill the Great Commission? How can we be a part of what God is doing overseas when we already have commitments here at home? What can we be doing right here and now to help other cultures and nations experience a life-changing relationship with God? Everyone can and must take part! There are five primary ways we can be a part of what God is doing around the world to bring people into a relationship with himself.

Changing the World for Christ

The biblical basis for each of these can be found in Matthew 6:19–21: *"Do not store up for yourselves treasures on earth, where moths and vermin destroy, and where thieves break in and steal. But store up for yourselves treasures in heaven, where moths and vermin do not destroy, and where thieves do not break in and steal. For where your treasure is, there your heart will be also."*

As we discussed earlier, two of our greatest earthly "treasures" are time and money. The key truth in this passage is that as we invest our time and our financial resources in things that are eternal, such as taking the gospel to the world, our hearts for eternal things grow. The five ways of changing the world for Christ are praying for the world, giving financially toward reaching the world for Christ, reaching the world's cultures in our own backyard, mobilizing others to reach the world, and traveling around the world to share the good news of Jesus. Let's look at each one in a bit more detail.

Praying for the World

As we discussed earlier in chapter 4, "A Conversation with the Creator," Jesus taught us to pray, *"Your kingdom come, your will be done, on earth as it is in heaven."* Because we know God loves the world, we know it's his will that every nation will get a chance to hear the good news of Jesus. We also know from Revelation 7:9 there is a great multitude in heaven no one can count, from every nation, tribe, people, and language, standing before the throne and in front of the Lamb. Therefore, to apply Jesus's teaching on how to pray, we must pray that every nation, tribe, and people would worship him here on earth as they do in heaven.

Jesus also challenges us to pray for the world in Matthew 9:36–38: *When he saw the crowds, he had compassion on them, because they were harassed and helpless, like sheep without a shepherd. Then he said to his disciples, "The harvest is plentiful but the workers are few. Ask the Lord of the harvest, therefore, to send out workers into his harvest field."* Jesus saw the huge number of people who were lost without him, and he felt great compassion for them.

God's desire to see the whole world experience his eternal love didn't start in the New Testament, either! We see God's heart for the whole world displayed in every book of the Bible, starting in

Genesis. Listen to God's promise to Abraham in Genesis 12:1–3: *"I will make you into a great nation, and I will bless you; I will make your name great, and you will be a blessing. I will bless those who bless you, and whoever curses you I will curse; and all peoples on earth will be blessed through you."*

We must pray for the world. If we don't feel like it, we must pray that we'll feel like praying for the world! God will answer and give us a heart for it!

There are also some practical ways you can grow in your heart for the nations. I'd suggest going online and learning about a country such as China or any other country that comes to your mind. Many organizations and resources such as Operation World (www.OperationWorld.org) have websites dedicated to sharing how you can be praying for that country. Visit one of those websites, and consider watching a documentary to learn more about that country, the challenges it faces, and the needs it has. Remember first and foremost to pray for their hearts, that the people of that nation will come to know Christ as their Lord and Savior.

Giving Financially toward Reaching the World for Christ

It takes two parties to reach the world with the good news of Jesus—those who physically go to the nations and those who pray and provide the financial resources for those who travel. The apostle Paul writes, *How, then, can they call on the one they have not believed in? And how can they believe in the one of whom they have not heard? And how can they hear without someone preaching to them? And how can anyone preach unless they are sent?*

In God's eyes, the role of sending is equivalent to the missionary's role of going. This principle is similar to the discovery of the polio vaccine. In the early 1900s, more and more polio outbreaks occurred worldwide, and by 1950 it became a widespread epidemic. More than 21,000 paralytic cases were reported by the CDC in the United States alone.

In 1955, Dr. Jonas Salk at the University of Pittsburg Medical School discovered the vaccine for polio with the help of his colleagues, and a countless number of people's lives have been saved as a result. Who was ultimately responsible for the breakthrough discovery that has eliminated polio in developed countries? Dr. Salk or the people who funded the grants that paid for his research? The obvious answer is both.

As we discussed in the previous chapter, "The Right Pit Crew," the body of Christ is made up of many parts. God calls some to go physically to the nations to share Christ, and God calls some to stay at home so they may send those who go. In the Great Commission, Jesus called all of us to play one of those roles and *make disciples of all nations.* " Pray about which role God is leading you to play. While you are here at home, give financially so that others may go.

In 1 Samuel 30:24, David, the leader of the Israelite army and their future king, made the following statute and ordinance for his people: *"The share of the man who stayed with the supplies is to be the same as that of him who went down to the battle. All will share alike."* It is the same in the kingdom of God.

Many people feel convicted when reading the Great Commission in Matthew 28, since they are not physically going to make disciples of all nations. To help reach all of the cultures of the world, however, we don't necessarily have to go overseas. God can use us to reach the nations by making it possible for others to go—or even by reaching our nation's different cultures right here in our own neighborhood, city, or state.

Reaching the World in Our Own Backyard

At the time of this writing in the early twenty-first century, more than 650,000 students attend college in the United States, originating from nearly every country of the world. There are also countless numbers of international students attending college in other parts of the world where many evangelical Christians live, such as South Korea. If we reach these international students, the future leaders of their countries, with the good news of Jesus, we can reach the world for Christ!

Because I work in college ministry and have built friendships with many international college students, I know from experience that internationals love to build friendships with Americans. Meeting Americans and experiencing American culture are part of the allure that brought them to our country in the first place. Because they are looking to meet Americans and practice their English by carrying on conversations, it is often very easy to engage in deep spiritual conversations. In fact, many times I find it easier to have a spiritual conversation with an international student than with an American student.

Sadly, on most college campuses in the United States, international students are overlooked by Christians. More than 80 percent of these international students will never be invited into the home of an American.[1] Many come to America from countries like Argentina, where hospitality is the norm, and they don't understand why Americans are so rude and inhospitable. They find themselves isolated, hanging out mostly with other international students, and then they return home.

All it takes is a little effort to reach out and build relationships with these students. On one of our college campuses in Charleston, there are a number of students from China. Celeste, one of the women on our staff team, has reached out to this community of Chinese students and has built meaningful friendships with them.

She often hosts these students for dinner, movies, and game nights, and spiritual conversations with them come easily. I write this at a time when Christians are being persecuted in China—it's amazing to think how hard it would be for Celeste to do the same thing in China that she's doing right now in Charleston!

Mobilizing Others to Reach the World

Leading a Bible study on world missions, inviting someone to give, and "raising the banner" for world missions all mobilize others to reach the world. Full-time ministry workers who organize trips or train and recruit others to impact the world for Christ certainly mobilize others. Ordinary, everyday Christians who love the Lord can as well. God *so loves* the world, and because we love God, we can *so love* the world as he does.

One student at Charleston Southern University, Jaimie Evans, has taken this to heart. She took a trip last summer to Argentina to help share Christ with Argentine college students. When she returned to campus this fall, she began mobilizing others to go by talking to her friends about the trip, sharing her experience, and challenging others to pray. She led a Bible study and encouraged everyone in her Bible study to go as well. Several of Jaimie's friends have caught the vision to share Christ in Argentina, and at least one of them has already applied to go on a mission trip to Argentina this summer.

All Jaimie needed to do to mobilize her friends was talk about what was already important to her heart and life! By sharing about God's heart for the world, we raise awareness that God is at work in other places besides our country. God will use our words to stir others' hearts and help them develop a heart for the world as well!

Traveling around the World and Sharing the Good News of Jesus

It is my heart's desire that every believer, health permitting, will make a trip to another area of the world at some point in his or her life to share Christ overseas. By spending precious time in another country and meeting the locals, we can more easily understand God's love for the people of the world. Also, it will be evident to us that people who don't know Jesus are *harassed and helpless* (Matthew 9:36), and our compassion for them will grow.

If you do go overseas, however, I would encourage you to find a church or an organization that doesn't just go to that country one time or once per year. If we go somewhere and lead someone to Christ, it's important to have Christians in that location year-round who can mentor the new believer and help him or her grow spiritually. We talked about the need to have more mature Christians help younger Christians to grow in chapter 11, "Please Help Me!"

For example, every college campus in America that has an active Campus Crusade for Christ ministry has a partnership country overseas. Our partnership country for our campuses in Charleston is Argentina. Each summer, college students take part in summer projects to go to Argentina and share Christ on college campuses in Buenos Aires, a city with more than a million college students. Many students in Buenos Aires have come to know the Lord these past few summers as a result of these summer projects, and there is also a STINT team (Short-Term INternational Team) made up of graduates who have committed one or two years of their lives to live in Argentina. These missionaries continue to share Christ and help young believers to grow in their faith long after the summer projects have ended.

Two years ago, the Lord provided me with an opportunity to fly to Buenos Aires for spring break with a group of American students.

We traveled there both to encourage the American missionaries and to be a little part of what God is doing in Buenos Aires.

One afternoon, we walked to the local medical university to pass out fliers advertising free English classes we would be teaching that same evening. Most Argentine students are required to take several years of English classes, but they rarely get to practice conversational English by spending time with Americans. It presented the perfect opportunity to meet students and build relationships with them.

I stood in the hot sun, passing out fliers, but the Argentine medical students were too busy to notice someone passing out pieces of paper. That's when I thought of a crazy idea to cut holes in a trash bag and wear it like a poncho as an attempt to draw people's attention. I looked silly, but it worked! As soon as I put the trash bag over my head and spoke in English, inviting students to the English classes, a crowd gathered around me as students came to find out why a crazy American was dressed in a trash bag. More than two hundred fliers were gone in an instant! (By the way, I don't recommend this tactic on American campuses—it probably wouldn't be so effective!)

A few hours later at our free English classes, a tremendous crowd of Argentine students attended. I spent an hour helping students with their grammar, and then a young medical student named Jorge asked me to go outside and take a walk with him. He said he wanted to get to know me better. Argentines are well known for being a hospitable, friendly people, and Jorge wanted to make a new friend.

Jorge and I spent the next several hours walking, sitting on benches or street corners, and talking as we got to know each other. He told me most of his life story as well as his spiritual background and personal beliefs. He then asked me why I came to Argentina for a visit. This was my opportunity to share my personal story.

I told Jorge I came to Argentina to talk to people about Jesus, who had changed my life for the better.

In a sincere voice with broken English, Jorge asked, "Why would you come all the way to Argentina from America just to talk to people about Jesus?"

I responded, "I don't know. Maybe God just wanted me to come here. Maybe God loves people in Argentina so much that he would turn the whole world upside down and bring people here to tell them about him."

Jorge stared at me for a moment as he thought to himself. Suddenly, his eyes lit up, and his lips broke into a giant smile as he said, "I believe maybe you're right. Tell me what you believe about Jesus."

I then shared with Jorge the good news that Jesus was sent to restore for all eternity a broken relationship with God.

That night, Jorge invited Jesus to be his Lord and Savior! A year later, tears came to my eyes when I received an e-mail from a friend in Buenos Aires telling me he mentored Jorge after my visit. Jorge had just become a student leader with Campus Crusade for Christ at his medical university. God's heart truly beats for every person in the world—how can *you* be part of God's rescue plan?

As we come to a close, just as I shared with Jorge, I want to encourage you that now is the time to give Christ control of your life. It's very simple. If you've never opened the door of your heart to Jesus and invited him to be your Savior, you may do so right now by praying a prayer similar to the one I prayed when I first invited Jesus into my life.

My prayer went something like this: "Lord Jesus, I want to know you personally. Thank you for dying on the cross for my sins. I open the door of my life and receive you as my Savior and Lord. Thank you for forgiving me of my sins and giving me eternal life.

Take control of my life. Make me the kind of person you want me to be."

If you've already opened the door of your life to Jesus but have been living on your own strength, I'd encourage you to reread chapter 3 and recommit your life to Christ by giving him control.

The basic fundamentals of Christianity we've explored in this book are the foundation for an authentic, intimate walk with God. I'm still growing in each of these challenging areas today. My prayer is that the Lord will help you to use these truths to build a solid foundation for authentic faith—a real faith in a phony, superficial world.

Epilogue

L iving an authentic relationship with God is the greatest adventure we can have. It's all about loving God, loving people, and being involved in the expansion of the kingdom of God throughout the world. The adventure is so much bigger than us, and it's an adventure that lasts for all of eternity.

My prayer is that this book has been an encouragement to you as you seek to grow spiritually. The principles in this book are principles the Lord and other believers have passed along to me during my spiritual journey. If these principles have encouraged you in your spiritual journey, please continue to pass them along to someone else.

It hasn't been an easy journey by any stretch of the imagination. As you can tell from my story, my search to find authentic Christianity has been a wild, crazy ride! I wish I could say that I've arrived at my destination and that I'm now an authentic Christian. However, I'm still in process and still hopeful that day will come.

I recently spent an evening with two dear friends, Josh Gale and Bob Monaco, on a pier at Waterfront Park in Charleston, South Carolina. We had a beautiful view of the Cooper River Bridge, with the water glistening beneath the moonlight. Josh is a senior at

Charleston Southern University, while Bob is a fifty-eight-year-old sage within the ministry of Campus Crusade for Christ.

Knowing I had written this book and that Bob is full of wisdom, Josh asked Bob what he had learned in all of his years as a believer about what it means to be an authentic Christian.

Bob responded, "Authentic Christianity isn't something you accumulate. Being authentic in your relationship with God is something you can have one day but then not have the next. You have to wake up every morning and decide you want to follow wholeheartedly after the Lord. If you don't, you can lose the authenticity."

Bob was right. Some days I experience that authenticity, and some days I don't. God always desires for me to have an intimate relationship with him, but that doesn't happen without daily intention, action, and—most of all—grace.

I hope that the fundamentals of authentic Christianity found in this book will help you experience a relationship with God that is real, sustaining, transformational, and full of love for those who don't know Jesus.

Notes

Introduction
1. David Kinnaman and Gabe Lyons, *unChristian* (Grand Rapids, MI: Baker Books, 2007), 11.
2. Ibid., 29–30.

Chapter 1 | Don't Drink and Mountain Climb
1. David Kinnaman and Gabe Lyons, *unChristian* (Grand Rapids, MI: Baker Books, 2007).

Chapter 3 | Striking It Rich!
1. Based on the true story of Ira Yates. J. J. Bowen, *Uncertain Riches: The Discovery and Exploitation of the Yates Oil Field* (Austin: Eakin Press, 1991).
2. Wayne Grudem, *Systematic Theology* (Grand Rapids, MI: Zondervan Publishing House, 1994), 782.
3. Bill Bright, "Have You Made the Wonderful Discovery of the Spirit-Filled Life?" (Orlando, FL: NewLife Publications, 1966).

Chapter 4 | A Conversation with the Creator
1. Bob Sjogren and Gerald Robison, *Cat and Dog Theology* (Waynesboro, GA: Authentic Media, 2003), 13–27.
2. Kenneth Boa, *Conformed to His Image* (Grand Rapids, MI: Zondervan, 2001), 65–66.

Chapter 5 | An Epic Fireworks Battle
1. Henry Cloud, *Changes That Heal* (Grand Rapids, MI: Zondervan Publishing House, 1992), 20–21.

Chapter 6 | Living in a Ditch

1. Henry Cloud, *Changes That Heal* (Grand Rapids, MI: Zondervan Publishing House, 1992), 20–21.

Chapter 7 | Roadblocks

1. Henry Cloud, *Changes That Heal* (Grand Rapids, MI: Zondervan Publishing House, 1992), 92.
2. Ibid., 97.
3. Stephen Arterburn and Fred Stoeker, *Every Young Man's Battle* (Colorado Springs, CO: WaterBrook Press, 2002), 45.
4. Ibid., 25.
5. Michael Leahy, *Porn Nation* (Chicago, IL: Northfield Publishing, 2008), 90–92.

Chapter 8 | Sometimes the Bedbugs Bite

1. Richard A. Easterlin, Laura Angelescu McVey, Malgorzata Switek, Onnicha Sawangfa, and Jacqueline Smith Zweig, "The happiness–income paradox revisited," *Proceedings of the National Academy of Sciences of the United States of America* 2010 107 (52) 22463-22468.
2. C. S. Lewis, *Mere Christianity* (New York, NY: HarperCollins, reprinted 2001), 143.

Chapter 10 | Just Talkin' about Jesus

1. Eddie Rasnake, *Following God: The Book of Romans* (Chattanooga, TN: AMG Publishers, 2005), 15–16.
2. David Kinnaman and Gabe Lyons, *unChristian* (Grand Rapids, MI: Baker Books, 2007), 26.
3. Randy Newman, *Questioning Evangelism* (Grand Rapids, MI: Kregel Publications, 2004), 14–15.

Chapter 12 | The Right Pit Crew

1. Wayne Grudem, *Systematic Theology* (Grand Rapids, MI: Zondervan Publishing House, 1994), 873–75.
2. Thom Rainer and Eric Geiger, *Simple Church* (Nashville, TN: B&H Publishing Group, 2006).

Chapter 13 | A Trip around the World

1. Statistic provided by the Traveling Team, an organization that mobilizes college students and churches to take the good news of Jesus to the world. http://www.thetravelingteam.org/?q=node/376/

Suggested Reading

Chapter 2 | Real Relationships Take Time

A good resource to use as you are learning to implement daily quiet times (or times with the Lord) is *Four Sevens*.

Four Sevens: http://crupress.campuscrusadeforchrist.com/discipleship/foursevens

Chapter 3 | Striking It Rich!

As you are learning to integrate the Spirit-filled life, the *Thirsty* devotional is a great resource.

Thirsty: http://crupress.campuscrusadeforchrist.com/discipleship/thirsty

Chapter 4 | A Conversation with the Creator

I highly recommend *Fireseeds of a Spiritual Awakening*, a great book on prayer!

Fireseeds of Spiritual Awakening: http://crupress.campuscrusadeforchrist.com/discipleship/fireseeds-of-spiritual-awakening

Chapter 5 | An Epic Fireworks Battle

Will Walker's *Kingdom of Couches* shares how we can foster the essential characteristic of community.

> *Kingdom of Couches*: http://crupress. campuscrusadeforchrist.com/discipleship/ the-kingdom-of-couches

Chapter 6 | Living in a Ditch

Keith Johnson's *White Paper* "Hearing the Music of the Gospel" discusses Christ-centered Bible study. The *White Papers* are a series of training articles that cover important spiritual and ministry concepts such as evangelism and the reliability of Scripture.

> *White Papers*: http://crupress.campuscrusadeforchrist.com/ discipleship/white_papers

Chapter 7 | Roadblocks

Flesh and *Fantasy* are two good resources to supplement the discussion of the sexual immorality roadblock.

> *Flesh*: http://crupress.campuscrusadeforchrist.com/discipleship/flesh

> *Fantasy*: http://crupress.campuscrusadeforchrist.com/discipleship/fantasy

Chapter 9 | Dancing with a Black Bear

A great resource on God's will is the *White Paper* called "The Art of Discerning the Will of God."

> *White Papers*: http://crupress.campuscrusadeforchrist.com/discipleship/white_papers

Chapter 10 | Just Talkin' about Jesus

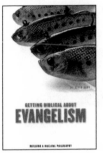

Keith Davy's article "CoJourners" and his booklet *Getting Biblical About Evangelism* are two great resources that encourage students in sharing their faith.

"CoJourners: A Transferable Concept": http://crupress.campuscrusadeforchrist.com/evangelism/cojourners_a_transferable_concept

Getting Biblical About Evangelism: http://crupress.campuscrusadeforchrist.com/evangelism/getting-biblical-about-evangelism

Chapter 11 | Please Help Me!

Keith Davy's *Design for Discipleship* as well as his resources in the *Life Concepts* series help beginning disciple-makers as well as new disciples in the next step of their journey.

Life Concepts: http://crupress.campuscrusadeforchrist.com/discipleship/life-concepts

Design for Discipleship: http://crupress.campuscrusadeforchrist.com/discipleship/design_discipleship

Chapter 13 | A Trip around the World

The *White Paper* "Mission Impossible" explains how to fulfill the Great Commission through missions.

White Papers: http://crupress.campuscrusadeforchrist.com/discipleship/white_papers

Think Up
to
Get Up

How to Break Free from
Destructive Ways of Thinking

ROBERT L. LOWERY III

Trilogy Christian Publishers
A Wholly Owned Subsidiary of Trinity Broadcasting Network
2442 Michelle Drive
Tustin, CA 92780

For information, address Trilogy Christian Publishing
Rights Department, 2442 Michelle Drive, Tustin, Ca 92780.
Trilogy Christian Publishing/ TBN and colophon are trademarks of Trinity Broadcasting Network.

For information about special discounts for bulk purchases, please contact Trilogy Christian Publishing.

Manufactured in the United States of America

10 9 8 7 6 5 4 3 2 1

Library of Congress Cataloging-in-Publication Data is available.

ISBN 978-1-64773-606-4 (Print Book)
ISBN 978-1-64773-607-1 (ebook)

To my dad, Robert Lowery Sr.
(February 5, 1946–January 27, 2018).
He gave me the strength to do and be
more than I see in myself.
Love you!

Contents

Introduction

For as he thinks in his heart, so is he. "Eat
and drink!" he says to you, but his heart
is not with you.
                    —Proverbs 23:7 (NKJV)

King Solomon gave a timeless principle when he shared
those words. Your thinking determines who you are, and
James Allen, in the book As a Man Thinketh, added, "And as
he continues to think, so he remains." Unfortunately, there
are countless people who chart their course in life based on
what's been said about who they are and what they're capable
of. Thoughts like this are just how it is: "I can't get ahead,"
"My parents struggle with depression, anger, poverty, etc., so
it's just in my genes." These are a few examples of thoughts
that have been accepted most likely at a young age and have
taken root in your heart.

Believing you are a certain way because of genetics or
any other reason that places you in the seat of a victim is
exactly what the enemy wants you to think. Why? Because if
this lie is accepted, you will go throughout life forever reacting to your circumstances and never overcoming them. This
book will help you understand and apply biblical principles
that will help you begin your path to freedom that is rightfully yours through the blood of Jesus Christ! The power of
God is more than able to deliver you from any emotional

or psychological stronghold that the enemy has been using to control your peace, your joy, your purpose, and your life! As you read this book, pray and ask God to give you wisdom and revelation on how to break the specific strongholds in your life. Also read this book along with your Bible, and if this book helps you to broaden your understanding of a scripture, I suggest you pause reading this book and begin to study that scripture, because revelation of scripture comes from God, and if He is releasing a greater wisdom, it is always for your benefit and should not be ignored.

In the following chapters, I intend to expose the tactics of the devil to keep you in a defeated, impoverished mindset and to help you break free from this stronghold. I am not an expert on psychology, nor am I an Ivy League scholar giving you points I think are simply good ideas that can help you; I am just a person who struggled to overcome depression, low self-worth, and all the unspoken principles those methods of thinking taught me. I am just a guy that is, to this day, still thinking and getting up myself.

This book is to the person who is afraid to courageously go forward and embrace who God has created you to be because of the fears your past has taught you through bad experiences. To the person who is afraid to live and afraid to die. To the person who submissively accepts what people say about you rather than what you say about you! The content in this book is comprised of principles I have grown to understand and apply to my life as I fought through my fears, poverty, low self-worth, and every thought that you can think of that represents defeat. This book was written to help you discover the abundant life Jesus died for, but just like with any other gift, in order to enjoy it, you first must accept it. I was drowning in depression and low self-esteem, and God gave me the grace to change just as He is giving you.

The observations and principles in this book, I have grown (and am still growing) to learn and apply to my life. I pray that this book will help you overcome destructive thinking just as these principles are helping me overcome mine. Let go of whatever it is you need to let go of and embrace whatever it is you need to embrace to be all God is calling you to be! I have learned that it is more beneficial to first identify and break free from destructive thinking habits that you have adopted over the years before you embrace the principles that will help you come out of destructive thinking.

Just as you can't pour new wine in old wineskins (see Mark 2:19–22), you also cannot apply new ways of thinking without first disregarding the old ways of thinking. When you let go of a destructive belief, you, within the same action, cut off the life blood that is supplying all the destructive thoughts connected to that belief. This frees you to go forward and be all God has called you to be, one thought at a time. Let's do as Hebrews 12:1 (NKJV) instructs us to do, which is to "break free from every weight and sin," together, as we journey through this book.

Thanks for your support!

What Does It Mean to Think Up?

If you focus on the storms and frustrating situations that you are involved in, you will continually produce that same end, perpetuating those feelings in your thoughts. Betrayal, physical or emotional abuse, etc. If you're not careful, paying too much attention to your past has the potential to cause you to continually be drawn to future circumstances that reinforce that same abuse you have suffered in your past even though that abuse was years ago.

Mephibosheth, King Saul's grandson, is a clear example of this. The story of Mephibosheth is told in 2 Samuel chapter 4, verse 4, and chapter 9. He was dropped as a child and crippled. Because of this handicap, he could not provide for his family. He was clearly in a position to accept help if it was offered, right? King David one day decided to honor the family of King Saul, the former king, for the sake of Johnathan, King David's best friend (see 1 Samuel 18:1–3), and reinstate all the property owned by King Saul to his family. Mephibosheth was the only person King David could find. But when he informed Mephibosheth that he could now stay in the palace and be taken care of and receive his inheritance, which was rightfully his, Mephibosheth's response was, "Why do you look upon a dead dog as I?" (See 2 Samuel 9:8 NKJV.)

Like Mephibosheth, so many people today are so defeated in their mentality that no circumstance will change the low opinion they have of themselves. It takes the power of God unto salvation to awaken your spirit and for you to begin to see what God sees about you. King David giving Mephibosheth an opportunity to take his rightful place according to his birthright only stirred up feelings of confusion. Why? Because when you think low of yourself, you expect and unconsciously demand the people around you to do the same. Expectations will always resemble the level of self-worth you possess. Mephibosheth allowed his poor beliefs about himself to be a pillar of his thoughts. Whenever you allow impure thoughts to be a cornerstone in your thinking, you will reject who God is molding you to be.

Don't Allow Your Bad Past Experiences to Be the Thermometer of Your Value

Many people today fall victims to the worthless thoughts they unknowingly accept, forcing themselves to be a slave to the circumstances those thoughts create. Your environment, to a certain extent, influences your beliefs, your beliefs influence your thinking, and out of your thinking, your character, attitude, and mindset are shaped. Your ability to think is a blessing given by God, but unfortunately, many people have turned this blessing into a curse by allowing their bad past experiences or the words of destructive people to create limited and oppressive beliefs about themselves.

This was my struggle for many years.

When this happens, there can be no other result but to embrace the mindset of a victim. Out of this victim mindset, thoughts of depression, low self-esteem, and inferiority complexes are birthed. These thoughts can cause you to believe it is impossible to overcome inferior thoughts and embrace your full potential of who God called you to be.

Think Up to Get Up: How to Break Free from Destructive Ways of Thinking is my attempt to help you see that you can rise above any circumstance if your thoughts are above that circumstance. This principle is nothing new, but I have found that the simplest truths that can transform your life are usually the principles that are easily forgotten. Our culture is determined to make you and me a victim, a statistic, to make you doubt, to make you fear, to make you assume the worst, to make you dependent on things outside of God, rather than believe and think in agreement with what God says about you.

"Think Up to Get Up" Means to Discipline Your Thoughts

> When we are no longer able to change a situation, we are challenged to change ourselves. (Victor Frankl)

> If your thoughts become a victim of circumstance the circumstance wins! (Dr. Myles Munroe, YouTube, "Change with Dr. Munroe")

When I say "Think up," I don't mean simply to think positive. It is a short way of saying, "Discipline your thoughts to rise above defeat in all forms." I believe weakness or strength is first manifested in thought before it is expressed in an attitude, emotion, or circumstance. You will not stand against an adversity if you do not first stand within. Evolving within your heart from believing you are strong to embracing biblical knowledge, wisdom, and principles that make you strong is my prayer for you as you read this book. God empowered each one of us with the grace to change any circumstance by changing what you think about that circumstance. This truth is the underlining narrative of this book.

Defeat Is Spelled
S-E-L-F L-I-M-I-T-I-N-G
B-E-L-I-E-F-S

I don't think I can rises from a deeper I don't think I am.

—John Maxwell
Intentional Living

Suffering is the byproduct of dysfunctional beliefs.

—Albert Ellis, PhD

Your circumstances reflect what you believe.

—Earl Nightingale

What Are Self-Limiting Beliefs

Self-limiting-beliefs are an idea or principle that is held within your heart and acts as a wall or roadblock to the path of manifesting your God-given purpose and potential. The limitation is created when what you believe to be true negatively contradicts what is actually true, which forces your actions to work against you. I believe, when you understand the destructive power of limited beliefs, you will more diligently resist its vices and break free from the lies it has created. It's easy to assume that the fix to overcome self-limiting beliefs is to just try harder, do more, have more faith, pray more, etc. This was what I thought for years. What I found is, putting more effort into actions that are not yielding fruit will always produce a hopeless attitude because with each fruitless act, your faith diminishes. More effort mixed with a self-limiting belief system equals stagnation. Placing faith, prayer, or any other spiritual discipline on top of self-limiting beliefs will not change the results. That's the same as praying for an apple tree to produce oranges. If the seed isn't right, the fruit will not be right. Your beliefs are seeds that will only produce the fruit, good or bad, that's contained within. I found that I was progressing at a slow pace because I had the limiting belief that I did not deserve spiritual, emotional, and financial freedom, that I did not deserve to be 100 percent free to do all and be all God has called me to be. To my surprise, this belief had more power to direct my life than my efforts to break free from it. Why? Because beliefs are the road and your efforts are the vehicle. Changing the vehicle (efforts) does not change the road (beliefs). I had to come to the reality that though I had the right heart and intention to not embrace limitation, it was still manifesting in my life through low self-worth and the fear of success because my efforts did not transform the self-limiting image I had of myself.

Your Beliefs Are the Foundation of Your Thoughts

Believe with unwavering conviction that you have something to give to the world, or the world will believe with unwavering conviction that you don't.

Selling yourself short of your potential is one of the most common side effects of limiting beliefs. Being easily persuaded to see your ideas, your vision, and your goals in a manner that fits the narrative of what others think you are is toxic. Why? Because your beliefs and values are the reservoirs that your thoughts are drawn from. We all know that if you draw water from a well that is filled with dirt and bacteria, that same water will produce sickness if it is consumed. So it is with limited beliefs. Your thoughts, when turned into actions, will produce a limited life, so if you change your beliefs, you will change your life. Your beliefs are the foundation of your thoughts, and your thoughts are the pillars of your life. Who you are is the fruit of who you believe yourself to be. Your beliefs are directly or indirectly connected to the foundation of every triumph or downfall in your life. You cannot hold on to any belief that is connected to indecision, fear, doubt, or insecurity and get up.

What you believe creates thought patterns that enable you to embrace or reject what God wants to birth within you, whether that is a closer intimacy with Jesus Christ, growth in your character, or a greater understanding of your purpose. The beliefs you have of yourself can be the most empowering force against the enemy's lies, or the beliefs you have of yourself can be the glue that keeps every destructive criticism and disappointment in your heart. Letting go of self-destructive beliefs is the first step before overcoming any obstacle that you face.

What Empowers Our Limiting Beliefs?

In this subchapter, I'm going to list the three main destructive ways of thinking that encouraged me to limit myself. I'm sure there are many things that can empower the limiting beliefs and convictions that a person could have. Limited beliefs can be acquired by many ways, but I'm only listing these three because they are the ones that limited me the most. When limited beliefs are accepted as truth, it becomes a part of who you are, which, in turn, becomes a normal or natural way of thinking for you, although this way of thinking is not serving you.

What helped me better understand the importance of our thoughts is to view what we think as a road that leads to a destination. This is true in the negative, like thinking on the road of rejection, which leads you to a destination of self-doubt and lack of faith, or positive, like thinking on the road of acceptances, which leads to the discovery of your true identity and self-worth.

Fear

Fear, when it is accepted, becomes a part of who you are, which, in turn, becomes a normal or natural way of thinking for you. In order to get the most out of this chapter, insert the method you came to know limited beliefs. It is important to find out what you are sowing into that empowers the limiting beliefs you have so you can expose your limited thinking and break free from a limited life. Let's go deeper into how the three areas limited me and how you can break that limitation.

> Be of good courage, and he shall strengthen your heart, all ye that hope in the Lord. (Ps. 31:24)

I think we all know and have heard of the dangers of fear. I don't need to go in-depth for you to understand why fear is destructive, but what I want to emphasize is that what you do or do not believe about fear can intentionally or unintentionally cause fear to produce a self-limiting belief that you cannot do all and be all God has created you to be. It is easy to suppress the life God is blessing you to embrace, because of the disappointments of your past and the self-defeating habits those disappointments created. I love Jesus Christ and His saving grace because He still gives us opportunity to get up, grow up, and change even though we may have withdrawn from life. I must admit, I understand why people withdraw; I have done the same thing. For me, I withdraw because of fears of the unknown, fears about how people will respond to my actions, the lack of confidence in God to finish the good work He has begun within me, and the lack of faith in my ability to be effective in my purpose. These fears prompt me to wait, to pray, to get direction from others, or to wait on God to give me strength rather than take the next step toward my purpose. I am not suggesting that you naively run headlong into whatever vision you have. Praying, getting advice from others, and seeking God for revelation to ensure your vision is from God and in alignment with your purpose is not only important but also biblical. But I am saying that any spiritual discipline can potentially be an act of disobedience of the Spirit of God's leading when you use that discipline to disobey what God has already spoken to your heart. King Saul is an example of this (read 1 Samuel 15).

I was waiting to act on what God put in my heart because of fear, and waiting on God for direction was really a mask to cover up my fears with spiritual disciplines. God already revealed to my spirit the direction he wanted me to go, but I was fearful to embrace that revelation. Only when I began to face my fear and do what I believed God was calling me to do did I discover that even good things like prayer can become a stumbling block when they are used to disobey what God already gave you clarity of direction in. Obedience is better than sacrifice!

Fear brings unnecessary pain, because it introduces the heart to thoughts and ideas that lead to paths that are destructive.

Tips on breaking limitations-based fear: Awareness. Acknowledge that fear is limiting your potential. Self-awareness precedes growth! I became aware that fear was limiting me when every time I thought of myself as the leader God is calling me to be, fearful thoughts clouded my mind. What is God calling you to be?

Rejection

> And we know that all things work together for good to them that love God, to them who are the called according to his purpose. For whom he did foreknow, he also did predestinate to be conformed to the image of his Son, that he might be the firstborn among many brethren. Moreover whom he did predestinate, them he also called: and whom he called, them he also justified: and whom he justified, them he also glorified. What shall we then say to these things? If God be for us, who can be against us? (Rom. 8:28–31 KJV)

Past experiences of rejection are the primary way I began to accept an attitude of low self-worth. I was born in Clearwater, Florida, and raised in Largo, Florida. I remember when I moved to a new neighborhood in Largo, Florida, I was focused on being accepted. Within a couple of months of attempting to find friends, I got into a disagreement with two of the neighborhood brawlers and I got jumped. Though I didn't get hurt, I felt rejected by the whole neighborhood, and this attitude birthed a strong feeling of rejection that I did not know how to couple with because of my immature thinking, as we all are as a teenager. This experience birthed within me an attitude of rejection. No matter how you arrived into the seat of rejection, you cannot stay there and get up.

When you feel rejected, you go down a path of thinking that causes you to assume that you are worth less than the people who are rejecting you. This is the primary lie that causes you to think and live a life that is way beneath your potential. I have learned that there will always be people who will attempt to give or take away your self-worth and value for their benefit. You must be sober, as 1 Peter 5:8 tells us, because giving others the authority to marginalize your value will, within the same action, take away your God-given ability to be all God has called you to be. How? Because you cannot trust in the heart of a person who does not have the God-sent vision for your life. I believe value comes directly from God and is downloaded into your heart through His Spirit. You must seek God to embrace your true self-worth. Getting your self-worth from materialistic things, people, praise, or accomplishments will feel good for the moment, but God did not design these things to give you value.

Ignorance

> Wherefore be ye not unwise, but under-
> standing what the will of the Lord is.
> (Eph. 5:17)

Being *ignorant* is a state of being uninformed (lack of knowledge). The word *ignorant* is an adjective describing a person in the state of being unaware and is often used as an insult to describe individuals who deliberately ignore or disregard important information or facts.

Ignorance is destructive not primarily from the lack of knowledge but also from the illusion it gives a person of knowledge. The person who perishes because of ignorance always has a strong sense of intelligence; this is how true wisdom evades them, because they already know. Have you met a person that you were trying to share some information with and they cut you off and said, "I know that already," without hearing what you had to say?

Ignorance is innocent and not destructive for a season, but once your ignorance is uncovered, you must choose to accept the truth or reject it. Rejecting truth is also accomplished by doing nothing to become informed, as so many do. Once this is done, you are no longer ignorant; ignorance has now matured to a foolish heart, as the Bible claims.

Ignorance is fortified or matured to become truth to an individual by circumstance and the opinions of others. These circumstances and opinions of others become the ignorant person's confidence of accepting and applying the principles ignorance is giving. Ignorance of your worth will, without a doubt, inevitably result in you thinking, acting, and living beneath your purpose.

To understand something takes desire and effort. It takes more energy to understand a thing than to just be knowledgeable about it. It takes just a couple of minutes to read about the importance of a good diet. But when you learn the importance of a good diet through experience, pains in your body, physical ailments due to the lack of dieting, you can now understand why that knowledge is important. When knowledge meets application, understanding will be achieved.

How to Break Limiting Beliefs

Acknowledge the fact that you have limiting beliefs.

Whether your limiting beliefs came from the failures of your past, the rejection of your peers, or ignorance of the belief systems you allowed to guide your life, the failure to prayerfully confront and expose limiting beliefs in your life will always result in the failure to be all God has called you to be.

I found that to break a limiting belief, you must act on new knowledge that exposes limiting beliefs as the lie that they really are. Acting in agreement with what you know builds faith, courage, and confidence to view your limiting beliefs as a block that can be moved instead of a stone wall that cannot.

Beliefs I Acted on to Eliminate My Limiting Beliefs

I can't think how I'm thinking going where I'm going—this statement reminds me that a change in my thoughts is a requirement to grow, not a choice. Attempting to push yourself to be all God has called you to be will reveal weaknesses in your thinking that I call mental roadblocks. These roadblocks, if entertained, will cause you to question or doubt your actions.

When these roadblocks arise, I will tell myself I can't think how I'm thinking going where I'm going. This statement reminds me that it is a requirement to trust God to believe, to act and to think on the level that God is taking me.

Your Desire to Get Up Must Be Greater Than Your Desire to Stay the Same

Desire is required for change of any kind. It is the foundation from which one builds their relationship with Christ, their character, their marriage, their wealth, and in the negative sense, your desire can ruin your marriage, cause you to lose your job, burn bridges with those who love you, or leave you homeless. Desire is one of the God-given character traits that He gives us full responsibility for. God will birth a desire in you that will bring you closer to Him, like interest in the Word of God. But He will not make you perfect or mature that desire; that is left up to you. Without desire, your honor unto God will not come from your heart.

No one who loves their child is forced to provide for them; it naturally comes from your heart to be the best provider you can. It's the same with God. When your love and appreciation come from your heart, it is authentic, not artificial, religious, or dependent on what He can do for you. It is God who works in you both to will and to do for His good pleasure (Phil. 2:13). I was inspired to write this book because I see Christians today using their faith in God to compensate for their lack of desire, ambition, drive, and fight that is required in order to possess their promised land. Forgetting that action is what brings faith to life. Many "name it and claim it" or believe they will overcome their obstacles because "I'm a nice person." Passive faith is the normal of many people today. Believing in something until an obstacle comes and challenges that belief, which then causes you to no longer hold to what you believe. I am not writing this book to simply help you reach a goal or higher standard of living; this book will help you identify false beliefs that have quietly crept into your heart, which are the source of all stagnation. Faithfully adhering to false principles that appear to be sound can give you or strengthen your confidence and belief in that false principle. Once it is uncovered as a lie or unethical, let it go!

Struggling with an addiction or a certain sin that they want to break free from, but the problem is they don't want to stop committing the sin. They only want the bad side effects to stop, the depression or anxiety after they indulge. So they pray and ask God to help them overcome this issue, but they sincerely do not want to change. Not realizing the major role their desire plays in God's master plan. When you have little desire to want a specific circumstance to change by nature, you put your faith in action and ask God to change the situation, but when God reveals to you something He wants you to do as a seed toward your change, you omit it because you only wanted it bad enough to pray about it not act on what you desired. They pray and ask God to take away that drug addiction, that sexual tendency, that depression or anxiety, but with only enough desire to ask God to change them, putting full responsibility for change on God as if He has sowed those bad seeds that are now coming forth.

This book will help you clearly see the difference between your faith and your desire. "Be not deceived; God has not mocked: for whatsoever a man soweth, that shall he also reap" (Gal. 6:7). He is the author and finisher of our faith, but you are the author and finisher of your desires.

Your Environment Feeds Your Desires

Desire is naturally in every person and is the motivation to change, positive or negative.

When I was growing up in Largo, Florida, we didn't have much money, so it was a desire to have a new home and a car I didn't have to check before every drive. These desires were inspired by lack, embarrassment, and anger of circumstance. The desire for a more financially stable life was birthed out of the environment I was in.

Your environment plays a major role in what you desire, but not what you will become. Only those with little or no desire allow their environment to tell them who they are and what to become, because little desire is connected to little faith in your God-given authority to change your circumstances for the better. It is important to expose and eliminate the contradicting desires that may be holding you back from your purpose, your potential, your destiny. One will only apply faith to what you desire, which is what God intended. Your desire must come out of your own heart in order to put forth the necessary efforts to grow. This desire cannot be some artificial, implanted feeling to make you serve God or do His commandments. God will not make you desire His Word; He only plants the seed and leaves it to you and me to direct our desire toward His Word.

> As newborn babes, desire the sincere milk
> of the word, that ye may grow thereby. (1
> Pet. 2:2 KJV)

God will not make you desire His Word. "Out of the abundance of the heart, the mouth speaks" (Luke 6:43–46 KJV). What you desire will dictate what abundance will come out of your heart, whether good or corrupt. Do you want to change, or do you want to change your circumstances? Many people today are reaping the bad seeds they have sown and think simply becoming more spiritual (praying or going to church consistently) will change their life for the better. They seem to forget that if you want to change what you're reaping, you must change what you sow (Gal. 6:7 KJV). Too many people are buying into the idea that this simple but powerful scripture is *not* true.

In the book *As a Man Thinketh* by James Allen, he writes that men are eager to change their circumstances but not themselves. All accomplishments and failures can be connected to your level of desire to accomplish that goal. The people who live their lives to Christ and sincerely commit themselves to bringing their lives to alignment with His Word first had a desire to change before they had faith in God. This desire motivated them to seek out an answer to that empty space they had in their heart. People with no desire to be set free from sin, get an education, or confront stagnation have one thing in common: no desire.

As I help people overcome issues, giving them scripture to increase their faith, giving them books on their area of defeat, I do all I can to pull them up out of the slump they are in, putting all my time, resources, and effort to bring change in their lives. But I have noticed something that's caused me to rethink my approach. It is a key that Jesus knew was important before He performed certain miracles. At the pool of Bethesda, he asked a man, "Wilt thou be made whole?" (John 5:6 KJV). At first, I believed this is a strange question. Of course, he wants to be made whole—he had had this problem for thirty-eight years. The man didn't answer with a simple yes; he answered with the results of his failed attempts. His actions answered the question. This scripture reveals that not everyone who is in bondage has a desire to change. They say things like, "I'm tired of going through this," or "I'm doing the best I can." Though they say they want to change, their actions are inconsistent with their words. This is a person that only wants help from others and does not take responsibility for their part for a change, for which no other result but stagnation can be reaped.

Desire, or the lack thereof, is the primary cause of success or failure on all levels. No desire breeds no faith. No faith in God that He can change you, and no faith in your ability to effectively carry out His plan for change. Desire is the twin of faith; you must have both. But many are attempting to break free from bad habits or accomplish goals with little desire to change, which breeds no faith, not just in God, but in themselves as well. This book will help you see your desire and your faith in the proper perspective, which in turn will help you with thus:

1. Identify the source of your stagnation.
2. Identify false and unrealistic beliefs that are producing worthless and unrealistic results.
3. No longer put full responsibility on God to receive your promised land.
4. Identify your responsibilities and God's promises.
5. Expose how no desire hiders God's purpose for your life.
6. Not to accept what you don't desire.
7. Understand that faith is a seed, and desire is the hand that plants it.
8. Understand that desire directs your faith.
9. Understand that no desire births traits of laziness, procrastination, fear, in which you will attempt to use your faith in God to overcome.

Desire Matures to Faith, and Faith Matures to Belief And Beliefs Acted on Daily Become a Reality

People with no desire will pray prayers like, "God, take this sin out of me," or they say, "When my season comes, I will change," not knowing all change, for better or worse, starts with a desire, not faith.

> The soul of the sluggard desireth, and
> hath nothing: but the soul of the diligent
> shall be made fat. (Prov. 13:4 KJV)

Because of the character trait of laziness, your desire will never be transformed into faith, simply because laziness hinders action, and faith without works is dead. So many think, just because they have faith in Jesus Christ, they will automatically prosper. I blame this mindset on false teachers, which the Bible says to beware of (see 1 Timothy 4:1 NLT). We are saved through faith. This does not mean I continue doing and thinking the way I did before Christ. We must be transformed by the renewing of the mind. This is a process of bringing God's principles into the way you think. This takes consistent application, not just thought. God wants His Word to be a part of who you are, not just what you believe. Those with no desire to be conformed to God's Word will never effectively sow into His Word with the intent of application; it will only be to comfort grief or frustration. But God's Word is meant to change your life, not your mood. Desire and faith are twins, but they are not the same. Let's look at the definitions of the two.

The difference between desire and faith. *Desire* is a strong feeling of wanting to have something or wishing for something to happen. *Faith* is the evidence of things hoped for, the evidence of things not seen. No desire forces you to want to understand the evidence before you act, which cannot happen. The truth will always escape the mind of the man with no passion, no desire, no drive, because whenever he is confronted with a problem, a wall, or a giant, laziness, doubt, fear, and indecision will seem to be waiting right there to tear down any thoughts of acting on that truth that greater is He that is within him than he that's in the world (1 John 4:4 KJV), acting on what he knows is right and will change his life, but the character traits that follows, a man with no desire, is too accurate to him. His doubt, fears, and indecision have matured from being just a thought he should have cast down if he had the strength to now a heart of no desire.

One can have foolish thoughts, and each thought can be confronted by the wisdom he has accepted as truth, which, in turn, will push out that foolish thought. Notice that the person who has accepted God's Word as truth to the point that he acts on it can only clearly identify traits of fear, failure, and laziness, which have the tendency to creep in the mind that is idle even for a second.

One man reads in the Bible, "As a man thinketh in his heart, so is he" (Prov. 23:7). He meditates daily about this scripture. What is God's intent when He birthed these words in Saul's heart? How does it affect me? How can I apply this scripture in my life? These thoughts trigger him to not only be more aware of what he is thinking but, surprisingly, also shocked by what he has been accepting as truth now exposed as the very seeds of all his insecurities. This inspires him to diligently continue to read God's Word, in which he comes across another scripture that says, "The soul of the sluggard desireth, and hath nothing: but the soul of the diligent shall be made fat" (Prov. 13:4). He then begins to meditate on this scripture. In his meditation, he easily connects as he thinks, "So am I to his desire to be diligent?" and discovers a fact he never thought about or even noticed. He has a lot of desires and has nothing except an apartment, a car, and bills. Through just these two scriptures, he finds out a fact about himself that changes his life: he is lazy. Eagerly shocked, he thinks over the past thirty-five years; most of the failures he suffered were from laziness, which is a trait of no desire. He never tried hard enough to overcome because, knowing what it takes to win, he accepted losing with a "positive attitude" and thought it was because of some unknown reason for his failure. At the time of the failure, he was right—it was unknown because Albert Einstein Quote. His mind had to be elevated the day those two scriptures elevated his thinking only when he, by faith, accepted them as truth. This is an example of how truth of God's Word changes you, but it is only to those that accept his Word as truth.

God's Word, as in this story, reveals areas of defeat you may never discover, which is a sad reality for so many Christians today, all because they resisted their mind renewal process that Ephesians 4:23 speaks of. Many reinforce the attitude of no desire when they reject God's wisdom and understanding, in which He already declared that His people are destroyed because of this (Hosea 4:6). One only acts on the reality of their thoughts. So many have so-called Christian beliefs but do not act on them, which means they have not accepted the Bible as truth.

This is the first step of freedom from all bondage. It is impossible to overcome a habit of bondage, an addiction, without believing in a truth that enables change. No desire, no motivation goes deeper than simply not having the will to persevere. It is a mindset, not a habit. Truth is hidden from the ignorant not because the ability to comprehend is imma- ture but because it does not agree with an ignorant man's val- ues. One man believes he is a failure, and so he begins to stop attempting to please the boss at work and does just enough to keep his job. He starts to focus on all his insecurities, and every comment of constructive criticism is perceived as a personal attack. You see, his insecurities have turned into action. You cannot control what people say about you, but you can control the way you receive what is said. Looking for an easy way to get what we want has been, and I believe it will always be, in our nature. Looking at the world today, many people have made billions of dollars making products that bring eye-opening results with little effort. Today's society wants everything easy, with little to no effort. This type of thinking is the source of the laziness that is causing many to believe that what you sow and what you reap do not correspond to each other. Many people set low bars for their lives because their level of diligence is small.

The Bible has several scriptures of the results of a person who is diligent and the consequences of the lazy:

> He becometh poor that dealeth with a slack hand: but the hand of the diligent maketh rich. (Prov. 10:4 kjv)

> The soul of the sluggard desireth, and hath nothing: but the soul of the diligent shall be made fat. (Prov. 13:4)

Nothing Is Overcome without a Diligent Spirit

This point is also emphasized in the parable of the talents told in Matthew 25:14–30. Three servants were given money to multiply while their master was gone. When he returned, two servants multiplied what was given, and one hid their money in the ground. Their master returned and examined what they had done. The servants who were given five talents and two talents, respectively, gave their master a return, but the servant who was given one talent hid his lord's money in the ground, thinking this was the safest place to keep it, only to return and find out there was a responsibility connected to the talent that was given, but it was neglected. His master called him wicked and lazy (Matt. 25:26). This servant was not grateful for the opportunity he was given, so he did the only thing that made sense, which is to maintain his talent and not multiply it. This is a mistake many people make today. We are all given gifts and talents that we squander because of an ungrateful heart. This mindset blinds one's ability to see an opportunity as a blessing. A blessing to an ungrateful person is something given to them that takes no cultivation to discover the value. Ungratefulness produces a spirit of laziness, not necessarily because one refuses to labor, but because of their inability to see what can come out of the talent that is given, they simply allow their gift from God to be buried.

Breaking free from laziness is required for you to unlock your potential. Physical and mental laziness reinforces every addiction, every ungodly character trait, and works against God's method to bring a change of mind.

Defeat Is a Mindset

Your life today is the result of your attitudes and choices in the past. Your life tomorrow will be the result of your attitudes and the choices you make today.
—unknown

Don't allow the destructive mentality you have adopted through terrible past experiences influence your thinking. I have learned this can only be accomplished by developing an unwavering focus on embracing who you are, not focusing on letting go of where you've been. We understand we can walk in only one direction. No one disputes this truth. You also must realize you can only think effectively in one direction. The double-minded man is unstable in all his ways, but why? Because indecision is the cancer of growth. Begin writing a list of who God is calling you to be. Defeat is a mindset that you accept before it's an event that you experience. Your environment influences your thinking, your thinking influences your beliefs, and out of your beliefs, your character, attitude, and mindset are shaped. We cannot always control our environment, but we do have the ability to control our thinking. This ability is a blessing given by God. Still, I'm writing this book because today, many people have turned this blessing into a curse, allowing others' words and bad past or present experiences to create limiting beliefs about themselves and their future, or, even worse, completely reject the purpose God has created them for. Because of this, many people fall into depression and low self-esteem, believing it is impossible to come out because they have allowed those labels to define who they are.

Destructive Thoughts Lead to a Destructive Life

Destructive thoughts can send you down a path of thinking that deteriorates your self-worth, creates doubt and unbelief in yourself, God, and even those who believe in you. Destructive thoughts force you to accept your circumstance as an affirmation of your self-worth. Destructive thinking is such a cancer in your belief system that I want to be clear on what I mean when using this term. My definition of *destructive thinking* is thinking about a object, a person, a situation, a circumstance, your past, or your future in a way that leads to frustration, anger, self-pity, powerlessness, or confusion. If how you think about anything leads you to see yourself as less than, that is destructive thinking. I believe destructive thoughts are directly connected to defeated, victimized belief systems.

For years, I was paralyzed within my own stinking thinking because I based my potential off others opinions of me and accepted whatever life threw at me as God's perfect will, whether it was good or bad. I failed to examine my circumstances in the light of God's Word and did not stop to ask myself if the bad situations I found myself in the fruit of what I had sown. I found that asking yourself this one question alone could help you become more solution-oriented in your thinking. I assumed that whatever happened to me was ordained by God. I had this destructive thought that what God does not prevent He orders. But I have now come to believe this is not true. I have now grown to think that God does not ordain all the negative things in your life, but what He does through His Spirit is to use what we are going through to make us stronger.

As I write this book, I still fight against destructive thoughts and beliefs that are counterproductive to my purpose, my goals, and God's will for my life. Please don't make the mistake I made by thinking that you are losing because you're in a fight. We all grow weary of the daily disciplines you must have to go forward. The only thing we can do to stand and be the strong men and women that we know we are and think and focus on the vision God placed on your heart. Focus on where you're going, and soon you will discover that where you are is a loose garment that can't hold you. I believe, if you do not identify the lies you tell yourself, grabbing ahold to the truth that can change your life will not help you as much as it can. Thinking above destructive thoughts rather than sinking in them takes a relentless attitude, which will take courage and faith to embrace.

As the twig is bent, so the tree grows.
(Alexander Pope)

Destructive thinking can paralyze you by causing you to

1. think about a problem or circumstance in a way that does not create a clear and compelling path to a resolution;
2. create or focus on passive or ineffective methods to bring about a solution;
3. have a strong doubt or disbelief in your ideas and creativity, which only can result in an attitude of confusion or uncertainty;

4. believe unto conviction that you deserve poor results and a poor life.
5. focus on how your past limited you and what you don't have.

These are just some of the things that attempted to paralyze me. I believe the ways you overcome these traps are to

1. focus on your first step to come out of the problem or circumstance, not the entire situation;
2. affirm your belief that you are more significant than any event that comes your way, which can be done by consistently reading the Bible and listening to thought leaders who overcame the same areas;
3. allow all your frustration and the uncomfortableness of your current season to create a strong diligence to reach the next step out of your circumstances.
4. seek qualified counsel (Prov. 11:14).

You cannot walk into your purpose on your own. Ensure the wise counsel you receive is from people who love you. This is important because we tend to seek counsel from people we are comfortable with, not necessarily people who are qualified to speak into our life.

It's easy to think about the entire problem, how it was created, who's to blame, etc., and not focus on the first thing you need to do to come out of the problem, when you focus on the first step, which may clarify the issue, or get a greater understanding of the issue. When you focus wholeheartedly on how to think up, being stuck has less and less power.

Prolonged Tolerance Will Lead to Accepting Destructive Circumstances

Tolerance is a passive emotion that, once birthed, will grow into a cornerstone in your thinking. You cannot break free from destructive thinking until you decide that you are not going to accept whatever form of oppression has kept you from receiving the abundant life Jesus died for. Today, many people tolerate fear, intimidation, poverty, low self-esteem, failure, and depression without understanding whatever you accept becomes a pillar of your life.

I believe oppressed thinking is tolerated far more than physical forms of oppression, like physical abuse, because of the consequences of allowing physical abuse to continue can easily be seen by the abused. I pray that this book will help you see the results of oppressed thinking. Before you can benefit from the principles that the Word of God teaches, you first must make up in your mind that you will *not* tolerate this bondage any longer! This is the first step to change. If you fail to reject who the enemy is trying to make you, all truth that sheds light on your bondage will frustrate and even anger you, because the natural man does not receive the things of God. (See 1 Corinthians 2:14 NKJV.)

As I grew in my understanding of the Word of God, I started to notice I ceased to tolerate defeated thoughts. The verse "As a man thinketh in his heart so is he" (Prov. 23:7) became the main reason I began to monitor my thoughts. As I did this, I became grieved at what I tolerated due to fear and low self-esteem. What you accept is connected to how you perceive yourself, and how you perceive yourself has been formed up to this point in your life by what people say about you and what you say about you. One of the most destructive character traits that a person with low self-worth develops is a high tolerance of physical, emotional, and spir-

41

itual pain. Tolerance is a defense mechanism that is designed to give you hope in oppressive circumstances. Tolerance keeps the human spirit full of hope despite the stresses of life. Emotional tolerance is a defense mechanism that is a blessing in cases of oppression. The ability to tolerate hardships and the pressures of providing for your family, raising children, being a husband/wife, and not allowing that stress to influence your beliefs negatively is a blessing from God.

The adversary attempts to take this blessing and use it to your detriment. The devil attempts this in trying to transform your tolerance to acceptance. The devil attempts this by trying to make the challenges you face seem unbearable and too much for you to handle. Once you accept this belief, you can no longer focus clearly on the vision God has given you and your family. You now attempt to focus on unimportant things.

Many people accept defeat not because they want to but because of the circumstances in their life that steal their faith in the fact that defeat is not a representation of who you are. No one wants to go through seasons of weakness. I know for me, those seasons make me feel like I'm failing in managing the opportunities God has given me, because I feel like I'm not making progress, but what helps me is the truth that I feel weak because God is stretching me in areas that were, in the last season, untouched. Each time He said, "My grace is all you need. My power works best in weakness." So now I am glad to boast about my weaknesses so that Christ's power can work through me. "That's why I take pleasure in my weaknesses and the hardships, persecutions, and troubles that I suffer for Christ. For when I am weak, then I am strong" (2 Cor. 12:9–10).

I believe that Paul felt the same way. Whether Paul's weakness was a life experience or a physical infirmity, Paul knew to turn to God for strength, which he could not manifest through himself. What is the difference? Tolerance will cause you to fight for what you believe, and acceptance will make you change what you believe! This is always the enemy's motive in every attack he brings.

> Again there was a day when the sons of God came to present themselves before the Lord, and Satan also came among them to present himself before the Lord.
>
> And the Lord said to Satan, "From where do you come?" Satan answered the Lord and said, "From going to and fro on the earth, and from walking back and forth on it."
>
> Then the Lord said to Satan, "Have you considered My servant Job, that there is none like him on the earth, a blameless and upright man, one who fears God and shuns evil? And still he holds fast to his integrity, although you incited Me against him, to destroy him without cause."
>
> So Satan answered the Lord and said, "Skin for skin! Yes, all that a man has he will give for his life.
>
> But stretch out Your hand now, and touch his bone and his flesh, and he will surely curse You to Your face!" (Job 2:1–5 NKJV)

The book of Job teaches us a valuable lesson about what motivates our adversary. To change what you believe. I think when anyone is faced with hard times, we discover a new fashion of who we are and what really matters. Hard times force us to stand on what we believe about God and ourself.

When hard times hit Job's life, he was forced (like everyone is) to interpret those devastating events. In the midst of that, his wife, who was supposed to be his primary support, told him to do the very thing the devil wanted him to do, curse God. When you go through something that makes you feel defeated or worthless, be sober and vigilant, because your adversary, the devil, is right there, tempting you to curse God. Job had no choice but to tolerate what God allowed to strengthen him. God will not place more on you than you can bear.

Truth Must Be Matured unto Personal Convictions

Truth Plus Acceptance of Truth Equals Beliefs That Grow into Convictions

> And ye shall know the truth, and the truth shall make you free. (John 8:32 KJV)

> If we live truly, we shall see truly. It is as easy for a strong man to be strong as it is for a weak man to be weak. (Ralph Waldo Emerson)

I believe your life is the fruit of your convictions. Whether your convictions are making you stronger or weaker, faithful or faithless, courageous or fearful is based on the beliefs you allow to become a part of your character. When I say truth must be matured into convictions, I mean what you believe about yourself that is in agreement with your true identity cannot and will not produce a positive change you can see until those true beliefs become a part of who you are. My goal in this chapter is to help you understand that what you believe must be transformed into action in order to think up to get up. We all have a truth that were living by. Whether it's a truth that empowers you or a truth that demoralizes you is a choice that you have full control of.

God enabled truth to have the ability to make you free, but it is not truth alone that makes you free; it is the acceptance of the truth. Without the acceptance of truth, the truth cannot be matured and become a part of who you are. Wisdom, knowledge, information, or principles, no matter how true they are, and no matter how helpful the benefits are when applied, their ability to change your life cannot be activated until you accept it as truth. This point was one of the keys that helped me see myself as greater than my circumstances. I knew what God's Word said about me, but I did not accept it.

I want to help you understand that what you believe to be true will act as an empowerment tool to push you through the most challenging times of your life or a one thousand-pound weight that will make even the smallest step forward seem impossible. When you are convicted of the truth, you resist contrary beliefs with more resistance and faith to stand firm.

You cannot change the direction you are going if you will not humble yourself and examine your current path. Someone who knows not to steal may steal, dependent on the circumstance. Someone who is strongly convicted that honesty is everything, that person will not steal under any circumstances. The only difference is, one knows the truth, and the other is convicted of the truth. In order to think up, you must be convicted of the truth. Most people accept any thought that goes unconfronted as truth no matter if that thought is building you up or breaking you down. Knowing what thoughts to accept or reject is critical for you to realize all that God is calling you to be. This is why it's important to examine your thoughts

Remember, you become what you think.
Think discouraging thoughts, and you'll
get discouraged. (Joyce Meyer)

Thoughts have the potential to become a reality if that thought gets enough attention. People who think poor, for example, do not mean that they are or deserve poverty; poverty, whether spiritually, financially, or emotionally, is the result of ignorance of what it takes to be wealthy in any or all the previously mentioned areas.

My point is that there may be only one bad character trait holding you back from all God has for you.

Don't Allow the Lies You Have Accepted as Truth in Your Past Remain True in Your Future

You cannot progress or change any aspect of your life without rejecting the current information you allowed to shape your life. There must be a pause to reject the old information before growing to learn and changing from the new information. Many people accept whatever life throws at them because they feel they have no choice, but accepting or rejecting circumstances is just the iceberg's tip. The circumstance is the result of what you believe inwardly. So if you believe in your heart you are a fool, whether it's true or not, you will find yourself in countless circumstances that echo this inner truth. But why is it that what we believe about ourselves becomes a reality even if what you believe is not true? Because even though you may not agree with a name someone or some circumstance points out to you, the real damage is done when you accept it as truth.

I believe all experiences are accepted and downloaded into your memory and used as a point of reference to contribute to evaluating future experiences. What you believe about yourself that is actually false has the potential to be more destructive than what you think. Why? You cannot be changed in the spirit of your mind (See Ephesians 4:23) if you do not first reject what you have allowed to shape your mind.

To repeat the point I raised in the introduction, you cannot apply new ways of thinking without first disregarding the old ways of thinking. When you let go of a destructive belief, you, within the same action, cut off the life blood that is supplying all the destructive thoughts connected to that belief.

When I was addicted to marijuana and slept around, I lived at the door of deliverance, but I never fully accepted my healing. Month after month, I talked about reasons I needed to change my life, but those talks did not lead me to open the door of deliverance. The reason I never opened the door was I was not committed to change. I would get high while watching sermon messages! I knew there was a life beyond addiction, but at the time, I was comfortable thinking and hearing about that life but not experiencing it. Thankfully, the prayers of the righteous avails much! As I write this book, I stand free from alcoholism, drug addiction, and pornography for twelve years! In April of 2008, I accepted Christ into my life and my life hasn't been the same since.

I've met people who knew their drinking was an issue, or their promiscuous tendencies, but they lived at the door of deliverance, never walking through and accepting their healing. Month after month, talking about how they need to change, especially after a night of feeding their issue, but never opening the door. The reason they never open the door is that it's a commitment that they are not willing to pay. Don't let that be you.

You see, the only reason a kid drops the loose change in his hand is to grab $20. He knows what he's reaching for is more valuable than what he has in his hand. So he, without a hesitant thought, lets go of the chump change. Knowing the value of what you're reaching for will help you let go of what you once viewed as valuable. But to many, opening the door while holding on to their old mind to evaluate is what they see more than what they have. Prolonged tolerance always leads to acceptance. Sadly, many people today tolerate physical and emotional abuse at an increasing rate because they tolerated the abuse for a long enough time to accept it as a part of their identity. I believe the people who stay in their abusive situation have allowed their identity to be connected to abuse. It is harder to become free from bondage when the value you place on yourself has been influenced by people or circumstances you tolerated. What you tolerate is connected to how you perceive yourself, and how you perceive yourself has been formed up to this point in your life primarily by what you say about you and to an extent by what the people you allow to speak into your heart say about you.

> God's word about you must become your
> word about you. (Bishop TD Jakes)

If God's Word about you does not become your word about you, you will never be who God has intended for you to be. What I mean is, the truth of who Jesus is and the truth of who He says you are must be the foundation of how you think and perceive your circumstance, so when the enemy comes in like a flood, you will, without thinking about it, utter out of your spirit, then out of your mouth, "I am more than a conqueror" (See Romans 8:37 NKJV). This is a result of His Word ceasing to become a good principle to live by. His Word has been crystalized to a reality. When the enemy attempts to tell you lies about how you must see your situation as never changing your reality, God's Word will cause false thoughts to be cast down so quickly that you won't even waste time acknowledging the lie; you will just simply keep moving forward. I am not saying that you will not have struggles, valleys, or roadblocks; I am simply saying that you will no longer waste excessive time going back and forth in your heart, whether to believe the devil's lies or the truth of God's Word. I am saying, even if the circumstance is not lining up with God's expected end, retreat no longer is on the table as an option. You boldly go before the throne of grace and stand in agreement with who God says you are!

> The first thing that changes in any situation is your mind. Your life becomes a byproduct of that change. (Robert L. Lowery III)

> It is not hard to find the truth. What is hard is not to run away from it once you found it. (Etienne Gilson)

Accepting your circumstances guarantees that tomorrow will not get better. God enabled truth to have the ability to make His people free, but it is not truth alone that makes you free; it is the acceptance of the truth. Wisdom, knowledge, information, and principles, no matter how true they are, and no matter how clear the benefits are when applied, their ability to change your life cannot be activated until you accept it as truth that cannot be ignored. I believe tolerance leads to acceptance. Whatever you allow to persist in your life without you taking 100 percent responsibility for the effects it causes will end in no other result. Still, you are accepting what you have allowed to persist. I have learned that you must first think on the level you are striving toward before that level can be attained.

This is an inner fight that forces you to believe you are worth more, you are better than, and you are not limited to the restraints of your daily frustrations.

The level of your convictions determines
the level of your obedience

What you believe must mature into a strong conviction.

You will not change what you accept. Acceptance acts as a glue to stay satisfied with what you're reaping, spiritually and emotionally. It can also act as a barrier to shield you from what you need to receive, the truth.

Acceptance—the action of consenting to receive or undertake something offered.

What you accept is a direct reflection of what you believe. Accepting a thought birthed out of fear, anger, jealousy, worthlessness, or any other debilitating thought will, if not confronted, create an attitude that will limit your God-given potential. A limitation is wrapped in the skin of acceptance. The only time you gather enough strength and willpower to think above your fears is when you first begin to not accept your fears as truth for your life. How can the truth set you free? By first accepting it as truth.

What the eye sees, what the ear hears is
already in mind. (Unknown)

You must examine the circumstances that cause you to indulge in your defeated thoughts. This process is done on an unconscious level, so you can't simply stop thinking about how people think you're foolish, for example. The beliefs you have of yourself can be the most empowering force against the enemy's lies, or the beliefs you have of yourself can be the glue that keeps every criticism and disappointment in your heart. What you accept is also a reflection of what you believe you deserve. Some make the assumption that they must accept their circumstances. This is a character trait of the victim mentality. Thinking like a victim will guarantee failure and insulate yourself from wisdom that will pull you out of your unwanted circumstance. The problem isn't accepting what is given to you; the problem is believing you deserve what has been given. The difference is, in order to accept that you're a failure, you must agree with the principles of failure. Remember, you cannot get up unless you think up.

It is easy to forget that not doing what it takes to come out of your circumstance is the same as accepting your circumstance. Some people think *poor* does not mean that they are or deserve poverty; poverty, whether financial, emotional, or poor health, is the result of ignorance of what it takes to be wealthy in any or all the previously mentioned areas. If I am ignorant of the fact that my laziness will produce poverty, I will be poor, and if I know laziness will produce poverty and I continue being lazy, I will be poor. Both desires to avoid the end result, but it is inevitable because of one character trait, no matter how it was reached, laziness. An ignorant person and a foolish person are sometimes put in the same category since ignorance of any sort is needed to be so. But the most important difference is, a fool cannot get out of whatever state they've fallen in, but an ignorant person can, because the ignorant is still teachable, but the fool has already made up their mind to reject knowledge.

Truth only makes one free when it is accepted. I have found through experience that a principle that you need in order to break free from your past or a wrong way of thinking is hard to accept because you believe that you have been conditioned to believe you deserve what you're reaping. For years.

You must believe you are more than a conqueror (Rom. 8:37). God's will is for His Word about you to become your word about you. If you have kids, you know the value of telling your child they are smart. You speak into your child what is true, with the hope that your truth will be manifested in their actions, by their becoming a straight-A student. Your child's belief in your word matures to belief within himself or herself, and his/her belief is manifested by his/her grades. You do not act on what you believe; you act on what you are. Sometimes, what we believe does not grow into what we act out in our lives. It's easy to believe one thing but do another. This is why I believe it is important to seek God to understand who you are because out of identity comes your convictions.

I made the mistake of not examining what I allowed to enter my heart. Proverbs 4:23 (KJV) reads, "Keep thy heart with all diligence; for out of it are the issues of life." You will not guard what you don't value. Tolerating oppressed thoughts leads to you not valuing your heart. Life and death are in the power of the tongue. When someone is speaking death over you, respond with life! If you don't, you will accept the death that's spoken because an idle mind cannot stand against another whose mind is focused on making you accept their thought of you. This is where the fight starts. A person who cast down vain imaginations must first disagree with that imagination.

You may be saying to yourself, "I don't accept people's views of me. I'm a strong-minded person who stands against any wrong thought of me." Look at it this way: what you believe about yourself is not determined only by disagreeing with what is said about you. To stay above critical labels and stereotypes, I've learned that affirming who you are and reading and listening to content that provokes you to be the highest expression of who you are daily. For example, you can disagree that you're not beautiful or handsome enough to get married. You know that you have what it takes to get a mate but, at the same time, believe that your past relationships do not encourage your belief since all your relationships did not end well. So the emotional part of your brain will connect the results of your past relationships and the results of the criticism of not being married. Now, you do not believe that you are not married because of your looks, but you do believe you are not married because something is wrong with you based on your past relationships. This is an example of how you can disagree with a criticism of yourself but still allow that criticism to chip away your self-esteem because you believe the result the criticism is suggesting.

The principles of the Word of God cannot be forced into your heart. All truth must be accepted. This is why many people become wealthy. They simply don't accept poverty for their family. The attitude of acceptance can be birthed in multiple ways. One way is by the truth of what The Word of God says about you, "You shall know the truth, and the truth shall make you free" (John 8:32). How can it truly make you free? By giving you more wisdom than the circumstance. It is easy to see a problem when you understand all the issues surrounding it.

On the other hand, your circumstances can become frustrating, and a vice, if the only wisdom you have to solve your problem does not work. Another way of developing an attitude of acceptance is by pure emotion, fear, anger, frustration. The problems you consistently find yourself in year after year are a good indicator of what you accept. "Wherefore lay apart all filthiness and superfluity of naughtiness, and receive with meekness the engrafted word, which is able to save your souls" (James 1:21).

Receive with Meekness

Once a thought is accepted, your mind starts to convince yourself that you have no choice, that it's not that bad, that everything will work out. Most people accept any thought that is consistently spoken to them: "You will never get on your feet," "Everyone is against you," "You're not smart enough." Thoughts and criticisms will always come. The question is, Will you accept them as your reality? Any thought has the potential to become a reality if that thought gets enough attention. Light reveals what cannot be seen; understanding reveals the truth that is affecting your character traits that leads to depression.

Bondage starts from without and when persisted that bondage can come within and alter your vision for the worst. As you allow Gods truth to grow within you heart you will be one step closer to thinking up!

Vision Is the Starting Place of Thinking Up

The Height of Your Vision Is Intertwined With the Depth of the Value You Have of Yourself

Earl Nightingale, in his best-selling speech, *The Strangest Secret*, told the story of two boys who were raised by their alcoholic father. When they became adults, they were interviewed by a psychologist who were studying the effects of drunkenness in the home. One did not drink and the other was an alcoholic like his father. Both was asked why did they turn out the way they did. And both gave an identical answer—"What do you expect when you have a father like mine?" When I heard of this story, it confirmed the uncomfortable truth which is you choose to allow your past experiences to keep you down or build you up. Choose the latter! Our past has the ability to give or take away your value depending on how it's perceived.

Your path of growth must be slightly ahead of your path of problems. Your thinking will follow which ever path is leading. I've learned when you see your past as a problem you will tend to look to your future in fear not to repeat it. But when you see your past as a tool which made you able to embrace your future, you will look to your past only to withdraw lessons and principles to thrive. This is a mindset shift that may be challenging but worth the fight to embrace because just like the two sons you can use your bad past experiences as a vice to keep you stuck or a tool to add value to your self and those around you!

As I began to become more serious about breaking out of the destructive ways of thinking that I have adopted, I began to see the relationship between the vision I have of my future and the value I place in myself. I placed no value in myself because of my shortcomings. If you cannot see yourself stronger than what you're fighting to overcome, you will allow what you're fighting to overcome to dominate you! This domination will reveal itself in subtle ways, like these:

1. An attitude of avoidance when confronting the uncomfortable facts of your reality
2. Faith in things that God did not ordain you to have faith in, like hope, time, or anything that omits any responsibility on your part to act
3. A double-minded attitude toward the direction you believe you should take to get up

As I began to see my past as preparation for my future, I began to appreciate and value who God is calling me to become. To be greater than what He has called me out of. The reason I believe vision is the starting place of thinking up is that the direction you are thinking is the direction that you will go. I struggle with trying to attain a God-given vision for myself and for my family. It has been a struggle because of the fear of making mistakes. I don't want to be out of the will of God and do something I just have the ambition to do but am not called to do, and at the same time, I don't want to live beneath my God-given potential and spend a lot of time striving to achieve a goal that is way beneath my potential. I've learned that your vision cannot be embraced out of fear.

My vision was clear in my heart but my past failures birthed a timid attitude toward my future.

It is important to see your past circumstances as experiences required to make you into the man or woman today than allowing yourself to see your past as an anchor that will forever keep you stuck. The Bible says to write the vision and make it plain (Hab. 2:2 KJV). It also says, without vision, the people perish (Prov 29:18). I'm only saying that you don't get a clear, God-given vision until you are clear on who you are and who you are not.

The value I place on myself is directly correlated to the amount of faith I have in the God-given potential I allow God to manifest through my life. Vision misdirected is the same as having no vision. Focusing on who you are not rather than striving toward who you are and who God is through you can manifest no other result than more of what you are not. This is the same as a farmer who devotes all their time studying the almanac but never sowing a seed.

As I began to become more serious about breaking out of the destructive ways of thinking that I have adopted, I began to see the relationship between the vision I have of my future and the value I place in myself. I placed no value in myself because of my shortcomings. As I began to see my past as preparation for my future, I began to appreciate and value who God is calling me to become, to be greater than what He has called me out of. When I didn't value myself, it was hard to see even one year into my future. I did not connect what I like or am passionate about with where I'm going. When I began to see the value in who I am, I became more concerned about whom I was around and my purpose. Value is determined by how rare a thing is.

Seeing value in yourself is required to produce the faith and courage that is needed to step out of your comfort zone and embrace the vision that fits your true worth.

Every time I heard the word *vision*, I almost always related it to the famous scripture "Where there is no vision, the people perish: but he that keepeth the law, happy is he" (Prov. 29:18). I had an idea of what having a vision meant, but I never thought my vision had a lot to do with my growth in my relationship with Christ and my purpose.

If you're a prisoner of fear, you will not attain your goals, because you are really not trying to attain them. Your fears then become a self-fulfilling prophecy.

> The quality of your thinking determines
> the quality of your life. (A. R. Bernard)

It seems so common and natural to shape a vision around your problems, but it's not effective. Casting a vision for your life that is centered around problems and daily frustrations may be disconnected from your purpose. When I adopted a vision that was centered around my problems, it became easier to include new problems based on how I felt at the time.

What happens when you have a vision but it is focused on goals that are centered on proving those who dismissed you wrong or how you do not have the support you think you need to embrace your purpose, so you adopt a vision that leads you into isolation?

We live in a society today where terms do not mean what they state. Statements like "I'm moving forward" may not necessarily mean that they are no longer going to stay in a current situation; it may mean that they are simply not going to worry about it anymore. The allusion of forward progress may be the very thing stopping you from actually making forward progress. The scripture that puts all responsibilities on God to change a situation is more readily believed than the scripture that says faith without work is dead.

The height of your vision is intertwined with the depth of the value you have of yourself. I've learned that having a small value in yourself can open the door to you falsely believing that you have no power to change your circumstance.

You will only see as far as you believe yourself to be valuable. It is more important to see your past circumstances as experiences that were required to make you into the man or woman you are today than focusing on having a clear vision for the future. Don't misunderstand me. I am not saying that you should not think about and plan for your future. The Bible says to write the vision and make it plain (Hab. 2:2 KJV). It also says, without vision, the people perish. I'm only saying that you don't get a clear, God-given vision until you are clear on who you are and who you are not. This is very important, because if you do not find who you genuinely are, your vision will be tainted with other people's vision or with the negative criticism and belittling that you have accepted. But when you seek the face of God to understand who you are, your fear, your thoughts, and your beliefs that do not serve you will be exposed, and then you can begin to eliminate them.

Don't live your life trying to just be a better person. First, understand the person you are today. If you do not believe yourself to be valuable, you will then not allow your imagination to see yourself greater than that value. I think you would agree that what you are unaware of you cannot change. For years I was unaware of the principles I needed to embrace my true value. God valued the children of Israel enough to give them their promise land but the children of Israel only valued themselves enough to just be free. Don't let that be you. Allow the value that God placed on you to grow the value you place on yourself.

It is easy to be a dreamer. It gives you immediate gratification; it raises your self-esteem and gives you hope. But unfortunately, these same benefits, if you allow them, can cause you to be content with just staying a dreamer. Staying in the realm of dreaming does nothing for the level of value you have in yourself. Why? Because there's no risk being taken, and there is no sacrifice. Mephibosheth could not freely receive the fact that David saw him worthy of embracing what was rightfully his. It is common for people with low self-worth to reject compliments from others when those compliments do not reflect the image the receiver has for themselves. How you see yourself cannot be hidden. It is revealed in the way you speak, dress, and act. You will not receive freedom if the value you place on yourself is chained to bondage!

When I didn't value myself, it was hard to see even one year into my future. I did not connect what I like or am passionate about with where I'm going. When I began to see the value in who I am, I became more concerned about whom I was around and my purpose.

I learned through, unfortunately, bad experiences that you would only see as far as you believe yourself to be valuable. If you have little value in yourself, your vision for your life and what you believe you were put on this earth to accomplish will inevitably reflect that value, or if you believe you are more than a conqueror and believe that you are priceless and God put you on this earth for a reason greater than simply to exist. Though you may not fully understand what that may be, your value in yourself will naturally lead you to add value in yourself and grow in your understanding of who God is and who you are, which will lead you to think thoughts greater than other people's opinions or even your own limiting beliefs.

A dream is the desired outcome you want, but the steps to manifest that dream may be unclear. A vision is a dream that has been matured to develop the next step to manifest that dream. Without a vision, the people perish (Prov. 29:18). It is healthy and recommended to have big dreams for your life, but where your life really begins to change is when your dream is such a joy and passion of yours that you allow your dream to be matured into the next step that you take today! Your growth spiritually, intellectually, and emotionally is set by your vision, and your vision is fueled by your desire. A vision can be described in many ways, having a plan, goals, or a strategy. Having no vision can make you unequipped to even realistically strive toward any goal you have. Someone who believes they are worthless will never even attempt to envision themselves as priceless and has the potential to add value to a relationship.

Since vision comes from within, our adversary fights us from within.

Everyone, from a child to an adult, has a vision for where they see themselves going, even if they're ignorant of the result they are sowing toward. The way that seems right to a man is his vision. This way may have the approval of men. Your vision can be good for society and even highly religious (Saul wanted to sacrifice the very animals God told him to kill; Saul's vision was influenced by people's vision), yet the end will always lead to destruction if it's not God's will for you (Prov. 16:25).

Protect yourself from the way that seems right.

What seems right about the wrong way? Little or no understanding of the right way. The serpent influenced Eve not by showing her the wrong way but by finding out what she understood about the right way then by giving her more information that seemed right. The enemy's weapon isn't always a lie. It is also information that seems right enough for you to accept its vision. Telling you information that you are ignorant of is the foundation that the enemy attempts to build his lies on. In this way, the lie appears true. Bad information can be received as wisdom and accepted by you if you are ignorant of the understanding that information stands on. Be not unwise but understand the will of the Lord (Eph. 5:17 KJV). You learn

God's will for you when you prayerfully study God's Word. The entrance of his Word gives light (Ps. 119:130).

"Where there is no vision, the people perish: but he that keepeth the law, happy is he" (Prov. 29:18). The people perish without a vision because your vision is directly connected to the direction you are speaking, and what you speak to yourself can be life, leading to spiritual awakening, or death, leading to oppression and self-condemnation.

"There is a way which seemeth right unto a man, but the end thereof are the ways of death" (Prov. 14:12). This is why when the enemy attacks us, he does it with a thought he knows he cannot make you reject, the promises of God, but he can present an image that lures you into a way of thinking that appears right, but the end is destruction. The circumstances you find yourself in are speaking something into your spirit, whether you realize it or not. If you are consistently looking up, you will consistently speak up, not because you believe you should, but because that is what you see. Your vision is the foundation of what you speak.

> Death and life are in the power of the
> tongue: and they that love it shall eat the
> fruit thereof. (Prov. 18:21 KJV)

You cannot walk straight if you do not see straight. Many people today have high hopes and dreams for their future, but there is a difference between hope and a vision. A *vision* is a clear and written step-by-step plan that focuses on where you want to be in the future. *Hope* is just an idea of where you will like to be. The problem with the latter is, it is so passive that it can never make it past your beliefs of yourself. Some believe they must change their environment before changing their speech, not realizing their environment is one of the primary influences of their speech.

Wherefore be ye not unwise, but understanding what the will of the Lord is.
(Eph. 5:17)

Vision and Your Surroundings

The people you surround yourself with, and the circumstances you are consistently in, is a reflection of how you
see yourself. Envision yourself as stronger than any limited
circumstance. This is accomplished by thus:

1. Know your worth it. Belief that you are valuable is, I
    believe, the most important quality to have, because
    it turns within the way you think, limiting circum-
    stances into small problems that are expected.
2. Write down where you are going.

Stand at the Door

I believe God opens doors. He rises, and He takes down,
but I believe that it's our personal responsibility to at least be
standing at the door when He opens it. This means to pre-
pare your heart and stir up the gift that's in you for you to
have the discernment and awareness of the season that you're
in to even know that a door has opened. It's sad to see God
open doors only for people to not realize it because they're
not standing at the door. They allow discouragement, fear,
and insecurity to cause them to not even believe that God
will open a door, so they focus all their energy on surviving.
Your daily actions should reflect your vision. If it doesn't,
your actions will still reflect your vision, just not the vision
given by God.

Don't Allow What You're Ignorant of to Control You

The ignorance I'm referring to in this chapter is the mentality that a person develops when they intentionally or unintentionally choose to live beneath their potential. I've learned that accepting a life that is far beneath what is possible for you births a unawareness of what you can become.

You Can Be Alienated from the Life God Has for You Through Ignorance

> The power of the oppressor is the maintenance of ignorance. Oppression breeds ignorance. (Dr. Myles Munroe)

> This I say, therefore, and testify in the Lord, that you should no longer walk as the rest of the Gentiles walk, in the futility of their mind, having their understanding darkened, being alienated from the life of God, because of the ignorance that is in them, because of the blindness of their heart. (Eph. 4:17–18 NKJV)

You will always be controlled to the degree of your ignorance. When you are unaware of who God is, that will ensure that you will not come into the realization of who you are.

> Now we have received, not the spirit of the world, but the spirit who is from God, that we might know the things that have been freely given to us by God. (1 Cor. 2:12 NKJV)

God has freely given you and me things that make our lives more fulfilling and purposeful, but when you're ignorant of the truth that it's God's will that works in you and me to embrace the abundant life, you run the risk of interpreting every undesired circumstance as a limitation that cannot be overcome. I'm not here to tell you it's easy to step out of bondage, but I can tell you that it's worth it! When you are ignorant of the peace, the joy, the wisdom, the authority that God has freely given you, you force yourself to assume or guess what belongs to you and what doesn't.

Have an Open Mind to Examine Truth Before It Is Accepted or Rejected

> And the people of Berea were more open-minded than those in Thessalonica, and they listened eagerly to Paul's message. They searched the Scriptures day after day to see if Paul and Silas were teaching the truth. (Acts 17:11 NLT)

Paul and Silas went to Thessalonica and Berea, preaching the gospel (see Acts chapter 17). The Jews in Thessalonica were envious and rejected the gospel. I want to emphasize that they did not take the time to examine what was preached in light of God's Word. They allowed the truth to frustrate and anger them to the point that they wanted to harm Paul and Silas. This is an attitude I believe is still alive today.

How many times has unexamined truth allowed you to get frustrated? I'm not just referring to your spiritual maturity but relationally. How many relationships were started or cut off prematurely based on unexamined "facts" you blindly accepted as truth? Emotionally? How many times have you allowed your emotions to get the best of you? We all have played the fool in one category or another (I know I have!), but I am learning that having an open mind to examine truth before it is accepted or rejected will serve you in a much greater way than if you simply assume what is accurate or not based solely off how you feel at the time. I believe the attitude of accepting or rejecting information based only on how you feel is one of the character traits of a double-minded person mentioned in James chapter 1, verses 5–8. The point is, all these examples are feelings that manifest when you are confronted with the task of increasing what you know in order to overcome what you see and feel. The truth you may need in this current season of your life may produce feelings of fear or doubt. Im here to tell you that those feelings will push you to reject what you need by creating a alternate truth (according to your feelings) which will cause you to stay in your comfort zone. Don't let this happen to you!

Ignorance is only a stopping force when you allow what you are misinformed about to be accepted as truth without examining the principles that make it true and then turning that misinformation into the primary source of your decision-making. Ignorance can make you feel lazy: "It will take too much time to learn this." Ignorance will make you feel stupid: "I'm not smart enough to understand this." Ignorance will make you diminish your motivation: "I'm too tired to learn that." A yoke is destroyed by growing out of it, not learning to adapt to it! This way, when the enemy comes back to attempt to put it back on, no matter how hard he tries, he cannot place that bondage on you, because it does not fit!

Coming out of ignorance takes effort. You cannot confront anything when you are unaware that it is a destructive device over your life. Sometimes you can be aware that something is a problem, but at the same time, unaware that it is producing most of the bad fruit in your life. Oppression can only be perpetuated if the oppressed are ignorant of their rightful place in Christ and accept the belittling and condescending comments and destructive criticisms they hear about themselves as a true reflection of who they are. When you are ignorant, you, without any force, accept whatever happens to you as if your circumstances control your life. This type of thinking can quickly mature into an attitude of a victim (see chapter 11). No one with a victim mentality will develop the faith and courage required to believe that you are more than a conqueror! You cannot fight against what you are unaware of, and you will not take by faith what you do not believe is yours! It is not enough to just be aware of your shortcomings. What may also motivate you is being aware of the rotten fruit it's producing.

Ignorance is like a two-edged sword; it can destroy your life through what you don't know and through what you are misinformed about that you believe as the truth. I am not saying you must know everything in order to protect yourself from the shackles of ignorance—that is impossible. I am saying that you must develop a habit of always searching out and examining the facts of what you hear, like the Bereans, in order to make sure that the knowledge you are accepting as truth, is truth. This way, what you are unaware of won't have the ability to control you.

Ignorance of Who God Is
Will Result in Ignorance of Who You Are

Like the children of Israel, they knew that continuing as a slave in Egypt was a bondage that they wanted to be free of. But after God freed them from bondage and they began to journey to the promised land, they were learning a second type of bondage, bondage that, to them, didn't really appear threatening; after all, they were free, something they prayed for, I'm sure, for years! This bondage was ignorance. The children of Israel for years connected their identity to a slave which suppressed their true identity. God blessed them to discover their rightful place but in order to do so they had to redefine themselves as the head and no longer the tail! Ignorance of the strength, ignorance of their authority, ignorance of their potential, and ignorance about the power of their God even after they had seen God deliver them from one of the most powerful rulers of that time. This ignorance caused most of them to stay a slave in their thinking which manifest in their low opinion of themselves.

What the Holy Spirit Does Not Do
Control Your Response to the Holy Spirit's Leading

> Therefore lay apart all filthiness and superfluity of naughtiness, and receive with meekness the engrafted word, which is able to save your souls. (James 1:21)

The Spirit of God is our helper. God gives us the strength and the faith. Many Christians believe that the Spirit of God forces the believer to live holy only through confessing with their mouth and believing in their heart (Rom. 10:9). The ability to live holy is given through His Spirit but also works alongside the believer's desire and will to embrace the salvation of the Lord. Without your desire to allow God to have His way in your life, the Spirit of God will be hindered in His ability to sanctify and lead you to your complete deliverance.

Bring Conviction without the Ability to Submit

Suppose God is convicting you about an area in your life. The convictions of God come standard with the grace to obey. Many Christians do not submit to the convictions of God because they believe God has not matured their faith to submit. They say things like, "I will change in God's season," "I'm just taking this walk one day at a time." If God, for example, is convicting you to get out of a relationship because it is a hindrance to your deliverance, He also is giving you the strength and power to obey. A powerless Christian is the enemy's goal, and assuming you don't have any authority to act on God's leading is a form of ignorance that is the most dangerous.

> Wherefore is there a price in the hand of
> a fool to get wisdom, seeing he hath no
> heart to it? (Prov. 17:16 KJV)

I believe that your ignorance, when you first become aware that you are one, must be confronted or your heart will become callus to truth. The way that I guard myself from this device is to read or listen to the Word of God daily. This reminds me that the little that I know is nothing and rekindles my fire to go after the knowledge of God and put great value on His wisdom. The Word of God says to desire the sincere milk of the Word that you may grow. Thereby, the Spirit of God blesses us with a desire to know His will, but it is up to you to feed that desire.

Power Over Principles of Ignorance

1. It is your responsibility, not God's, to feed the desires He put in you.
2. Reading or listening to God's Word is the cure for ignorance when mixed with a heart to apply His Word to your life.
3. The longer you delay confronting an area that you have discovered you are ignorant of, the harder you make it on yourself to break free.
4. Pray and ask God for wisdom. He does not hoard it for special people; it is for all to benefit.
5. God omits your ignorance only for a season. Don't allow your season of ignorance to turn into disobedience.
6. Knowledge that is not rooted in truth will bear the same fruit of the foolish man.

> The fool hath said in his heart, There is no God. Corrupt are they, and have done abominable iniquity: there is none that doeth good. (Ps. 53:15)

When you are ignorant, you, without any force, accept whatever comes, as if your circumstances control your life.

This type of thinking is matured into the attitude of a victim. You cannot fight against what you are unaware of, and you will not take by faith what you do not believe is yours! Peace is yours (Phil. 4:6–7); deliverance is yours (Luke 4:18).

Ignorance is a state of being uninformed (lack of knowledge). The word *ignorant* is an adjective describing a person in the state of being unaware and is often used as an insult to describe individuals who deliberately ignore or disregard important information or facts.

Ignorance is destructive, not primarily from the lack of knowledge, but also from the illusion it gives a person of knowledge. The person who perishes because of ignorance always has a strong sense of intelligence; this is how true wisdom evades them, because they already know. Have you met a person with whom you were trying to share some information and they cut you off and said, "I know that already," without hearing what you had to say?

Ignorance is innocent and not destructive for a season, but once your ignorance is uncovered, you must choose to accept the truth or reject it. Rejecting truth is also accomplished by doing nothing to become informed, as so many do. Once this is done, you are no longer ignorant; ignorance has now matured to a foolish heart, as the Bible claims (Prov 1:7).

Ignorance is fortified or matured to become true to an individual by circumstance and the opinions of others. These circumstances and opinions of others become the ignorant person's confidence in accepting and applying the principles ignorance is giving.

Every demonic spirit must carry along with it the spirit of ignorance to ensure you stay bound. I believe at the foundation of every form of bondage is ignorance. A person is only bound to the degree of their ignorance.

> Wherefore be ye not unwise, but understanding what the will of the Lord is. (Eph. 5:17)

> My people are destroyed for lack of knowledge: because thou hast rejected knowledge, I will also reject thee, that thou shalt be no priest to me: seeing thou

hast forgotten the law of thy God, I will
also forget thy children. (Hosea 4:6)

The Power of Ignorance

The intelligence behind the enemy's attacks will always
influence a mind ignorant of God's will (Hosea 4:6).

The problem with not knowing the information is not
that you do not know but that when God gives you the
grace to see that you are uninformed, you now choose to
not know.

Innocent Ignorance Matured to a Foolish Heart

Ignorance is innocent and not destructive for a season,
but once your ignorance is uncovered, you must choose to
accept the truth that exposed your ignorance or reject the
truth that exposed your ignorance. Rejecting truth is also
accomplished by not doing anything, as so many do. Once
this is done, you are no longer ignorant. You are now a fool,
as the Bible claims.

> The way of a fool is right in his own eyes:
> but he that hearkened unto counsel is
> wise. (Prov. 12:15)

> Wherefore is there a price in the hand of
> a fool to get wisdom, seeing he hath no
> heart to it? (Prov. 17:16)

A fool hath no delight in understanding,
but that his heart may discover itself.
(Prov. 18:2)

Speak not in the ears of a fool: for he will
despise the wisdom of thy words. (Prov.
23:9)

But as it is written, Eye hath not seen,
nor ear heard, neither have entered into
the heart of man, the things which God
hath prepared for them that love him.
But God hath revealed them unto us
by his Spirit: for the Spirit searcheth all
things, yea, the deep things of God. For
what man knoweth the things of a man,
save the spirit of man which is in him?
Even, so the things of God knoweth no
man, but the Spirit of God. Now we have
received, not the spirit of the world, but
the spirit which is of God; that we might
know the things that are freely given to
us of God. (1 Cor. 2:9–12)

Only God knows how and where in your life you are
to apply a biblical principle. Many today are applying God's
Word to their life without the Spirit of God, which may produce results according to the purpose of the spirit of man
but not the purpose of the Spirit of God. No man knows the
things of God but the Spirit of God (1 Cor 2:11).

It does not matter if you're ignorant of the fact that a
gun can kill you; if you pull the trigger, you're dead. Action
will always reap a result even if you are ignorant of the result.

Prayerfully ask God how to apply His word to your life. Ive learned that seeking God for direction creates a heart posture that enables you to shut out feelings that can potentially stump your growth. (Proverbs 2:1-5)

1. My child, listen to what I say, and treasure my commands.
2. Tune your ears to wisdom, and concentrate on understanding.
3. Cry out for insight, and ask for understanding.
4. Search for them as you would for silver; seek them like hidden treasures.
5. Then you will understand what it means to fear the Lord, and you will gain knowledge of God.

The Difference between Thinking Up and Thinking Arrogantly of Yourself

Seeing Yourself Clearly Protects You
From People or Circumstances Defining You

> Before you set things right, you must see
> things right. (John Maxwell)

The purpose of this chapter is to expose the fact that at times you may be tempted to retreat into your limited view of yourself because of a small, subtle lie that, I believe, has robbed the destiny of millions. That lie is, you are thinking arrogantly of yourself or are prideful when you think you're worth more than what you've been accepting. As I began my journey to let go of my fears and embrace who God is calling me to be, there was a limiting or self-defeating thought that hindered my growth. Since I never seen myself as better than my circumstance when I began to value myself, there was a part of me that struggled to fully accept my new perception of myself. Therefore, seeing past your limited view of yourself is so important.

> For I say, through the grace given to me,
> to everyone who is among you, not to

> think of himself more highly than he
> ought to think but to think soberly, as
> God has dealt with each one a measure of
> faith. (Rom. 12:3 NKJV)

I believe that one of the main traps people fall into is misinterpreting what the Word of God says about how we should see our circumstances and ourselves. The scripture above is one of the scriptures I misunderstood for years, which caused me to feel a false sense of conviction every time I set a goal that forced me to have vision above my self-imposed limitations. Limited thinking was so normal for me that I began to accept it as my normal. I was so afraid of "thinking highly of myself" and indulging in prideful thoughts that I ended up developing a mentality that is a direct opposite, which is a pessimistic attitude toward my God-given potential and what I can accomplish. To assure that I did not engage with the attitude of pride, I thought low of myself and labeled it humility. This was my unconscious attempt to make sure I did not entertain the vicious sin of pride. Thinking up forced me to deal with my clouded definition I developed of pride. I allowed my past to inject the false belief that only prideful, selfish people take what's theres out of life. I was so focused on not being prideful that it indirectly birthed and matured an attitude of fear of my own potential. This is dangerous, because limiting who you are to preserve or prevent yourself from becoming a person of poor character is unwise. I now know that having the courage to embrace all of who God is calling you to be takes more character than to sit on the sidelines of life and taking what's rightfully yours is required because no one is going to give you anything worth having!

As John Maxwell clearly stated, seeing things right is very important. Many people are so afraid of thinking too highly of themselves that they end up thinking way lower than they should. Low self-worth is the primary route to mediocracy. I struggle with the question of, Am I being prideful or arrogant because I see myself greater than the limitations that are being presented to me? Am I prideful because I want to be wealthy enough to be able to support more than just me and my immediate family? Am I prideful because I now believe that I am greater than just the neighborhood I grew up in or the opportunities that come my way? These were some of the thoughts that I had as I fought to let go of my limited beliefs of myself and embrace the vision that God gives me through His Word.

It took years for me to believe that I can earn one hundred thousand dollars a year. Not to earn it, but to believe I could earn that amount. I had to let go of the brakes before I could move forward. For me, letting go of the brakes meant letting go of the limiting beliefs that influenced me to expect what I always had been given. Nothing more. When I learned about the dangers of low self-worth and how that mentality can rob you of your purpose, your joy, and your peace, I began to search out all the destructive beliefs I had of myself. As I replaced those limiting beliefs with new and empowering beliefs, like, "I am more than a conqueror," "I am priceless," and "I am royalty because the God I serve is royal," I began to believe unto conviction that this was my true identity. I began to notice that I triggered or activated a sense of disdain in the people around me, especially those who see me as insignificant. I heard things like, "You're thinking too highly of yourself, you should think realistically." As I heard these things, I began to ask myself, "Am I prideful for believing that I'm more than a conqueror?"

That question was what birthed this chapter.

It is not prideful or arrogant to believe that you are great. I believe you are great because you are the only you in the world. The purpose connected to your life is of great importance so why would the person assigned to carry out that purpose be insignificant? God put you on this earth for a purpose, and it is every man and woman's responsibility to search out and fulfill that purpose. And in doing so, you will make people feel uncomfortable. You will make people think that you are too good for them, but the unfortunate truth is, if you are around people that want you to minimize your vision for your life, they are not the people you should stay around. As I learned this truth, it was very uncomfortable for me because I was very concerned about how people perceive me and I didn't want to be perceived as being too good, but over time, I had come to the realization that it's not my responsibility to clarify people's perception; it's my responsibility to be all that God has called me to be, no matter how others may feel about it.

You Will Not Rise Above Any Limiting Circumstance Or Belief If You Do Not Believe You Can

The purpose of this chapter is to help you understand that there is a clear difference between speaking confidently and authoritatively and speaking arrogantly and being consumed in yourself. As I fought and continue to fight to understand God's will for my life, there are many times I was uncomfortable because I had goals that seemed to be higher than those around me. Because I didn't want to feel out of place, I lowered the standards for my life, even felt ashamed to share the vision that God put on my heart, in order to ensure that the spirit of pride was not being entertained. I have found this way of thinking to be very destructive. The Word of God declares, God has not given us a spirit of fear, but peace and a sound mind (2 Tim 1:7). Fear of all kinds does not produce righteousness, diligence, perseverance. You cannot go in the right direction by only making sure you are not going in the wrong direction.

When I say "a false sense of conviction," I mean I felt uncomfortable thinking I was better than what I was going through that came from my limited view of who I believed I was. I believe, in order to think up, you must understand God is calling you out of mediocracy. The children of Israel were given the measure of faith to think of themselves as free citizens. I'm sure there were many Jews that spoke against Moses, mocking their freedom as a dream (see Exodus 3:9). Their cries to the Lord were a representation that they did not belong there. There are numerous scriptures that warn us against the attitude of pride. There will always be someone to tell you you're a dreamer, but rare are the people who will speak to where you are going, not where you have been.

> And ye shall know the truth, and the truth shall make you free. (John 8:32 KJV)

First, let's examine what it means to accept something. To *accept* is to receive (something offered) willingly (*Merriam-Webster*), to take or receive (something offered), to receive with approval or favor (dictionary.com). *Tolerance* is the ability or willingness to tolerate something; in particular, the existence of opinions or behavior that one does not necessarily agree with.

As I look back over my life, I notice an important fact about my attitude when I felt defeated or taken advantage of. At that time, I did not think this attitude was destructive. Plus, I felt much stronger emotions that focused my attention on the injustice of the circumstance rather than the unstable character I displayed. The attitude is a high tolerance for defeat. This attitude was birthed because I perceived my failures, rejections, disappointments, and lost opportunities like an affirmation to myself, confirming my worthlessness. This type of thinking leads to low self-esteem and many other psychological dysfunctions. Though you may not have become oppressed through the way I have, but look back over your life. What do you think started your poor thinking or depression? Write it down.

Knowing when you started feeling oppressed will help you identify the people who, without knowing, may have agreed with your oppression. These people are usually close family members, childhood friends, or anyone you have grown to respect and value their opinion. Usually, the opinion of those close to you, even if it is not true, has the potential to be received by you as a fact if you do not guard your heart, as Proverbs 4:23 reminds us. It is important to know when and how your oppressed thought started. Why? Because if you do not know why you think in agreement with poor thoughts, you cannot confront future thoughts of oppression, leaving you vulnerable to the enemy's attack.

> When an unclean spirit goes out of a man, he goes through dry places, seeking rest, and finds none. Then he says, "I will return to my house from which I came." And when he comes, he finds it empty, swept, and put in order. Then he goes and takes with him seven other spirits more wicked than himself, and they enter and dwell there, and the last state of that man is worse than the first. So shall it also be with this wicked generation. (Matt. 12:43–45 NKJV)

This scripture reminds me that its equally important to fill your house with things that empowers you rather than things that cause you to doubt yourself.

Building Relationships That Support You

Healing Begins with God
And Continues Through Relationships

> You are saved, called, purposed, and graced
> to make a difference here on earth now
> among your friends, family, neighbors, and
> coworkers, and through every opportunity
> God brings your way. (Brian Houston)

I believe healing begins with surrendering your life to Jesus Christ. He can heal you from past hurts and emotional bondage that a man or woman cannot. However, in your healing process, God does use people to continue what He, through the Spirit, began. God strategically places people around you to help you mature into a healthy and strong servant of Christ. I learned through bad experiences that the truth that you live by is directly or indirectly connected to the truth of those around you, good or bad. For example, if your truth is, "I'm a second-class citizen and people like me never get ahead in life," you will tend to get along with and befriend others who believe they're a second-class citizen and cannot get ahead.

There's a type of dysfunctional joy in sharing stories about how their life has been failure after failure without the intent to identify why they failed in order to change, as if they receive a prize if they have the worst story. Don't misunderstand me; we all go through circumstances that may make us feel like we cannot get ahead, feel overlooked, or rejected, but the primary problem is not being treated badly—that is secondary. The primary problem is when you believe you deserve to be treated badly. This mindset seems to perpetuate a life of weakness and insecurity, which is the direct opposite of God's purpose for your life.

When you are striving to think up, the people in your circle of influence will support the change in your thinking and your renewed commitment to break free from all forms of limitation or make your change of thinking harder by labeling your new path as a dream, pride, or thinking highly of yourself. Although I realize the importance of the people God blesses me to come in contact with and to be an important part of my growth, I must admit, this is an area of biblical truth that I am immature in. I put my trust in people too easily, and I assume people have my best interest at heart even though I see clear signs that they don't. I will consider myself to be the last person to give relationship advice because of the fears and social anxiety I struggled with as a child. But the reason I had to write this chapter is that you, me, or anyone who wants to come out of destructive thinking cannot be healed on their own.

> As iron sharpens iron, so a friend sharpens a friend. (Prov. 27:17 KJV)

Iron requires iron to be sharpened, and with the help of the Lord and with emotionally and spiritually healthy people around you, the iron in them will wake up and bloom the iron within you. This principle also works in the negative; if you are around emotionally and spiritually unhealthy people, they will also stir up and grow the dysfunctions within you. Therefore, the Bible tells us evil company corrupts good habits (1 Cor. 15:33 NKJV).

The People You Surround Yourself With Are the People You Will Become

> You are the average of the five people you
> spend the most time with. (Jim Rohn)

People only surround themselves with people they feel comfortable with. If you feel comfortable only around people who believe they will never achieve anything in life, there is something within you that connects to their truth. It may or may not be the same worldview, but whatever it is in you that connects to that oppressive mindset, it is important for you to find and let it go! If you are comfortable around people who believe that they're priceless and respect themselves and those around them, there is something within you that connects to their worldview. The point is, never assume you connect with people just because you both like football, baking, family activities, etc. I believe there's a deeper truth that connects you to the people you befriend. You need Godly people around you that do not support your defeated state.

You must identify and separate yourself from people who take advantage of your insecurities and discourage your desire to change for the better. Whether you, or I, like it or not, if you are to be strong iron, you must then require yourself to be around strong iron, or you will be dull. This is common sense, but through experience, I found I will feel guilty for wanting to be around strong iron because I felt like

I was deserting the people who may have seen me as strong. I have learned that your true strength is revealed when you allow yourself to be vulnerable and confront the relational issues you have.

You Are Only as Strong As You Allow Yourself to Be Weak

Forgiveness is a character trait that is required for you to break free from destructive ways of thinking. Being able to let go of the pains in your past is a sign of emotional and spiritual maturity that I believe is a process to attain. I have learned that it takes strength to become vulnerable enough to examine your weaknesses, with the intention to change. The easiest thing to do is view your weaknesses as an accurate estimation of your value. If you allow your weaknesses and the insecurities and weaknesses of others to be the primary influence of your thinking, you will not value yourself. We are created to serve others, and no matter how badly someone has hurt you, whether through a friendship or a spouse, you cannot become spiritually and emotionally mature and be all God is calling you to be while harboring unforgiveness in your heart.

The reason I believe you are only as strong as you allow yourself to be weak is that spiritual strength and emotional maturity are directly connected to your ability to learn and grow from your weaknesses. People who view their weaknesses as an affirmation of their insignificance curse themselves with no other choice but to accept their circumstances as unchangeable, which guarantees that tomorrow will not get better. When you walk around with that mentality, insignificance becomes a self-fulfilling prophecy. No one can break free from the limitations they accept. Acceptance is another form of retreat. Sometimes we accept failure when we don't know how to succeed. You may accept destructive relationships when you're ignorant of the destructive nature of the relationship and the knowledge of how to build healthy relationships. You may accept poverty for your future simply because poverty has always been in your past. Most people tend to accept what they believe they cannot change. The activating word is *believe*!

We tend to get out of life what we expect. Beginning today, embrace the belief that you have authority over your circumstance through Christ, who strengthens you. (See Philippians 4:13 NKJV.) If you are involved in a relationship that encourages you to hide your God-given personality, creativity, talent, insight, wisdom, understanding, and ideas that represent the whole of who you are, you're in an unhealthy relationship. Unspoken rules that fuel low self-esteem, insecurity, anger, strife, and discord, you are in an unhealthy relationship. If unspoken rules are needed for that relationship to keep the peace, the relationship will grow in a dysfunctional manner. Dysfunctional growth in relationships means the emotions that are consistently called out, whether intentionally or unintentionally, are the same emotions that are used to keep you recycling the destructive behavior.

There is no such thing as a healthy relationship without sacrifice, openness, and honesty on both sides. Low self-esteem or low self-worth can be incubated and matured by being involved in a relationship that emphasizes unhealthy boundaries. These boundaries will not be easily seen, because the boundaries are a by-product of manipulation, deceit, and control. People who struggle with low self-worth are drawn to people who need them in order to feel a sense of self-worth or value. When someone is trying to control you, their primary goal is to gain your trust, because they know that their control cannot be enforced if their ideas and requests do not go directly to the heart. Ironically, isn't this the same tactic the devil uses to lead you down a path that seems right? It is only when the dysfunction grows to a stage where it is easily seen that it is discovered. People with low self-esteem are more prone to gravitate toward codependent relationships. This is a cycle that must be identified, confronted, and broken by the power of God.

Signs of an Unhealthy Relationship

There is more in you than what people need from you. I have learned that when it comes to protecting yourself from piranha-like people, you have to be selfish when it comes to guarding your heart. I know the word *selfish* has taken on a negative character trait in our culture. When I think of selfishness, I think of someone who cares only about themselves at the expense of tearing down others. But I have grown in my understanding and relationship with that word. I've found that there are some areas where you must put yourself, your family, your peace, your joy, your purpose as priority in your life. And you will not put the most important things that are close to your heart a priority if you carelessly allow people who do not have your best interest at heart to steal your future By stealing your time, emotional energy, and resources. The only way I learn to make sure that I am prioritizing things in my life is being selfish when it comes to protecting what's rightfully mine. I believe David had the same attitude; he heard that there was someone speaking against the people of God. He immediately went up and asked who this man was, as if to say he had no authority. (1 Sam 17:26)

90

> Guard your heart above all else, for it
> determines the course of your life. (Prov.
> 4:23 NLT)

Make guarding your heart a priority, which Proverbs teaches is important. You must go beyond freedom into inheritance.

Many people make the mistake of believing that coming out of a burdensome situation is a form of thinking highly of yourself. When this happens, the usual mindset is, if God wanted you to come out of this circumstance, He would bring you out. So therefore, diligently seeking the will of God for a strategy can be considered by some as pride. I guess Joshua and Caleb were operating in pride when they declared that the land God had given then could be easily attained (Num ch 13). Having the courage and faith to move forward can be an offense to the people around you because it exposes their lack of faith. Joshua and Caleb's faith was criticized by all the people who accepted just being free. Many believers today just accept salvation and never inherit their rightful place in the kingdom of God. It is God's will for you to move forward. Nowhere in the Bible does God bless stagnation, yet many people resist the nudge of the Holy Spirit, prompting them to study more, go on a consecration, or let go of that person who is contaminating their faith. Why do we resist? The first line of opposition is, "What's wrong with where I'm at?"

Seven Signs That You Are in an Unhealthy Relationship

1. You spend most of your time and energy attempting to maintain peace in the relationship than building open lines of communication.

2. You are always giving or pouring into the relationship, but you do not feel a steady pouring into you.
3. You stay connected because you feel guilty if you were to disconnect.
4. You are only connected because you believe friendship can benefit or help you.
5. No trust.
6. Indirect communication.
7. Speaks to who they think you are rather than who you are becoming.

> But you, dear friends, carefully build yourselves up in this holiest faith by praying in the Holy Spirit. (Jude 1:20)

Valuing yourself starts with letting go of people's opinions of what your worth. You will not build yourself up on your most holy faith if you do not see yourself as worth building. It is quite natural to want to connect with people who make you feel comfortable in your current state. The unfortunate reality is that comfortableness can easily lead to codependent relationships. Examine the people you are around the most. Do they add value to your life? In what way? Do you add value to their life? In what way? "As iron sharpens iron, so a friend sharpens a friend" (Prov. 27:17).

Change Your Goals into Requirements

The Difference Between a Goal and a Required Goal

> If you do not intentionally put yourself through the pain of growing, you will unintentionally put yourself through the pain of stagnation. (Robert L. Lowery III)

This is a major mentality change, but a change that will have a major positive impact on your life! Let's look at the characteristics of a goal and a requirement. A *goal* is an idea of the future or the desired result you would like to accomplish at a set future date. A *requirement* is something essential to the existence or occurrence of something else (*Merriam-Webster*). A goal gives the impression that it is important but not a big deal if you don't achieve it to accomplish your vision. A requirement lets you and anyone else know that this is important and needed for the vision. Think with me for a second. Try to remember two or three goals you have or had in your life. Were they achieved? Why did you make it a goal? Now, think of two or three things you presently require, or in the past required, yourself to accomplish. Chances are, you met your required goals. Why? It was most likely because not achieving those requirements meant a great deal of emotional or financial pain to you or someone you love. Goals and disciplines you require yourself to achieve will get achieved faster than a goal or discipline that you just hope to achieve in the future. The way you accomplish this mentality shift is simple but not easy.

Consistency is key.

Certain things are constant in your life. You must be one of them.

To change a goal into a requirement, you simply work on achieving that goal every day. Not every week, not every other day, not every time you feel like it's important. Work at it every day. You may be saying to yourself, "I'm already working on my goal every day, and I'm not achieving it." That may be because you are performing an action that you perceive to be moving you toward your goal but it's not. Don't confuse busyness with effectiveness.

I learned this lesson while writing this book. It has been a goal of mine for five years to write a book. Every time I thought of starting, I told myself I couldn't write a book, I don't know how to write, I don't have a following, I'm not a phycologist, I'm not a pastor, and I don't have a platform. All these were true. Then one day, I just decided to start writing one chapter at a time. It still took me a year to finish just a chapter because I was so critical of myself. I kept erasing and adding paragraphs, changing the title, and so on. Then one day, I came to the resolution that I must write every day to finish this book. If I didn't, I would never finish. I was so frustrated with myself that I knew I had to go to the extreme to win. I began writing before work, during lunch breaks, and after work. I tell you this to understand that the minute I gave all myself to complete this book was when my life changed. You generally don't give your whole self to accomplish goals, but you give your whole self to accomplish requirements. If your goal is not worth your time every day for you to achieve it, it may not be a goal you genuinely want to achieve.

Fight Tired

> Wait on the Lord: be of good courage,
> and he shall strengthen thine heart: wait,
> I say, on the Lord. (Ps. 27:14 KJV)

To break the enemy's stronghold, it will undoubtedly take strength that you may or may not believe you possess. Everyone is motivated to fight when you have strength. In heavyweight boxing events, notice before the main event, boxers have a lot to say. They talk about their training, how their opponent is no match for them. Even in their arrogance, some predict how many rounds the fight will go, but all this talk is given before the fight. Fight night is here. Notice most fighters do not like to talk. Why? Because they're focused. The disciplines they had to acquire to compete in the fight increased their focus level, which can be offset by talking too much on fight night. Why? Because they want to win, and you will not defeat anything talking about it!

I've observed that the winner is determined by how much strength a fighter has when tired. Some fighters like Muhammad Ali save their strength until their opponent is tired, because when you're tired, you have no defense. I am not a boxing expert, but I bet you have a greater chance to beat a tired opponent than a well-rested one. This is how most of us are defeated! When you're tired. Tired of trying to change. Tired of trying to overcome your past. Tired of striving to be who God called you to be. So what do most people do when they're tired? You talk about how tired you are and complain that you have it harder than anyone else because of how you were raised or because you were abandoned or lacked opportunity. All those events may have contributed to your frustrations, but don't allow your fatigue to be the nails to your coffin; instead, allow it to be the foundation of your strength.

> You never know how strong you are until being strong is your only choice. (Bob Marley)

Weak-willed people are always tired because they believe the world owes them something, so everything they do, they put forth little effort and expect a big return. This type of thinking is the norm of today's society; that's why the lottery is so popular. If you're going to get up from where you are, you must ask yourself these questions:

1. Do I talk about change instead of doing what it takes to change?
2. Do I complain that my circumstances are a result of someone else's efforts?
3. Do I allow others to directly or indirectly control my life?

If you answered yes to one or more of these questions, then most likely there's a defect in your thinking, causing you to stay where you're at. Some of your greatest battles will be fought tired. Accept it and embrace it. Comfortable fights are battles that have no reward. When you're tired, you question your every action as if rest is the better alternative. If I believe rest is more important than the fight for my purpose, I will not be vigilant and stand within my God-given authority. Rest is manifested in different forms, not just sleep. It comes in the form of submitting to temptation, not being as diligent as God put it in your spirit to be, or running from your purpose like Jonah (Jon. 1:1–3). I believe sometimes I trust God's power to change a situation as if that same God is not within me. Sometimes the change that becomes the seed to your growth starts with you! "I can do all things in Christ that strengthens me" (Phil. 4:13).

You Are Not a Victim Even If You Have Been Victimized

A Victim's Mentality Is a Learned Behavior

> We are victims anytime we give another
> person the power to define our worth.
> (Margaret Paul, PhD)

It's fair to say that we all have been in the victim chair in one way or the other. I have two energetic boys named Isaiah and Joshua, which are six and two years old. As everyone with kids know, a fight over toys is bound to happen. A constant back-and-forth battle over who gets the fire truck or the PJ masks car is normal in our home. My wife Shantrelle or I will remind our boys, primarily Isaiah of the hundreds of toys their blessed to own encouraging them to either share or get another toy. This pep talk falls on deaf ears because as soon as the toy has to be taken because they chose not to share, they began to pout and sit in isolation. As my boys easily forgets about the hundred toys they can play with and focus on the one they can't, the victim mentality causes you to forget the numerous empowering responses you can choose and instead focus your attention on the one destructive response that perpetuate your helplessness. You become a victim any time you allow a thought, person, circumstance, fear, or insecurity stop you from moving forward.

In the late 1960s, Martin Seligman and Steven Maier conducted a study while researching depression. He and his colleagues discovered that dogs and, after further studies, humans also could learn how to be helpless when placed in environments that taught them helplessness. *Learned helplessness* is a phycological term referring to people who have learned to stay in a bad situation or environment because their past has taught them that they have no control over their environment. I believe this is an important discovery, because it reveals that if you learned to be helpless, knowing the destructive nature of this mentality, you could now learn that you have authority over your circumstances by the grace of God. I learned through experience that your circumstances will always attempt to define you in a way that does not reflect the true essence of who you are. If you relinquish your God-given right to speak those things that be not as though they were, you will slowly allow your circumstances to define you.

Character Traits of the Victim Mentality

A victim tends to always have things happen to them rather than them affecting or happening to things. They take on the character of a hopeless person who is afraid to act or defend themselves with their best interest in mind. A person with the victim mentality tends to be uncomfortable speaking and acting like the victorious conqueror God created them to be. Why must the victim mentality be exposed and defeated? Because you will not rise above any form of limitation when you see yourself as a victim every time life happens to you.

I learned that the victim mentality is birthed not when bad things happen to you or someone you love; the victim mentality is birthed and conquered in the way you choose to respond. Psychologists have proved that events do not create stress but how the person chooses to respond to that event. The victim mentality paralyzes you to respond in a way that defeats you. I believe the healthiest response to fear, doubt, and limiting beliefs is to courageously move forward. To see beyond your walls, you must believe the promises of God beyond your doubts.

The victim mentality empowers the attitude of low expectations. You tend to get out of life what you expect, but why is that true? Because wrapped within your expectation is what you believe unto conviction, what is possible for you to accomplish. The victim mentality acts as cancer, eating away what you believe is possible for you and, in turn, killing your level of expectation. This is why the victim mentality is imperative for you to let go of before you can think up to get up. We become victims by allowing circumstances, people, your past, or how you perceive yourself to define you in a way that does not reflect who God created you to be.

The Danger of Masking Dysfunctions with Scripture

We've all been victimized by someone or some experience. As my boss calls me in the office to discuss some changes to work procedures, I couldn't help but think about how my manager consistently places a certain employee I will call Brad in a position to make more money and have better opportunities to advance. I wanted to say something about this imbalance, but a second thought consumed my attention. Maybe God is attempting to teach me something. Yes, that's right; He is doing a greater work in me, and I must hold my peace and submit to His will. Around that time, I just began learning the importance of godly character and being in the will of God. This situation seemed like the perfect opportunity to grow. "Obedience is better than sacrifice!" (1 Sam. 15:22). This scripture had nothing to do with the way I perceived that circumstance, but it did sound spiritual enough for me to overlook the fact that I was fearful of confrontation.

I had a bad habit of focusing on a spiritual principle that could be learned in every circumstance and omitting the character flaws I am entertaining by doing so. I discovered later that spiritualizing circumstances was my way of having a good conscience, by letting those destructive circumstances persist. I allowed a destructive character trait to persist unconfronted because I was so focused on the spiritual blessing being taught within the circumstance. The truth was, I was fearful of confrontation, and I did not want to discuss anything with my manager that would make him angry and potentially fire me, so instead of being honest with how I felt, to avoid confrontation, I spiritualized my dysfunction.

It's a whole lot easier to say, "God wants me to hold my peace, which agrees with my personality," than to confront my fear and risk pain. I believe spiritualizing dysfunctions is another facet of a victim mentality. There are many ways to arrive in the victim chair, but the way that killed me was persisting in this destructive mindset by throwing Jesus in my mess versus allowing Jesus to expose and break me free from my mess. We've all heard the saying "Knowing is half the battle," but what happens when you tell yourself that God wants you to not know or not get to the bottom of a situation? That's what I was indirectly telling myself by avoiding the root cause of my attitude of neglect. The consequences are endless. Because you can live your life thinking that putting scripture on top of dysfunction okays the dysfunction. We all heard them. You say, "God wants me to hold my peace" (Eph. 4:3) when you are fearful to speak your heart.

When you're jealous of a friend or coworker for getting the promotion, you say, "The last shall be first and the first shall be last" (Matt. 20:16). When you're angry with your wife or husband because you feel they are not listening, say, "It's okay to be angry, but sin not." It's amazing how we can use the Word of God to bring healing into our lives, but only when we want to be healed. What's tricky is that the Word of God is true and shines the light on all darkness, but we can choose to use that light to make us just feel better rather than use that light to become better. The victim will always want to assume there's something good coming out of their pain, not realizing that the pain may be their own doing. You run the risk of becoming helpless to change your circumstance the second you believe the scripture you are using to mask your dysfunction agrees with your interpretation. Search the scriptures to heal your heart not to express your heart.

When you assume that God is afflicting you, you can easily assume that God will strengthen you. But will God strengthen you when you choose to inflict pain on yourself? This was the question I had to answer. I was so fearful of being honest with how I truly felt that I chose the road less traveled, which is telling myself this is for my good and this is why that behavior is okay. I was forced to see that this attitude is wrong by the bad fruit that was manifested in my life, which was a short temper, frustration, selfishness, and lack of a heart to help others. Now, ask yourself, Are these reasons given good enough for you to allow your peace, your joy, and your purpose to be hindered? If your answer is no, that's great; you are ready to break free from your victim mentality. If your answer is, "Yes, the reasons I have are good enough to hold me in the victim mentality," then, unfortunately, you will not be able to grow much further beyond this suppressive mentality. I strongly recommend you stop here and prayerfully ask yourself what is the foundation of your victimized mentality. When I began to see how my victim mentality was causing me to accept a life way beneath my potential, I began to go through the uncomfortable process of getting out of the victim chair.

Step 1: Proclaim out loud the scripture "I am more than a conqueror" (Rom 8:37) daily.

As you proclaim the scripture over your life, you may get uncomfortable feelings or emotions that may take time to come out of. Pray and ask God, "Why do these feelings arise when I proclaim the truth of God's Word over my life?" For me, I found contradictory feelings that arose because of the insignificant vision I had of myself. I did not believe I was more than a conqueror, so I prayed and ask God that whatever beliefs that may be harbored in my heart that is doubting my true identity be exposed and broken. This takes time; a victim mentality is not developed overnight. The majority of the time, it comes from things you accepted years ago. After God has blessed you with the understanding and ability to identify the lies and break free from them, submit yourself and break free! The most destructive act is to feel unsafe, unappreciated, used, or any emotion that devalues you and causes you to be afraid to express that inner broken-ness in a way that brings healing to your heart. I understand for most people, who identify themselves with the label of a victim, this will be a difficult chapter. I believe overcoming the victim mentality is a continual effort, not just one event. You would never be able to see yourself as the strong man or woman that you are if you continually look at yourself as a problem.

The easiest thing to do is to express or relieve yourself of your emotional frustration in a destructive way. It is human nature to allow your past experiences to be the determining factor of how you interpret your present circumstance. If you unknowingly touched a hot oven when you were seven years old, chances are, you have a heightened level of caution when you're around hot items, even though you may not know why. That early experience taught you that fire hurts and to never do that again. From then on, every time you come around fire, you may be overly cautious and for a good reason, you don't want to get burned. This is an example of your past helping you to stay safe in the future. The belief that fire can harm you was grafted into your memory through the pain you experienced. Well, just as past innocent mistakes can graft a predetermined response to present circumstances, past insults, ridicule, abuse, and belittling will also graft predetermined thought patterns with your present circumstances, opportunities, or relationships.

Many wrong thinking patterns may not come from the devil; some may have been formed by the way you interpreted an insult. You see, our past has a way of making us believe we are what we are because our present circumstance is bringing to surface the same destructive thoughts we felt in the past. You are not what people say you are; you are what the Bible says you will be, who God says you are, which is fearfully and wonderfully made (Ps. 139:14). You are more than a conqueror (Rom. 8:37); you are greater than your circumstances, because greater is He that is in you than He that is in the world (1 John 4:4). If you allow God's Word about you to consume you and it becomes your word about you, as TD Jakes quoted, your environment will began to reflect the inner beliefs you have. If you're in a circumstance that makes you feel weak, lo and behold, you begin to think weak, and you become weak. Your circumstances the next day make you feel defeated; you begin to feel defeated, then think defeated, and lo and behold, you are defeated. This is why you must be renewed in the spirit of your mind. Your feeling can fuel what God's Word says about you, especially when what you feel is contradictory. Thinking up is more than just being positive about what you are going through. Minimizing or overlooking the present facts of what you are going through in the name of positive thinking is foolish.

Your Response Determines Your Victory

> Many motivations or driving forces are not our fought. But this does not mean that our behavior is not our responsibility. (Dr. Henry Cloud)

Drs. Henry Cloud and John Townsend give many great insights on winning on the path to spiritual and emotional growth in their book *How People Grow*. One point they make that I believe is key is to not allow yourself to stay in a perpetual cycle of dysfunction by rationalizing or justifying an unhealthy response to your present problems due to your past. This is a vice that claims the destiny of many people. Dr. Cloud went on to say, having a background that may justify your current response does not explain why you chose to deal destructively with that hurt.

> Our past may explain why we're suffering but we must not use it as an excuse to stay in bondage. (Joyce Meyer)

Don't allow the lies you have accepted as truth in your past to remain true in your future. Insecurities, fears, doubts, and rejections from your past regrets from missed opportunities seem to have this powerful ability to get you to assume that your identity is wrapped up within these failures. Limitation is wrapped in the skin of acceptance. Your past only has the power to make you a victim when you accept the lies as your truth. Redefining what is true may be a painful process, but it is required in order to get out of the victim chair.

Sometimes the lies you have accepted were birthed at the most immature stage in your life and since you may feel a sense of protection, since the lie may help you cope with your reality, it can't help you grow beyond your reality.

> If your thoughts become a victim of circumstance, the circumstance wins! (Dr. Myles Munroe, YouTube, "Change with Dr. Munroe")

When you play the role of a victim, whether it is being taken advantage of by manipulation, someone close to you refusing to give you the love you deserve, from a parent not being in your life or a spouse having an affair, no matter how you may find yourself in the seat of a victim, you must see yourself stronger than the position you're in, by not allowing the victim mentality to be accepted. If a person keeps accepting defeat over and over, defeat becomes apart of the character of that individual. This adoption of the new character is unavoidable.

Two character traits affect your level of acceptance greatly; they are fear and passiveness.

Fear

Fear is an emotion that everyone deals with. The Bible tells us, "For God hath not given us the spirit of fear, but of power, and of love, and of a sound mind" (2 Tim. 1:7). Fear paralyzes all intentions to act. If you're not intentional about being strong you will unintentionally be weak. As I strive to face my fears and grow in my belief of what I'm capable of, I tend to always stumble across this one truth that encourages me to fight on! It's Weakness or strength are first manifest in thought before it is expressed in a attitude, emotion or circumstance. Don't allow your fears to empower your weaknesses, allow them to empower your resilience to stand strong!

Passiveness

The passive attitude is expressed by taking excessive amounts of time to confront the victim mentality. Passive people accept defeat as long as it doesn't bother them that bad, but once they get angry about the situation, they will confront anything with a vengeance. The problem is this: the days, weeks, or months spent accepting defeat, they are molding their minds to stay defeated. Being passive about overcoming the victim mentality will cause you to spiral downward into low self worth.

When you think low of yourself, you easily accept anything that happens to you and over spiritualize it, telling yourself it must be God's will for this or that to happen, quoting scriptures like Romans 8:28, "And we know that all things work together for good to them that love God, to them who are the called according to his purpose." By nature, we want to understand everything that happens to us. So quoting this scripture to the Christian helps them accept the circumstance as a blessing in disguise. The problem is when you think low of yourself; it is a part of your nature to accept everything without reviewing all scriptures about God's will for you. Just because something heartbreaking or disappointing happens to you that does not give you the right to feel defeated after your heart heals. If you put all your focus on your problems, you will never recognize your heart is healed, and it is you that is desperately holding on to the false identity of a victim your circumstance has given you.

Don't confuse your choice to be weak with an external influence causing your weakness.

Dr. Henry Cloud, in his book co-authored with Dr. John Townsend, tells of a couple who had relational issues. The husband would snap and get angry, causing excessive grief in their marriage. After months of progress, he snapped again and had gotten into an intense argument. Feeling empathetic, Dr. Cloud thought, What made him snap? Maybe he was just caught in sin (Gal. 6:1). As Dr. Cloud listened to his response, he became angry because he realized nothing snapped within him or triggered his anger. Though the husband blamed his anger on external influences, Dr. Cloud revealed that his anger was a conscious choice. This was not a weakness. This was a choice.

When you play the victim role, you surrender all power to change to someone or something outside of you. This is dangerous because if you tell yourself that someone other than you must take full responsibility in your growth you will only progress as far as other peoples vision of you. Theres a old story about a farmer who while planting pumpkins decided to place a pumpkin plant in a jug just to see what will happen. When harvest season came the farmer went out to collect his harvest. When he came across the pumpkin he put in the jug he noticed it was much smaller than all of the other pumpkins and it grown to the exact size of the jug. Just like this pumpkin only grew to the size of its environment, the victim mentality forces you to grow only to the size of the limitations people place on you. This limitation only has the ability to stump your growth to the extent you believe you have no control of your growth. Don't let this be you!

Overcoming the Victim Mindset

Consistent Action

This destructive way of thinking is so toxic that you must daily be intentional to sow seeds toward confidence.

> Finally, brethren, whatsoever things are true, whatsoever things are honest, whatsoever things are just, whatsoever things are pure, whatsoever things are lovely, whatsoever things are of good report; if there be any virtue, and if there be any praise, think on these things. (Phil. 4:8)

The Word of God tells us to think about the things that can free us from the limitations of circumstance. Truth, honesty, justice, purity, love, goodness, and moral excellence. I love the fact that the first thing that is mentioned is the truth. I have heard many people say the truth sets you free. I strongly disagree. Why? Well, if I told you, I will give you ten million dollars next week. The truth of that statement sets you free from all the responsibilities of working, but only to the extent of how you think. You have the choice to think, "That's nice, but I love to work, so I will continue working, just not as much." Or you may say to yourself, "Praise God you answered my prayers! I never have to work a day in my life!" Again, the truth of my statement sets you free from the responsibly to work, but only to the extent of how you perceive that truth. Well, the Bible says in John 8:32, "The truth *makes* you free!" What is the difference? In my example, you may have overlooked that I said "next week"; that means the thoughts you had were inspired by truth but unable to be acted on because it is not a reality until the money is in your bank account. When the money hits your account, now you have the power and freedom to make a choice to continue to work or not.

Some people look at truth as just setting them free. They look at all the things they could do or be as soon as something outside of them happens. Becoming stronger in their understanding of the Word of God, getting married, starting a business, and so on. These are some examples of allowing accomplished goals to be the start of their lives as if you are not living today.

"If my wife or husband will only be a better person, I wouldn't be like this." This is an example of you forcing the truth to have the ability to set you free in the future and not make you free now. When you know that you are the head and not the tail, it makes you respond to your circumstances with confidence and authority, but when you see that truth as just a good idea, you unconsciously give yourself the option to choose to believe it or not. Just as my previous example emphasized, you had a choice to work or not work based on your perception, but either option cannot be carried out because it is not yet a reality. But when the ten million is in your account, you not only have the grace to have the option to work or not but you now also have the power to carry out your plan. A truth that is not accepted is like someone telling you they will give you ten million dollars in the future, and all that statement has the power to do is give you joy and happiness only in thought because they have not given you the money. But the truth that is accepted is you actually having the money and now also having the power to act on your thoughts. Just because you understand or agree with the truth of God's Word does not mean you have accepted it as your truth.

God's word about you must become your
word about you. (Bishop TD Jakes)

If God's Word about you does not become your word
about you, you will never be who God has intended for you
to be. What I mean is, the truth of who Jesus is, and the truth
of who He says you are, must be the foundation of how you
think and perceive your circumstance. So when the enemy
comes in like a flood, you will, without thinking about it,
utter out of your spirit, then out of your mouth, "I am more
than a conqueror." This is a result of His Word ceasing to
become a good principle to live by, or even scripture but now
His word is apart of who you are! His Word has been crystalized to a reality. When the enemy attempts to tell you lies
about how you must see your situation as never changing,
your reality that is founded on the truth of God's word will
cause the false thoughts to be cast down so quickly that you
won't even waste time acknowledging the lie; you will just
simply keep moving forward.

Men are anxious to change their circumstances but unwilling to change themselves. (James Allen)

Oppression can only be perpetuated if the oppressed are
ignorant of their rightful place in Christ and accept the belittling, condescending comments and destructive criticisms as
the truth. Being a victim in your life is not normal. Until you
understand that truth with total conviction, you will never
break free from destructive thinking; you will always find a
reason to stay in your defeated state.

Many people love to overlook a principle or truth that is
causing their undesired outcome and assume that their prob-

lem is special and the principle does not apply to them; it applies to everyone else.

Not accepting defeat is an attitude, a character trait, not just something you say when you feel defeated. This mindset must be molded into your thought process. All the greats carry this attitude, and if you feel God is calling you to greatness, you're no different.

When you accept your present circumstance, you are telling yourself all the facts about where you are, as if those facts are confirmation that you're on the course of accomplishing your goal. "At least I'm not where I used to be, or it could be worse." These statements are signs of the acceptance of mediocrity. Focusing on the good of every situation is not bad, but sometimes what you see as good is really a poor excuse for the lack of progress you seem to overlook! I am not here to tell you getting out of bad positions is easy, but what I can tell you is that there's a God-given method of doing so.

The prodigal son's change came only when his circumstances no longer reflected the thoughts he had of himself. Ask yourself, "Do I believe I belong here in this state of poverty, in this state of depression, in this state of rejection?" I'm sure you probably answered no. Now, ask yourself, "Do the ways I view myself support or reject my circumstance?"

Poor self-esteem, uncontrolled anger, depression, jealousy, fear, pride, laziness, manipulation—these are some of the fruits of destructive thinking. We are under the illusion that how we feel is the primary reason for making decisions or accepting principles; this is not true. For example, let's say you are sitting on the couch, watching TV, and during a commercial, you want to get a snack out of the kitchen. Your mind focuses on the goal (a snack in the kitchen). Though you may be tired, stressed, depressed, angry, lonely, no matter how you feel, your feelings will not affect your set goal, because you perceive your goal to be easy to do despite your ill

ROBERT L. LOWERY III

feelings. So without hesitating, you start to accomplish your goal; despite all the mental strongholds, you still achieved your goal and you are no longer hungry. Unfortunately, many people today are stuck in depression, tortured by fear, angry at the world because they can't seem to get up. Not realizing the same tactics they used to get a snack out of the kitchen are the same tactics required to change their life. The only difference is you must set a goal that will bring you out of destructive thinking not. The principles in this book alone will not help you break free, your decision to allow these principles to be your first step towards freedom will! John 10:10 says, "The thief cometh not, but for to steal, and to kill, and to destroy: I come that they might have life and that they might have it more abundantly." When I read this scripture, I had to examine myself. Am I living an abundant life? What is the abundant life? How can I know if I'm living or just existing? These are questions I'm sure everyone asks themselves.

We are living at a time when knowledge is readily available but wisdom is scarce. Everybody has a word. If you do a survey asking people if they know Jesus as their Savior, many will profess that they have some type of "spiritual connection."

> This also knows that in the last days, perilous times shall come. For men shall be lovers of their own selves, covetous, boasters, proud, blasphemers, disobedient to parents, unthankful, unholy, Without natural affection, trucebreakers, false accusers, incontinent, fierce, despisers of those that are good, Traitors, heady, high-minded, lovers of pleasures more than lovers of God; Having a form of

> godliness, but denying the power thereof:
> from such turn away. For of this sort are
> they which creep into houses and lead
> silly captive women laden with sins, led
> away with divers lusts, Ever learning, and
> never able to come to the knowledge of
> the truth. (2 Tim. 3:1–7)

This is the time we are living in today. The part that jumps out at me is what will make someone have a desire to want to learn if they do not want the truth.

Fighting for what's yours isn't always easy, especially when you find out the sacrifice you're paying for it isn't enough.

God allows ignorance to consume you only after He sends a word of knowledge. The word He sends is your boat in the storms of life.

Power over Ignorance

> Take heed unto thyself, and unto the
> doctrine; continue in them: for in doing
> this thou shalt both save thyself, and
> them that hear thee. (1 Tim. 4:16)

The attitude of contentment, if you allow it, can act as the glue that keeps you stuck in the victim mentality. This mentality is not only cancerous; it is deceitful.

Once this mindset is accepted, you will become a slave to every situation, going whichever way people lead you because you believe everyone can help you except yourself. I'm here to tell you, you are the only person who has the power to break free from bondage, and you are the only person who can keep yourself in bondage. We are taken captive or set free through our thoughts, nothing else. Our environment, experiences, family, friends, and beliefs play a role in our decisions, but the only role they play is the role of a tool to shape, form, build, or tear down thoughts we have of ourselves, what we can do, what we can't do.

Through these experiences, we develop character traits that reinforce slavish thoughts that were hiding deep into our hearts. In order to break free from what's holding you, you must identify what's keeping you. People who carelessly accept whatever life throws at them eventually become content with unstable thinking. James 1:8 reads, "A double-minded man is unstable in all his ways." This means a man or woman whose beliefs are in disagreement with their thinking will be unstable. Double-minded faith is one of the primary sources of passive contentment, to be happy in one circumstance then feel powerless in another; each circumstance you experience produces an attitude of hopeless acceptance.

Thinking above Ignorance

When I wrote "thinking above ignorance" down for the first time, my first thought was, Does that make sense? Can you really think above ignorance, or is it just a catchy phrase that just sounds good to me? Then a second thought came. You think above ignorance by becoming a learner and understanding the areas where God reveals to you that you are defeated in. It's not about being a know-it-all or being able to quote scripture for every area of defeat; it's about humbling yourself and opening your heart to hear God as He leads you out of bondage. As I fought to believe in myself and value myself as God values me, my main struggle was overcoming the destructive belief that I am not smart enough to lead or to write. When I got married to my precious wife Shantrelle and started a family, I then had to overcome thoughts, believing I was not strong enough and man enough to be the foundation of my family. He gave me a beautiful, anointed wife, which, by the way, I prayed to have for over three years. So I chose to believe that because God blessed me to see it and have it, He will also bless me to be effective in it. From this belief came a strong conviction that I will. I will be all that God is calling out of me. But I went from being ignorant to being convicted by taking one step forward, one day at a time. I believe overcoming the victim mentality is a continual effort, not just one event. You would never be able to see yourself as the strong man or woman that you are if you continually look at yourself as a problem.

> A *victim mentality* is an acquired personality trait in which the person tends to recognize themselves as a victim of the negative actions of others and to behave as if this were the case in the face of contrary evidence of such circumstances. (Wikipedia)

> You can't be a victim if you don't relinquish power to someone capable of making you a victim. (M. J. DeMarco)

You are not the battles you lost, the temptations you gave into or the doubts you wrestle with. The fears and broken places in your life are not designed to make you fall into disparity but are meant to be a source of strength to draw from when faced with adversity. Strength comes out of weakness, and I have learned that God allows the weak moments in your life to create a passion that, I believe, no other experience can produce, which acts as the fuel to push you into your purpose. In order to not be defined by your frailties, you must allow your frailties to be defined as the pressure required to create the dimond that you are! It takes everything in you to go forward and be the man or woman that God is calling you to be. When you allow the low points in your life to define you, it becomes more of a challenge to redefine yourself as a victor. You will always see yourself as weak when your belief system is founded on principles that produce weakness and the victim mentality is one of those belief systems. When I say weakness, I'm referring to any attitude or emotion that causes you to see yourself as inferior, inadequate, worthless, not worthy or ashamed to embrace your God-given identity. That part of you that wants to accept the labels your past gave you, the part that wants to just accept whatever life throws at you and label it as God's will, I'm referring to that part of you that wants to believe someone else is going to make you strong without you putting forth any sacrificial effort on your part.

> Finally, my brethren, be strong in the
> Lord, and in the power of his might.
> (Eph. 6:10)

You don't become strong by focusing on not being weak. You become strong by embracing the principles of strength. But what are the principles of strength? Is it just having a positive attitude? Learning to see your circumstance no matter how good or bad as a blessing? I believe that question everyone must answer through their own experience, but the way God blessed me to see the answer is to first make strength as a way of thinking before it is a way of living. When the Word of God tells me to be strong, that lets me know that strength is a choice, not a result.

Strength Is Understanding

One of the hardest but most effective things I had to do to come out of my destructive ways of thinking was to examine and understand the walls I built around my life that kept me thinking within the limitations of my wisdom, my experiences, and my past. The walls I'm referring to are the destructive beliefs I developed about myself. We all have walls, roadblocks, fears, and uncertainties that, if allowed, will control your life for the worst. Seeing beyond your walls takes courage, faith, and vision. Courage to persevere past your hang-ups. Faith to believe that there's more than what you see and vision to effectively direct your courage and faith to a specific next step.

Limitation of all forms begins with faulty beliefs.

It is impossible for the truth of who you are to change your life when that truth must jump the hurdles of your truth (which is within the walls). What I learned is, your truth is intertwined within the walls you built to keep you safe. I fought within myself for about four years to believe I had what it took to write a book. Within my walls were beliefs of "I'm not smart enough," "I don't have a platform," "I don't have a following on Facebook, Twitter, and any other social media outlets," and "Oh yeah, I don't know how to write!" These walls kept me from not taking action for years, but as I continued to study the Bible, my notes on the scripture began to go from one paragraph to several pages. This little observation gave me the faith to just begin a chapter, then study how to write, then I disciplined myself to write every day. And after about two years, the truth that was within my walls became silent, and my new truth began to grow. Understanding is first established before God pours His wisdom into you. Without understanding, you will not have the proper vision to connect your wisdom from experience and

His wisdom from the Word of God and apply it to a specific circumstance.

At that time, all those things were true, but there was a greater truth that was unable to break through to trump my truth, which is, the Spirit of God never gives a prophetic understanding unless He wants to bring change.

Fear, anger, jealousy, pride, frustration, confusion, and self-doubt are emotions that force you to think destructive thoughts. We are living in a time when you have the greatest opportunities. We in the United States have the freedom to be a business owner and an education. Worship God without fear. With all the limitless possibilities we have as a society, there are millions of people suffering from depression, low self-esteem, and inferiority complexes

I have concluded that God has designed it for me, you, and any person who wants to know who they are to uncover purpose by pursuit.

The idle mind is forced to understand his or her world by only using their eyes and feelings (which, by the way, is a poor, inaccurate servant) to reveal who they are. When I came to Christ, I also had an idle mind. I allowed the circumstances I consistently found myself in to define me. I struggled with rejection as a child, so naturally, I felt worthless if I wasn't accepted by my peers. This book is for people who struggle with low self-esteem. Freedom from poor thinking begins when you decide to pursue the right thinking.

Get Out of Yourself

Anxiety in the heart of man causes depression, But a good word makes it glad. (Prov. 12:25 NKJV)

Self-Awareness Precedes Growth

When an experience is your best teacher, then progress is imprisoned. Consult your experience but never let it rule you. (Dr. Myles Munroe)

I believe there's a lot of truth in this statement. We tend to allow the experience in the past to become all we can accomplish in the future. This attitude came quite naturally for me. Since I didn't accomplish much in my past, I thought to myself, "I'm not going to accomplish as much in my future." I found when you allow your past to be the gauge for your future you severely limit your potential.

To be self-aware means to know and understand where you're going, who you are, what you want and don't want. That sounds simple but as I strived to understand who I was in Christ, there were a lot of things I thought I believed or values I lived by that, when I examined them closely, were just convictions stemming from my upbringing. If you are not self-aware enough to know that you do not value your-self, for example, you will be confused when you don't have the energy to grow in areas that God is calling you to grow in.

When I struggle with low self-worth, I never read any books on how to overcome that attitude. That was because, since I did not believe that was for me, I didn't strive to find what it took to break free. Once I became aware of that, I felt I was able to confront, expose, and most importantly, add value to myself by first realizing that how I was thinking was birthed out of insecurity, not the truth.

> You will never become what you could be
> until you become angry with what you
> are. (Myles Munroe)

> Before you complain that you're a slave
> to another first, be sure that you're not a
> slave to yourself. (Napoleon Hill)

Getting outside of yourself, I have learned, means to not assume everything you think, feel, and understand as truth without making sure your assessment isn't biased or laced with insecurity. You cannot lead or grow beyond personal transformation. I believe the easiest thing to do is assume how you perceive a situation is the most accurate way to see it, because along with that perception are feelings that enable your heart to readily accept your perception as truth. Getting outside of yourself means before you accept what you're thinking, cross-examine it with the Word of God and consult others you trust to speak into your life. This will help you to not become a victim of your thoughts.

We can all contest that sometimes we think and feel in ways that are not of God. I have learned that examining my thoughts and how I feel for the dysfunction in them gives me a more stable fighting stance against vain imaginations. Philippians 4:6 says to be careful for nothing, but in everything, in prayer and supplication, with thanksgiving, let your requests be made known unto God.

You will never think above your circumstances without getting outside the path of assumptions. God is always standing, waiting for you to consult Him about you, but you must have the heart to receive.

Before you accept a thought as truth, ask yourself these questions: Why am I thinking this way? Is this thought based on an insecurity? You help the weaker you by allowing oppressive thoughts to go unconfronted. Getting outside of yourself helps take that power back by first identifying the beliefs that empower the weaker you, and only then can you begin to manifest the stronger you.

I must admit, one of the hardest things for me to do was to see myself as an overcomer, as empowered, as strong, as the head and not the tail.

The problem was, I viewed myself as Mephibosheth did, which was as a dead dog. Buried beneath this statement carries the belief that my ideas and experiences are worthless because I'm worthless. I had to expose and eliminate the destructive belief of low self-worth to embrace my God-given identity.

Steps to Take to Get Outside of Yourself

Know that the answer is not in you.

I had to humble myself and seek the face of God.

> There is a way which seemeth right unto
> a man, but the end thereof are the ways
> of death. (Prov. 14:12 KJV)

What seems right about the wrong way? Little or no understanding of the right way. The serpent influenced Eve not by showing her the wrong way but by finding out what she understood about the right way, then giving her more information that seemed right. The enemy's weapon isn't always a lie; it is also information that seems right enough for you to accept its vision.

> You must know yourself to grow yourself.
> (John Maxwell)

Sometimes the easiest thing to do is to move forward, but you can complicate your next step with your fears of the unknown, doubts that stem from your past, or my biggest giant, the fear that you will succeed. The reason I said the easiest thing is to move forward is that many times God has already put the next step within our heart. We just battle within ourselves to receive it and act on it. Don't let that be you! I believe God has placed your next step within you. Quiet your heart and pray. Let God lead you into your next step. Believe. Until you value and appreciate the opportunities God gives you to change, to grow, to learn, chances are, you will remain the same. Not valuing the opportunities God gives to embrace your freedom only allows the psychological boundaries to persist.

You Will Rise or Fall
Only to the Level You Believe You Belong

Purpose of chapter: To help people understand that all growth, whether spiritual, emotional, or mental, will only be achieved by a person who believes they belong at the place of healing, spiritual maturity, and emotional maturity.

Thinking Roadblocks

The sad truth is, most people do not believe they belong in their rightful place of freedom. To be clear, I'm speaking of the individual personal definition of freedom, not mine, as it relates to this book. There is one thing I'm certain of, and that's if you do not fight for your definition of freedom, you will not intentionally go through the growing pains of discovering God's definition of freedom!

This is a chapter I put in at the last minute because as I studied the material I gathered to put in the book to help people and myself understand the value and importance of thinking on a level that best reflects the highest expression of who you are, I ran into some thinking roadblocks. Don't get me wrong; I strongly believe in the truth that this book gives. However, there were some deep-rooted beliefs that kept me from acting on the truth that I was discovering. I believe it is important to share them with you to help you see that you are not the only one that has roadblocks. Here is mine, which I uncovered as it relates to believing you belong in your purpose, your peace, your joy, and your gifting.

Thinking Roadblocks That Kept Me from Believing I Belong

1. Doubt. Can I really accomplish the vision God placed on my heart?
2. Learned helplessness. Lots of people tried to accomplish what I want to accomplish and failed. Why am I different?
3. Ignorance of direction. I don't know how to embrace my purpose, so I will just wait until the answer comes.

4. Fear. I will be attacked, and my flaws exposed! I will just withdraw from life; this way, I don't have to confront my fears and insecurities.

5. Self-deception. I am happy with where I am in life. Trying to achieve too much means that I'm ungrateful.

These five thinking roadblocks were at the foundation of my procrastination. I learned that procrastination is not a character flaw; it is a symptom or result of a hidden inner-thinking roadblock.

To discover yours, ask yourself these questions. I recommend you get a sheet of paper and write down your answers.

1. What do you believe God is calling out of you that will serve people?

2. What are the current limitations that are preventing you from serving in this capacity today?

3. Have you ever started something (not related to your job) that was very important to you but you never finished?

4. After you answer question 3, why didn't you finish?

5. Do you believe God has more for you than you are currently receiving?

6. If your answer is yes to question 5, why do you believe you are not currently receiving the more God has for you? If your answer is no to question 5, why do you believe you are currently experiencing all that God has for you?

7. Do you doubt yourself? If yes, in what ways?

8. Do you allow others to place value on your abilities? If yes, why?

Take all your answers and underline all the things you wrote that is a limitation. What do they have in common? For example, for question 7, if you answered, "Yes, because I don't believe I have what it takes," underline "Don't believe I have what it takes."

Prayerfully review all your limitations that are underlined and ask God to give you the strength, wisdom, and strategy to break these limitations. Begin to study your limitations. Find out who has broken these limitations, what the Bible says about your limitations, how your limitations keep producing its power to suppress you. Remember, once you find out the power source of your limitation, cut its power supply! It's more beneficial for you to take your foot off the brakes than to focus on pressing the gas with your foot on the brakes. Eliminating your roadblocks is like taking your foot off the brakes. There is no fear, no bondage, no insecurity that produces its power to suppress without your help. Whether knowingly or unknowingly, it is possible to feed your fears, insecurities, and doubts by allowing those thoughts to persist. We all have fears, insecurities, and doubts, but the second you allow those fears to control your life, that is also the moment you enable the suppressive power of that emotion to keep you stuck.

Move forward, despite your fears. Have faith, despite your doubts! As you do so, just do what the father did in Mark 9:24. He confessed that he believed Jesus could heal his son and, in the same breath, asked for help with what he didn't believe. I have learned that most of the answers to get out of our own way are within us, and God blesses us to discover our limitations by showing you you! In order to break free from your roadblocks, you must first want to. I know this sounds simple or even cliché, but you will be amazed at how many people know how to have a great marriage and don't. Know how to come out of poverty and don't. Know how to forgive and don't. Know how to control their anger and don't. It is rarely a lack of information that holds people back. It is a lack of desire to want to change. I make this point to say this: discovering your roadblocks is not easy but necessary to believe you belong in your healing. Embrace your full potential and walk into your purpose.

You see, if you are fearful of rejection, for example, you will procrastinate on trying out for the basketball team. Missing the last day of tryouts, you convince yourself it wasn't meant to be. The strange thing is, you must convince yourself that somehow fate played a role in your inability to act in order to keep protecting your ego. This example, I believe, is a common route to a life unfulfilled. If you spend all your time trying to get out, get out of depression, get out of anger, get out of low self-worth, when will you have the time to think up? I'm not saying that coming out of our fears and limitations is not important and therefore you should use only a small portion of your time, but what I am saying is, if you fall in a pit, yes, fight to get out of the pit, but once you get out of the pit and stand on solid ground, now fight to walk into your purpose and become the highest expression of who God is calling you to be. You cannot achieve the latter by only applying the principles you learned in the pit!

I believe it is possible to be addicted to deliverance. Being addicted to deliverance means you are so focused on breaking free from your pain that you omit the fact that you have a God-given purpose. I believe this happens when you spend the majority of your life trying to get to a place of spiritual and emotional health; you totally forget that you have potential that in order to be reached, you must let go of the lies of your past and embrace your future but not to spend your whole life letting go of the lies. This principle reminds me of the children of Israel. They spent most of their lives seeking and praying for freedom, just as we can easily spend the majority of our lives coming out of fears, rebuking the devil, coming out of insecurities. Once the children of Israel were free, they surprisingly did not have that same desire to walk into their promised land, as they had to be free from slavery. But why? I believe it was because they didn't want to fight to embrace what was theirs. I believe they wanted God to do another miracle. Wanting God to fight the battles that He wants you to fight is a form of spiritual immaturity that every believer must face and overcome to be all that God is calling you to be.

Here are some of the questions that kept me from fighting battles God wanted me to grow through.

1. I'm not spiritual enough to face this.
2. I don't know that God is with me in the fight, so I will just pray.
3. If I fight, I may appear that I'm the type of person that does not trust God to fight my battles.
4. If I fight, I may lose.

As you may have noticed, all the reasons given to just stay free in the wilderness may have been some of the same thoughts.

God's Truth Makes You Free!

> Finally, brethren, whatever things are true, whatever things are noble, whatever things are just, whatever things are pure, whatever things are lovely, whatever things are of good report if there is any virtue and if there is anything praiseworthy—meditate on these things. (Phil. 4:8 NKJV)

The Word of God tells us how to keep a pure heart, which is by being intentional about how you think. Truth, honesty, justice, purity, love, goodness, and moral excellence. I love the fact that the first thing that is mentioned is truth. I have heard many people say the truth sets you free. I strongly disagree. Why? Well, if I told you, I will give you one million dollars next week. The truth of that statement sets you free from all the responsibilities of working, but only to the extent of how you think. You have the choice to think, "That's nice, but I love to work, so I will continue working, just not as much." Or you may say to yourself, "Praise God you answered my prayers! I never have to work a day in my life!" Again, the truth of my statement sets you free from the responsibly to work, but only to the extent of how you perceive that truth.

Well, the Bible says in John 8:32, "The truth makes you free!" What is the difference? In my example, you may have overlooked that I said "Next week." That means the thoughts you had were inspired by truth but unable to be acted on because it is not a reality until the money is in your bank account. When the money hits your account, now you have the power and freedom to make a choice to continue to work or not. Some people look at truth as just setting them free. Meaning, their freedom is in the future, which is not connected to their reality today. They look at all the things they can do or be as soon as some future event happens, freeing them from their bondage. The truth you believe that only sets you free in the future is not the truth that God's Word refers to. His truth makes you free today, even within you, the unwanted circumstances you may be in, because only the truth that's in the Word of God leads you out of any darkness you may be standing in today. His freedom is not promised just for tomorrow. His truth leads to freedom that can be realized today!

Stand fast therefore in the liberty where-
with Christ hath made us free, and be not
entangled again with the yoke of bondage. (Gal. 5:1)

Poor thinking is a yoke, a mental manifestation of slavery. Why? Because it keeps you believing that you are what
your circumstances have defined you as.

Prosperity means something different to everyone. To
some, it means financial security. To others, it means food
on the table. To the poor in spirit, prosperity means surviving; people who are poor in spirit minimize the meaning of
prospering to just getting by. The problem with this mindset
is formed by your present situations, and staying in survival
mode too long births an attitude of acceptance of your present circumstance. I always thought poor people were simply
people with little or no money. Many today believe that if
you're broke, you're poor! This was what I thought for years.

I was raised with just enough to get by, so since my
parents worked so hard and had little to show for it, I was
convinced at an early age that poverty has everything to do
with the lack of money and being rich has everything to do
with the abundance of money. This viewpoint caused me to
believe that in order to come out of poverty, I must become
rich. Well, this may be true if your only goal is financial freedom, but as I got older, I began to realize that poverty comes
from poverty thoughts. I was thinking in agreement with the
principles of poverty because that was all I was exposed to.
For years, I struggled with a lack of desire, no belief in myself,
and low self-esteem. These destructive thoughts clouded my
mind as early as nine years old. Millions of people today
struggle with the same issues I struggled with. Defeat is a
mindset that you accept, not an event that you experience.
You can go through a period in your life that is devastating,

job loss, loss of a loved one, or a debilitating disease, but that experience does not give you the right to use that trial as a reason to fall into depression, low self-esteem. John 10:10 reads, "Thief cometh not, but for to steal, and to kill, and to destroy: I come that they might have life and that they might have it more abundantly."

Don't get me wrong. There are some circumstances that must be conquered by enduring them, but I'm speaking of an unwavering focus of overcoming rather than a focus on surviving. This book identifies patterns of destructive thinking and methods of how to overcome them. The reason I refer to poverty as a spirit is that the principles of poverty become a part of who you are, not simply what you believe. First Corinthians 2:11 (KJV) says, "For what man knoweth the things of a man, save the spirit of man which is in him? Even so the things of God knoweth no man, but the Spirit of God." The "spirit of man" refers to everything that makes you who you are. From the circumstances you encountered to the people you are around the most.

Thoughts, beliefs, and everything you went through to influence the principles you live by today.

> It's not that some people have will power and some don't, it's that some people are ready to change, and others are not.
> (James Gordon)

There is no such thing as a physical barrier or wall that is holding you back from walking into your purpose; the wall is set up and built high as your imagination can fathom in your mind. When you run into people or circumstances that challenge your faith, you view the walls they set before you as the only thing that is stopping you from being who God called you to be, and of course, you do what any sensible person does, attempt to knock it down.

As you use all your strength to knock down this wall and it does not budge, you then begin to think that it is impossible to move. So you give up and build your life, with this wall becoming a part of who you are.

Over time, this wall transforms from simply a mental insecurity or weakness that prevents you from moving forward to a default foundational method to how you interpret every circumstance in your life. At this stage is when a yoke or stronghold is formed!

The reason the wall does not come down as easily as you thought is that it was not built by that person you think is holding you back or that circumstance you feel is the source of your stagnation. The truth is, it is built by the strongholds you have in your mind!

Does this sound like you? Do you make every decision in a mental box that forces you to "color in the preset lines of your perception" rather than draw your own picture? If so, take your time reading through this chapter. Study each point, learn it until it becomes a part of how you think. This process can take up to three months, but don't be alarmed with the time. It is dependent on your desire to break free from this mindset.

Strongholds are formed through bad experiences that may or may not have anything to do with the devil's plan, along with demonic thoughts that are impressed on the way you interpret those experiences. God gave the enemy the authority to only attack us by our thoughts. He may attack you in your body, your family, or your money like he did the Job, but those are considered by the devil to be what I call manipulation strategies to bring to pass a specific end result, which is to get you to curse God to His face (Job 1:11).

Forms of Strongholds

> For the weapons of our warfare are not carnal, but mighty through God to the pulling down of strongholds. (2 Cor. 10:4 KJV)

Your perception of yourself is your biggest empowerment tool or greatest vice.

Believe with unwavering conviction that you have something to give to the world, or the world will believe with unwavering conviction that you don't.

Prayer changes things, but if you don't allow it to change you, you will not change.

> For we wrestle not against flesh and blood, but against principalities, against powers, against the rulers of the darkness of this world, against spiritual wickedness in high places. (Eph. 6:12 KJV)

> Between God, on the one hand, and the devil, on the other stands the praying man.
> Oswald Sanders. (*Spiritual Leadership 0*)

Self-limiting beliefs can cause you to accept lies that will keep you tolerating your bondage while praying for freedom.

Prayer is what keeps the heart full of faith and passion for seeing God manifest Himself in your life in a way that brings a clearer understanding of who you are and who God is.

After prayer, there must be a responsibility to do the things God gave you the ability to do.

Growth Is Just as Uncomfortable as Stagnation; The Only Difference Is One Is Intentional

When I began to understand that it is required for you to have a strong sense of belonging in order to thrive on the next level I confronted my fears more courageously. It's only the person that believes they belong that will not allow anything, anyone, or any circumstance to snatch away their God-given vision for their life.

When you know you belong, no one can deceive you in believing you don't.

For example, someone comes to your home and knocks on your door, accompanied by a sheriff, and tells you that there has been a big mistake, that the home you are paying the mortgage on is not your home, that it belongs to another person, so within the next twenty-four hours you must be out. You apologize to the person, "Sorry for the mis-understanding. I'll leave right away." Will you get angry and annoyed because there's no way possible that in all the years you've been paying your mortgage, this type of mistake can happen? Or would you ask, Who are you? And what company are you from? So you can immediately contact your lawyer to sue for fraud. I will probably just close the door. My point is, there are many people who are allowing someone they don't even know to tell them they don't belong with that vision that they have for themselves, or whatever represents freedom for. You allow that person's doubts to contaminate your growth. When you are not sure that you belong, you will give excessive attention to words of doubt and discour-agement spoken over your life.

The prodigal son's change came only when his circum-stances no longer reflected the thoughts he had of himself. Ask yourself, "Do I believe I belong here in this state of pov-erty, in this state of depression, in this state of rejection? I'm sure you probably answered no. Now, ask yourself, "Do the ways I view myself support or reject my circumstance?"

> The moment you settle in your mind, you
> do not belong in your mess no devil in hell
> can keep you in your mess. (TD Jakes)

> All God tells us is the next step. Take that
> one. And the one after that will appear,
> but not before. (Dr. Henry Cloud, *How
> People Grow*)

Remember, your thinking will always reflect the convictions you develop from the beliefs you have of yourself, God, and what you embrace as being possible. Your next step is to begin thinking about the impossible. What goals have you thrown away because you thought they were impossible? I believe if God blesses you to see into your future that blessing comes with the power to attain it! no matter how unrealistic that vision may seem at the time, if its in your heart, its possible for you.

Now that you are more aware of what is keeping you from thinking up. Now, let's talk about your next steps to apply the information in this book.

This chapter is designed to help you take everything in the chapters and give you a step-by-step guide to apply the information.

These steps are designed to focus your attention and energy on where you are going. In order for these steps to bear fruit in your life, you must set your heart to apply them diligently. TD Jakes said it best: diligence makes the difference (message: don't be poor in spirit).

First, seek God and focus on who you are. That means to pray and ask God what your purpose is and why you are here. Remember, Ephesians 5:17 (KJV) says to understand what the will of the Lord is. That means regardless of how you feel or what you believed until now, God wants you to understand His will for your life personally, not just for mankind. Since your thinking determines who you are, your response to what you received in this book, along with a receptive heart, will open the door to a sound mind and a sound life.

Second, take 100 percent ownership of your life. You are 100 percent responsible for your life. I know this may sound simple, but it took me years to stop being a victim, stop blaming people for my shortcomings, and decided in my heart to take 100 percent responsibility for my life. This simply means I will focus on changing the things that I have the God-given ability to change, and I will not allow things that I cannot change to make me feel sorry for myself or believe that I have a disadvantage. This took time for me to embrace and become a part of my mentality, so it may take some time for you. I did not believe I had the ability to take 100 percent responsibility for my life until I turned my life over to Jesus Christ in 2008.

This was the foundation that empowered me to seek God for my purpose. God birthed a new knowledge in me to understand that I was placed on this earth for a purpose, and reacting to my life as if I was an accident was a mentality that was birthed out of fear and insecurity. Knowing where that mentality was birthed made it easier to let go.

Write down your short-term and long-term goals.

"Thinking up" is a mindset, a mentality, not a method to use when you feel defeated.

To think up is to focus on what God is trying to teach you in the circumstance. This will help you turn your attention off how wrong or inconvenient your situation is to treating your circumstance as a seed that will bear fruit in some form; rather, it may be in the form of a more sound character or emotional or spiritual maturity. You cannot overcome anything when you wallow in anger, frustration, or confusion. If you allow it, these emotions are naturally (without any help of your own) going to attempt to consume your thoughts.

Know without a shadow of a doubt that this situation has come to make you wiser, stronger, and better, *period*.

This circumstance does not define who I am; this circumstance only reveals the strengths or weaknesses of the principles I chose to apply. This circumstance is the fruit of my principles, good or bad.

Steps That Helped Me to Think Up

1. I gave up my tunnel-vision attitude.
2. I developed the courage to confront my fears.
3. I cut off unhealthy relationships.
4. I became intentional about my growth
5. I developed the habit of examining what I think.

Misinterpreted scripture leads to misapplied faith to see your way clear.

> You are not truly free until your free to be yourself. (Joyce Myer)

> We do not grow because of will power or self-effort but because of God's provision. (Dr. Henry Cloud, *How People Grow*)

I believe, until you value and appreciate the opportunity God gives you to change, to grow, to learn, chances are, you will remain the same. Not valuing the opportunities God gives to embrace your freedom only allows the psychological boundaries that are forcing you to stay as you are to remain.

Fifty Principles That Will Inspire You to Think Up

These are principles I am growing to accept through my pursuit to be all God has called me to be. Each principle was revealed in difficult times in my life while I was struggling to let go of destructive beliefs, which were based only on my past experiences and fighting to embrace my identity in Christ. I believe we all must fight for our identity and that fight can produce internal struggles that may carry on further than we prepared to depending on each person's ability to let go of the lies their past may have produced. One of my favorite principles is this:

> Don't allow the lies you have accepted as truth in your past remain truth in your future. (Robert L. Lowery III)

My prayer is that these principles ignite questions within your heart that expose and cause you to break free from the limitations in your life. These principles, when revealed to me were harsh truths that at first, I really did not want to accept but in order to grow I knew I needed to embrace in order to let go of what I think and believe is possible, which, in turn, made room for me to embrace what God thinks and has made possible. These are life principles that work for me, and I pray that they will bless you. Thank you!

1. Your faith brings you to opportunities that your disciplines will only allow you to embrace. (Robert L. Lowery III)
2. Don't allow your bad past experiences to be the thermometer of your value. (Robert L. Lowery III)
3. Defeat is a mindset that you accept before it is a reality that you experience. (Robert L. Lowery III)
4. Weakness or strength are first manifested in thought before it is expressed in an attitude, emotion, or circumstance. (Robert L. Lowery III)
5. When you're intentional about your progress, your mentality grows to meet that intention. (Robert L. Lowery III)
6. Accepting your circumstances guarantees that tomorrow will not get better. (Robert L. Lowery III)
7. Don't allow yourself to act on a level lower than your God-given abilities. (Robert L. Lowery III)
8. While you are procrastinating, your opportunity may be fleeting. (Robert L. Lowery III)
9. Knowledge can only take you as far as your understanding can sustain you. (Robert L. Lowery III)
10. Believe with unwavering conviction that you have something to give to the world, or the world will believe with unwavering conviction that you don't. (Robert L. Lowery III)
11. Defeat or triumph starts with how you think. (Robert L. Lowery III)
12. There is no fear, no bondage, no insecurity that produces its power to suppress without your help. (Robert L. Lowery III)

13. You can't allow who you think you are to suppress who God created you to be. (Robert L. Lowery III)

14. Choosing to be strong is a foundation that enables you to become strong. (Robert L. Lowery III)

15. Your perception of yourself is your biggest empowerment tool or greatest vice. (Robert L. Lowery III)

16. It is a very passionate person's responsibility to be as informed as your passion can express. (Robert L. Lowery III)

17. You are not a victim even if you have been victimized. (Robert L. Lowery III)

18. Don't scrape the bottom of the emotional barrel and withdraw from life because of a problem. (Robert L. Lowery III)

19. It is more important to discover your value before you define your vision. (Robert L. Lowery III)

20. There are certain things that are constant in your life. You must be one of them. (Robert L. Lowery III)

21. Growth is just as uncomfortable as stagnation. The only difference is one is intentional. (Robert L. Lowery III)

22. You will never be stronger than your perception of yourself. (Robert L. Lowery III)

23. You will not rise above any form of limitation when you expect to be limited. (Robert L. Lowery III)

24. If your fears do not let you go as you walk into your purpose, they just will have to come. (Robert L. Lowery III)

25. If you do not intentionally put yourself through the pain of growing, you will unintentionally put yourself through the pain of stagnation. (Robert L. Lowery III)

26. Destructive fear is a form of ignorance at its highest expression. (Robert L. Lowery III)

27. Don't misinterpret what God is saying in this season because you were anxious for a specific word in the last season. (Robert L. Lowery III)

28. It's easy to allow your fears and insecurities to define you when you don't give yourself reasons to be defined otherwise. (Robert L. Lowery III)

29. You become a victim of your vision when your vision is birthed out of low self-worth. (Robert L. Lowery III)

30. Don't let whatever you're tired of taking you to a place of brokenness; allow it to take you to a place of victory. (Robert L. Lowery III)

31. You will rise only to the level you believe you belong to. (Robert L. Lowery III)

32. You can't think how your thinking going where you're going. (Robert L. Lowery III)

33. The height of your vision is intertwined with the depth of value you have of yourself. (Robert L. Lowery III)

34. If excellence does not become a standard, it will never be achieved. (Robert L. Lowery III)

35. What you believe is an expression of who you are. (Robert L. Lowery III)

36. Some of your greatest battles will be fought tired. Accept it and embrace it. Comfortable fights are battles that have no reward. (Robert L. Lowery III)

37. Strength or weakness is manifested through your interpretation of your circumstances. (Robert L. Lowery III)

38. Don't allow the lies you have accepted as truth in your past remain truth in your future. (Robert L. Lowery III)

39. People who do not have a clear vision for their life force themselves in the uncomfortable position of watching others achieve their vision. (Robert L. Lowery III)

40. It's not totally about finding the solutions to your problems; it's about finding the solutions to your problem that can be used within the time span of the opportunity that problem created. (Robert L. Lowery III)

41. Authority to be all and become all God has created you to be isn't something you ask for; it is something you submit to. (Robert L. Lowery III)

42. Your interpretation of your circumstances will sow seeds to empower you or cripple you. You choose. (Robert L. Lowery III)

43. What you tolerate is connected to how you perceive yourself, and how you perceive yourself has been formed up to this point by who you believe you are. (Robert L. Lowery III)

44. Are you going forward or standing still, looking at a sign that reads going forward? (Robert L. Lowery III)

45. Your beliefs empower or suffocate your vision. (Robert L. Lowery III)

46. You can rise above any circumstance if your thoughts are above that circumstance. (Robert L. Lowery III)

47. When you are ignorant of your God-given identity, you, without any force, accept whatever comes as if your circumstances control your life. (Robert L. Lowery III)

48. Ignorance is destructive primarily from the lack of knowledge, but from the illusion, it gives a person of knowledge. (Robert L. Lowery III)

49. Moving forward is the highest expression of a healing heart. (Robert L. Lowery III)
50. To see beyond your walls, you must believe the promises of God beyond your doubts. (Robert L. Lowery III)

CPSIA information can be obtained
at www.ICGtesting.com
Printed in the USA
JSHW061728150822
29247JS00001B/3

9 781647 736064